E-SUPPLY CHAIN

USING THE INTERNET TO REVOLUTIONIZE YOUR BUSINESS

E-SUPPLY CHAIN

USING THE INTERNET TO
REVOLUTIONIZE YOUR BUSINESS

How Market Leaders Focus Their Entire
Organization on Driving Value to Customers

CHARLES C. POIRIER & MICHAEL J. BAUER

BK

BERRETT-KOEHLER PUBLISHERS, INC.
San Francisco

Berrett-Koehler Publishers, Inc.
450 Sansome Street, Suite 1200
San Francisco, CA 94111-3320
Tel: (415) 288-0260
Fax: (415) 362-2512
www.bkconnection.com

ORDERING INFORMATION
Quantity sales. Special discounts are available on quantity purchases by corporations, associations, and others. For details, contact the "Special Sales Department" at the Berrett-Koehler address above.

Individual sales. Berrett-Koehler publications are available through most bookstores. They can also be ordered direct from Berrett-Koehler: Tel: (800) 929-2929; Fax: (802) 864-7626; www.bkconnection.com

Orders for college textbook/course adoption use. Please contact Berrett-Koehler:Tel: (800) 929-2929; Fax: (802) 864-7626.

Orders by U.S. trade bookstores and wholesalers. Please contact Publishers Group West, 1700 Fourth Street, Berkeley, CA 94710. Tel: (510) 528-1444; Fax: (510) 528-3444.

Production Management: Michael Bass & Associates

Printed in the United States of America
Printed on acid-free and recycled paper that is composed of 85% recovered fiber, including 15% post consumer waste.

Library of Congress Cataloging-in-Publication Data

First Edition
05   04   03   02   01   00   10   9   8   7   6   5   4   3   2   1

To Bill Read, Steve Keener, Mike Klaus, and Bruce Ferraro
for their continuing support

To Karen Schaefer
for her friendship, inspiration, support, and insight

Contents

re:
Oper 564

Ex 1.3.
hexagon
+
Ex 1.5.

Preface

Atsunami-like change is overtaking global business—an irresistible force of communication called the Internet. Over the World Wide Web, some companies are creating internal and external connections to establish new capabilities within their markets, changing the way business will be conducted and redefining roles and rules for how to direct a successful enterprise. This phenomenon is impacting every single part of a business, all functions and departments, and will eventually affect every consumer worldwide as well. The effect is dramatically influencing how business-to-business and business-to-consumer transactions will be conducted in the future.

The importance of this change, however, is generally not well understood in spite of the clear signs of its ultimate impact and the magnitude of the information being generated on its presence and applications. People who will be the most affected, the leaders of current business enterprises and their employees, fall into four categories as they perceive the implications of this unstoppable force.

In the first group are those who want to deny the Internet's importance, individuals who decry the magnitude of its force and pass off its impact as just another temporary trend that will leave little visible change in the way business is conducted. These people prefer focusing on improvement to internal operations, with or without an enabling Internet technical architecture. For this group, the cry seems to be "Keep making better products and offering new services, and the customers will keep buying." This approach overlooks the fundamental changes occurring in buying habits and the technological advances that are impacting buying and selling relationships, which are moving inexorably toward Web-based features. Those in this category, which includes many companies in the upstream (primary supply) portion of supply chains, fail to seek the advice that could help them withstand the onslaught of this wave of change.

The second group includes those who plan to ride out the impact of the Internet tsunami and repair the damage—individuals who refuse to invest the time or resources to take a leadership position. This category prefers to let others assume the lead, content in the dangerous assumption that their organizations can gain back any ground lost to the deluge after its extent has been determined. These people believe a sound strategy is foregoing investments and applications until the one best format is created for using the Web for their specific applications. Individuals in this group, including many currently successful retailers, are destined to find their organizations with a gap that will require years to close before they catch the leaders.

Taking a more precarious perspective, people in the third category want to run away and hide until the wave has passed. Unable to handle technology in a global environment, they want to fall back on current capabilities, even if the result is the distribution of products and services that are in constantly declining demand through conventional channels. For this group, the legacy computer systems installed decades ago are good enough to keep pace with the burgeoning use of the Web. Expensive, slow, and error-prone, these nonintegrated systems are an anchor on businesses forced to keep pace with swifter competitors. These people, including many manufacturing-oriented and distribution companies, will find their organizations consumed by those firms using technology to forge the new business responses demanded by the Internet.

Finally, there are those who are prepared to ride the Web's wave to new heights of accomplishment, using cutting-edge technology as the defining element of differentiation in a global business environment. Around the world, a new breed of business entrepreneurs is emerging, a group destined to establish leadership through applications conducted over the Internet. As these leaders of totally new businesses, led by those in high-technology and consumer distribution markets, raise enormous capital through the issuance of Web-based stock offerings, they are creating an impact on global commerce equal to that brought on by the industrial revolution. Indeed, we are witnessing a cyber revolution that will change forever the way business is conducted.

This new leadership is finding the way to link supply chain constituents into a tightly knit network of communication and functionality that is creating serious competitive advantages. It is this group that has assumed the role of pathfinder, forging the new business passages to future dominance of their chosen markets. Our intention in this book is to detail how these pathfinders are using the Internet to establish such an advantage. As we do, two conclusions will become evident. First, Internet technology has empowered business customers and final consumers to the point where businesses will have to go through profound changes to fully satisfy their customers and consumers. Second, these same businesses will be compelled to learn how to use all available technologies in collaboration with other businesses—members of their supply chain network—or risk failure in the new digital business environment.

The Internet's profound effect on business is already halfway through its course and has been given a name: *electronic commerce,* often referred to as *e-commerce* or the more encompassing *e-business.* This new tool will become the defining characteristic for those who understand its importance and impact and have the vision to combine its force with supply chain business processes. From a focus on continuous improvement, supply chain optimization has emerged as a major means of transforming an organization to better utilize assets and resources, generate profits and greater shareholder value, and positively react to customer and consumer demand. Leading business organizations are combining this technique with the Internet, to create the defining business discipline of the twenty-first century.

THE INTERNET'S TRANSFORMATION OF SUPPLY CHAIN EFFORTS

Supply chain is now the recognized discipline to shorten cycle times, transform purchasing from a tactical operation to strategic sourcing, reduce inventories, decrease logistics costs, and streamline communication processes across a total network, from initial supplies to final consumption and postsale service. It is the mechanism through which diverse organizations find the way to form alliances to meet a new form of Internet-oriented consumer demand. Constituents in a supply chain network share resources and benefits as levels of trust, absent in competing networks, are established and an advantage is created in particular industries and markets. It is the umbrella effort that brings focus to functional initiatives and binds partners together to add a critical dimension to business plans and responses to consumer demand.

Those leading their supply chains to positions of market leadership intend to add the force of the e-commerce wave to propel them beyond competing networks. As corporations redefine themselves as part of a total system of supply that responds to what a particular group of business customers or end consumers is demanding, *value chain constellations* are forming as the true means of differentiation in the eyes of those customers and consumers. These constellations are advanced networks, built around a nucleus organization that tends to guide its formation and direction. They have progressed collaboratively and share mutual resources to focus on eliminating redundant costs and reducing cycle times across the full supply chain system. They focus further on specific market segments, and business customers and consumers within those segments, so they can build new, profitable revenues together. These constellations move forward with their resources focused on bringing elements of e-commerce to the most advantageous position for the most highly prized customer and consumer groups, so their supply chain network will be that customer's or consumer's channel of choice, in order to dominate the chosen markets. They are establishing what we call *e–supply chain* systems to create the necessary links among data, communications, and network effectiveness.

We wrote this book for those who wish to be a part of this new wave of interactivity. Having found no definitive text to serve as a guidebook for both preparation and execution, we hope to fill that void with a clear and applicable text on the subjects of electronic commerce and advanced supply chain management, detailing how those powerful elements will converge, enhance business efforts, and lead to market dominance. We will define the concepts and principles behind e–supply chain and describe features that will enable networks to fulfill their missions.

OUR PURPOSES

This book builds on information contained in two previous Berrett-Koehler publications, *Supply Chain Optimization* and *Advanced Supply Chain Management*. We first review the pertinent supply chain concepts making the subject a timely issue and describe some of the noteworthy results, to establish a sufficient basis for making the connection suggested by our main topic. We then discuss definitions and applications of e-commerce and describe how it is the enabling feature of advanced supply chain networks. Case studies and personal activities with firms across the global spectrum of industries, markets, and countries will support our presentation. We will provide the information necessary to make the vital connection between an emerging business improvement process and the technology that makes its ultimate purposes feasible—optimization of the full supply chain network and satisfaction of a particular business customer or consumer group.

This book is necessary because of the large degree of misunderstanding about the subjects and the gap that exists between those who are knowledgeable but do not have responsibility for implementation and those who are not knowledgeable but must implement. Working with hundreds of firms in nearly all industries, we are amazed at the disparity in understanding and action concerning the application of electronic features that enhance supply chain efforts. The gap between leaders and followers is now measured in years.

This book is written for managers with interest in but limited understanding of electronic commerce and supply chain. It is for functional personnel curious about how e-commerce can help in their area of expertise, be it information technology and systems, design, procurement, planning, engineering, manufacturing, logistics, human resources, finance, or administration. It will be useful for technology specialists to help them sell e–supply chain features to their customers, internally and externally. For those who deal in hardware and software, it will help them better understand the interconnections between e-commerce and supply chain and better mitigate the risks in purchases, sales, and application. It is also for those engaged in marketing and sales to help them sell products and services through a modern value chain constellation that is fully technology enabled. Finally, this book is a training tool for anyone who wants to broaden his or her knowledge of e-commerce and supply chain. It will enable them to find the solutions needed to satisfy Internet-empowered customers and consumers and to learn how to apply all the technologies demanded in the new digital economy in collaboration with other organizations.

Acknowledgments

Many individuals have been most helpful in researching and preparing this book or giving us guidance in critical areas. They include Peter Blatman, Scott Bowman, Jerry Boltin, Owen Devlin, Chris Dials, Jim Erickson, Beth Feitinger, Lyn Ferrara, Ian Grimsley, Rob Guzak, Adam Hartung, David Hill, Jim Hine, Gary Jones, Mike Ledyard, Gary Moe, Mike Oliver, Gary Orosy, Peter Punwani, Jim Roche, Denise Senter-Loyola, Brad Scheller, Chris Slee, Chuck Troyer, and Chuck Weiss. Editorial guidance by Steven Piersanti led to the vital framework guiding the construction of the book.

Recognition would not be complete without thanking Deb Hageman and Marianne Harris for working through the many versions that led to a final draft and to Chris Dials for his editorial comments and help with graphics. We also appreciate the editorial comments and help received from Stanley Bass, Dr. Meichun Hsu, Catherine Dain, and Robert Novak. A special appreciation goes to Carol Kirsch, who brought the manuscript into its final format.

Introduction—A Guiding Framework

Supply chain is now a core business improvement effort for most companies, as senior management directives in that area are becoming commonplace. Supply chain optimization (SCO) has emerged as the central objective for these initiatives—an organized effort to enhance profitability and increase shareholder value as emphasis on cost cutting and quality moved logically to logistics and distribution, and then to total supply chain performance. What began as a look at how action teams could be focused on other areas of cost reduction has blossomed into a full-blown business improvement practice. It includes mapping, analyzing, and enhancing all the processes from ordering and receipt of beginning materials to final consumption and recycling of products and renewal of services.

With its growing importance, those companies pursuing supply chain improvement are discovering a new set of goals for its purposes: to improve economic value added (EVA), earnings per share (EPS), stakeholder value and customer satisfaction, or whatever primary objective a company has set for itself. As firms measure return on applied resources, the focus on total supply chain costs and benefits has led to applying SCO as the means to a necessary end, creating better overall business value. When this idea is taken to its ultimate conclusion, best use of total resources, the company is approaching optimization, and that becomes the central purpose for the supply chain effort.

The process then proceeds with the help of external constituents, companies that have also developed better supply chain practices. As firms find they have enhanced process steps in their supply chain, it is logical to share the best practices across their supply chain network. Now the firm works with a cadre of partners—suppliers, distributors, and customers—to achieve the next level of improvement. In this later development, the emphasis moves first to sharing best ideas and practices across what becomes a network of interaction, to finding the means to build together new, profitable revenues for all constituents of the network.

It is in this stage that the value of e-commerce comes into play, as the linked constituents of the supply chain discover an enormous opportunity to share information and skills electronically. Together they build the new e-business models that are distinguishing the leaders in the use of the Internet. A specific focus can be brought to gaining revenues with the best customers in a business-to-business (B2B) system. Eventually, they gain position with the best consumers in a business-to-consumer (B2C) system—working toward those who are truly in control of consumption today—by applying the best processes across the full linkage, from supply to consumption. The tremendous potential of the World Wide Web is then harnessed in a manner that helps the network succeed.

The convergence of an advanced supply chain effort with the total network use of e-commerce becomes the means to enhance the improvements generated from the SCO initiatives. This convergence must occur, however, across a full network of linked organizations dedicated to building business together. In this chapter, we'll provide a brief overview of where supply chain is headed, from SCO and beyond to the advanced techniques. We'll also present a framework for combining this powerful business tool with the use of the equally powerful Internet, as a means for achieving top-line results (new revenues), while continuing to improve bottom-line results (continuous cost improvement and better asset utilization). In Chapters 2 and 3, we'll further discuss the power and potential of e-commerce, detailing how it brings the ultimate enhancement to the supply chain effort.

SUPPLY CHAIN AS A PRECURSOR TO INTEGRATED NETWORK COLLABORATION

From leading retailers and industry manufacturers of consumer goods and high-technology products that pioneered the effort, supply chain has spread from product companies to service organizations such as banks, health care, and educational institutions. SCO is now a pervasive effort for businesses seeking the next level of progress with process improvement and customer satisfaction. Typically, these efforts are internally focused, and, although they usually result in enhanced earnings as the companies proceed with implementations, they also reach the point of diminishing returns as internal excellence peaks. Most firms then find an external orientation is necessary to continue the progress and to apply the benefits of e-commerce to the effort. Supply chain must be pursued, however, as a preparatory step toward full network cooperation.

A few definitions will help our discussion. In simple terms, *supply chain* refers to those core business processes that create and deliver a product or service, from concept through development and manufacturing or conversion, into a market for consumption. In typical supply chains, suppliers deliver raw materials (e.g., chemicals, grain, ores, and pigments) and necessary supplies (lubricants, parts, and computers) to manufacturers or producers who convert these incoming supplies into finished goods or services (cars, subassemblies, furniture, and appliance installation). The goods then move to a distributor (Fleming or Supervalu for wholesale grocery delivery) for further delivery to a business customer or directly to a consumer (through FedEx, UPS, or the U.S. Postal Service). The business customer could be another manufacturer (assembling subcomponents into a complete car or computer) in an extended supply chain that moves through several steps before reaching its final point of business consumption. The ultimate business customer is usually a retailer—a grocery chain (Kroger), department store (Dayton Hudson), club store (Sam's Club), or specialty outlet (Victoria's Secret)—that sells the goods to end consumers.

The linked processes in these supply chains can be continuously improved to bring significant enhancement to the firms connected to each other, from beginning to end of the total network. Process improvement typically starts with manufacturing and logistics and expands to supply of materials, order fulfillment, distribution of products, and customer satisfaction. No effort is complete, however, unless it includes improvement to cash and information flows.

Supply chain management (SCM) refers to the methods, systems, and leadership that continuously improve an organization's integrated processes for product and service design, sales forecasting, purchasing, inventory management, manufacturing or production, order management, logistics, distribution, and customer satisfaction. SCM involves optimizing the creation and delivery of goods, services, and information from suppliers to business customers and consumers. It is a means to improve the enterprise's competitive position within the market served by itself and the constituent members of its supply chain network. Typically, early SCM efforts are *internally* focused and dedicated to cutting costs and improving profits only for the company pursuing the effort.

SCM eventually requires the company to take an *external* view of its business environment and then collaboratively identify the vital supply chain processes that will differentiate the network, of which the company is just one part, in the eyes of the most desired business customers and end consumers. The partners can then set about to improve the competence of what will become their *value chain constellations*, the effectiveness of which will be measured by the ultimate customers and consumers in terms of their purchases and continued loyalty. These constellations—groupings of companies with a common dedication to a particular business customer or consumer group in a specific market segment or industry—will be the entities that dominate future businesses.

THE TRANSITION FROM SUPPLY CHAIN TO NETWORK TO CONSTELLATION AND FULL CONNECTIVITY

To help understand the transition being espoused, let's consider the formation of a supply chain network and its advancement to a fully enhanced e-commerce position. In this book, we will argue that a "nucleus firm" initiates such a formation best. A *nucleus firm* is a company that assumes the central role in bringing an external orientation to a supply chain and solicits the help of willing business partners on either side of its chain, so a full network effort can be generated.

Network Formation

Today's environment is so rich in information that the communication system has to bring the most important data—cash flow and order management—to those members of the network who are most in need, and it must do so more effectively than any competing network. The result is a supply chain network that has common objectives of satisfying the final customers or consumers and dominating specific markets or industries, supported by a powerful connectivity of information that enhances flexibility and response to actual consumer preferences.

- get going
- get real
- get business
- Phases

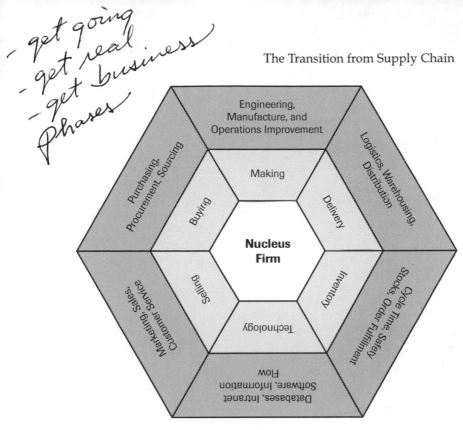

EXHIBIT 1.1   Network Formation

Exhibit 1.1 illustrates the movement from an internal environment to the beginnings of an external environment in which a network starts to take shape. We characterize this movement as the "get going" phase. Using the typical (but not exclusive) business elements of buying, making, delivery, selling, inventory, and technology, we outline how the network begins to coalesce and change focus from internal to external improvement. In Chapter 5, we present a ten-step process for making the full transition. Here, we will cover the fundamentals that are involved. This is a time when there will be a fair amount of probing, discussion, and partial sharing, as the need for trusting the selected partners quickly becomes apparent. There is no network, just the idea that one can be formed and the benefits can be mutual for all participants.

In the *buying* sector, a group representing the purchasing function will come together to discuss how the supply chain constituents can work to leverage their combined volumes and move sourcing to the next level of improvement. This does not mean just getting lower prices. It means determining how to cut order entry and payment costs, how to work with suppliers to develop nonprice features and

Looking ahead
+ ref. to Ch 2 & 3

benefits, and, most important, how to develop a better win-win situation in negotiations.

In the *making* sector, the firms form another team to look at how best operating practices can be shared. This will be a very difficult session, as most firms think they have a lock on the one best way to complete each process step. Experience, however, has shown us there is always room for greater improvement, even if the process steps enhanced are in an indirect area of manufacturing or production. At this time the constituents also begin looking at how they can share what's in their computer-aided design and manufacturing systems, so a preliminary form of collaborative design and planning can start.

In the *delivery* sector, a team will discuss best practices in logistics and begin looking at just how many assets the potential network operates and uses. The total amount of warehouse space is usually an enlightening piece of data, as is the amount of inventory residing throughout the total supply chain system. Now this team starts to seriously consider how just-in-time techniques can be enhanced and safety stocks reduced through better communication and delivery.

The *inventory* team will start looking at the cycle time from initial materials and supplies to customer or consumer consumption. The total days in most of these cycles are always shocking to the observers. Safety stocks are found that the partners did not know existed. The order fulfillment process is attacked to determine how best practices can bring the one best system to the network and save all parties time and costs while shortening the cash-to-cash cycle.

The *technology* team has to form its group and serve as an aid to each of the foregoing teams. Now the wealth of information residing in the collective databases is analyzed to find what can be shared for mutual advantage. The team starts to look at the software in use to determine how a communication network can be created to link all the disparate systems and legacy equipment in use. This team is crucial to success, as all other groups will have minimal effect without the vital information flows needed to support their networking.

Finally, the *selling* group turns its attention to how the constituents can share information on specific market segments and customers. Since most firms have done some form of segmentation analysis and created a meaningful database, they have a wealth of information to share, if the parties can overcome the normal distrust and aversion to sharing any information on customers. Pricing data rarely enter this preliminary stage of discussion.

The members of the emerging supply chain network find, as they go about accomplishing their tasks, that they must apply leading-edge technology and electronic commerce features to their information connections if the combined effort is to be successful. Supply chain defines the necessary linkages and interactive processes among companies that can form a network for a particular consumer group. That network will be helpless without the communication system that creates, disseminates, and uses the vital data that will enable the timely satisfaction of consumer demands. As these new electronic networks are fashioned, some of the leading firms will find their organizations in the midst of several value chain constellations, the next step in the progression.

Value Chain Constellation

Exhibit 1.2 takes us to the next level, which we characterize as "get real." Now the network has done some impressive work, perhaps made some preliminary improvements that help fund the balance of the effort, and is ready to get serious about the use of e-commerce

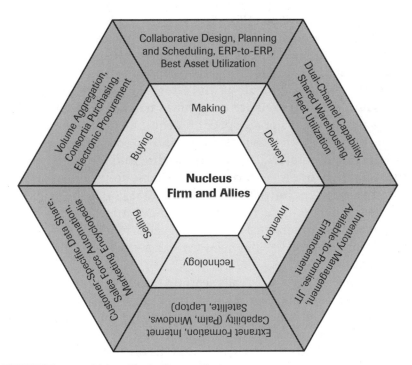

EXHIBIT 1.2 Value Chain Constellation

and the power of what can become a value chain constellation. The nucleus firm and its allies have developed a better level of trust and are determined to become an electronic network. With the introduction of activity-based costing information, the supply chain is now a "value chain" by virtue of knowing the cost of each process step, in the collective supply chain system. The effort moves to optimizing the value delivered and the cost of that delivery. The diagram shows how the six business elements now expand in importance and accomplishment.

The *buying* team is deep into aggregating the volume of purchases in key categories used by all companies in the network, and joint savings have been generated. They are developing the means to do consortia buying and definitely moving to Web-based procurement activities. A new level of savings is found as transaction costs are reduced and buying on a larger scale is accomplished.

The *making* team is into collaborative design, planning, and scheduling. They have linked their enterprise-wide resource planning (ERP) systems together, so there is online access to material and manufacturing flow, from beginning to end of the process steps. Together, the constituents are looking at who has the core competencies for each process step in the supply chain and how mutual assets can best be utilized.

The *delivery* team has rationalized some of the excess assets and is better using full network warehouse space, transportation equipment, and delivery capabilities. Elements of serious sharing are falling into place as a result of this effort. The use of joint warehouses and external logistics companies has reduced the money tied up in redundant storage space and equipment.

The *inventory* team has most likely shown some real savings in the reduction of safety stocks and is moving into the management of the total network inventories. An available-to-promise capability that accurately shows the customer what goods are where at any time is becoming a reality, and a new dimension is being brought to the partners' just-in-time (JIT) efforts, as access to much better information takes the need for extra stock out of the business equation.

The *technology* group is really leading the effort as an extranet is taking shape through a variety of current applications and equipment with an emphasis on creating value chain enhancements. An idea-sharing group is hard at work determining how to integrate the various software systems so a smooth flow of needed data is accomplished.

The *selling* team is now looking at customer-specific information, beginning to target market segments and several large joint customers. Using the data being shared, the sales forces are being automated (through direct access to important sales data), and a marketing encyclopedia showing the collective information the companies have on markets and customers is coming online.

As these constellations are formed, we prefer that they be focused on the end consumer, because that is where most supply chains culminate. Some companies, however, only focus as far as their ultimate business customer, and some firms will be part of multiple constellations. At this point, a form of customization to the terminology is in order. Hewlett-Packard, for example, has an e-commerce system dedicated to consumers who are serviced through its "shopping village." H-P also has an e-commerce system dedicated to business customers, serviced through its "business store." A particular business buyer could be simultaneously working with either system. It is for the nucleus firm and its allies to determine how it will define the eventual constellation concept for its advanced effort, particularly to designate the targeted end customer or consumer group that makes most sense.

Full Network Connectivity

In the final development, the value chain constellation solidifies as network allies move to a state that we characterize as "get business." Now the fruits of the effort go beyond saving money to finding new revenues together, by actively using e-commerce capability across a full network (see Exhibit 1.3). The value chain is discernibly different and better in the eyes of business customers and consumers by virtue of the total application of technology and the full connectivity of systems and information flow from beginning to end of the supply chain. E-business models have been jointly developed by network allies and are in use.

The *buying* team is deep into network sourcing through Internet applications. The connectivity includes appropriate auctions and portals, and the team has been actively involved in developing industry marketplaces. The *making* team is now into full network planning, using customer-centric measures to determine the results and efficiency of the effort. Asset utilization is nearing optimization as the arguments over core competencies are finished and the partners have the electronic capability to operate as one system for manufacturing and delivery. The *delivery* team has moved process steps to the best internal or external source, even to cyberproviders with few to no assets but the capability to optimize a full network system of transportation,

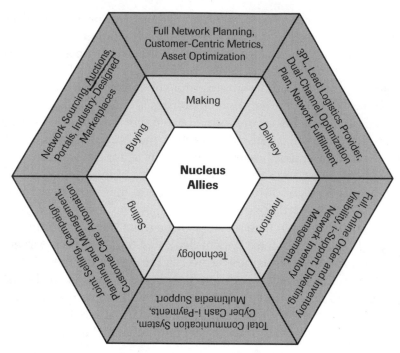

EXHIBIT 1.3   Full Network Connectivity

storage, and delivery. Online data systems are at the heart of making these systems function as a seamless operation, from delivery of the most basic raw materials to shipment of the final goods to consumers, and handling any returns that might occur.

The *inventory* team has implemented a full, online system showing the inventory in a "glass pipeline" of supply. Customers can now view what is in the total system, have access to the Internet support system, and divert flows to the most critical points of need. The total inventory in the full system will be under a network management system operating with a value chain extranet.

The *technology* team will be nearly exhausted but delighted with seeing the fruits of their efforts being documented. Total network communication systems will be in place and operating effectively. The financial side will include the use of cybercash for transactions and an Internet payment system will be in effect. Multimedia support for all teams to complete their work will be in place, as full network connectivity is not a dream but a reality.

The *selling* team will be armed with online access to whatever information they need to complete joint selling efforts. Campaign planning will be conducted by the value chain members and managed across all constituents. Customer care will be automated and matched with need and desire for attention.

The primary focus behind this supply chain transition and new electronic partnering will change from saving dollars to enhancing profitable revenue and satisfying business customers and consumers. Those networks that excel at managing the transition are destined to be the market leaders of the future. Already, companies that turned their attention early to supply chain and e-commerce as a means of getting ahead of the competition have established large leads. American Airlines, Amazon.com, Cisco Systems, Dayton Hudson, Dell Computer, Federal Express, Herman Miller SQA, Hewlett-Packard, L. L. Bean, Marks & Spencer, Nokia, Procter & Gamble, Sun Microsystems, Supervalu, Toyota, United Parcel Service, Vanity Fair Industries, Wal-Mart, and others are redefining partner relationships, channels of distribution, and communication networks to dominate their market segments.

A NEW LEVEL MUST BE ADDED TO THE SUPPLY CHAIN EVOLUTION

In a previous book, *Advanced Supply Chain Management,* we introduced the four levels of supply chain optimization depicted in Exhibit 1.4. This chart shows the evolutionary stages through which a supply chain effort progresses. A trip to the most advanced level must proceed through each of the preceding levels as stages cannot be skipped. The first two levels of progress are internally focused. It is in this area that most firms currently find themselves.

In Level I, the company pursues *sourcing* and *logistics* improvements, primarily by leveraging its total volume over a smaller base of suppliers. Lower prices, inventory reductions, lower transportation costs, and the elimination of some full-time equivalent personnel is accomplished in this level as people begin to learn how to apply supply chain techniques. The effort is typically started as an extension of current improvement efforts so a prioritized use of resources can be accomplished, focused on the most beneficial process changes. Cross-functional and cross-business unit cooperation is generally low in this level.

In Level II, the sophistication rises and an official sponsor is appointed to lead the process enhancements that create *internal excellence.* The sponsor and the chief information officer align to induce

Levels ⟶

	Sourcing and Logistics I	Internal Excellence II	Network Construction III	Industry Leadership IV
Driver	VP – Sourcing (under pressure), et al.	CIO supply chain leader	Business unit leaders	Management team
Benefits	Leveraged savings; FTE reduction	Prioritized improvements across network	Best partner performance	Network advantage; profitable revenue
Focus	Inventory: project logistics; freight: order fulfillment	Process redesign; systems improvement	Forecasting: planning: cust. services: interenterprise	Consumer: network
Tools	Teaming: functional excellence	Benchmarks; best practice; activity-based costing	Metrics; database mining; electronic commerce	Intranet: internet; virtual information systems
Action Area	Midlevel organization	Expanded levels	Total organization	Full enterprise
Guidance	Cost data: success funding	Process mapping	Advanced cost models; differentiating processes	Demand/supply linkage
Reach	Major cost (local) categories	Business unit	Enterprise	Global interface
Model	None ☐ - ☐ - ☐ - ☐	Supply chain – Intraenterprise	Interenterprise	Global market
Alliances	Supplier consolidation	Best partner	Partial alliances	Joint ventures
Training	Team	Leadership	Partnering	Holistic processing
	Internal		External	

EXHIBIT 1.4   Levels of Supply Chain Optimization

cross-functional cooperation and build a total prioritized list of potential improvements that spans the organization. Functional separation is banished in this level as cross-department and cross-business unit teams are sent off in pursuit of these improvements, combining the effort with existing initiatives that carry over from the previous stages. The seeds of e-commerce are planted in this level, as the firms begin in earnest to build point solutions and the internal information support system—the intranet—that enables further supply chain progress.

It is essential that a company complete Level II before it can proceed to the first stage of e–supply chain. Savings can be significant as a company completes this level. Our research shows savings typically of 8 to 10 percent in purchasing, another 8 to 10 percent in logistics, while inventory will decrease by 25 to 30 percent without hurting fill rates or on-time deliveries. The leaders surpass these percentages.

Unfortunately, most firms eventually hit a wall that inhibits further progress with supply chain—the wall that separates the internal from the external environment. Crossing that barrier has stymied many firms as they insist on continuing to focus on current, static business models and further internal excellence, even if it improves products and services that are in reduced demand in the marketplace. Firms with a high Level II orientation also continue to seek capital funds to improve operations that may add little value in the eyes of the consumer. When a product has reached the point where costs are close to optimum and the consumer has shown satisfaction with performance, more progress can be made when the firm turns its attention to building further enhancements that get those products to the intended consumers. A better orientation moves to a dynamic business model and balancing internal improvement with the external needs of the full supply chain network.

Only with strong senior management endorsement does a firm vault over the cultural wall and move to an external environment in which supply chain improvement and e-commerce applications really blossom. As external resources are added to internal teams seeking network improvement, the potential benefits escalate. The network's purpose now truly emerges: the satisfaction of the ultimate consumer. With new, profitable revenues being created, all members of the network benefit. With direct input from business customers and consumers, the information systems can be designed so the supply chain makes the necessary transition from a "push" toward the consumer, to a condition in which the consumer is "pulling" the product via actual demand.

Our experiences clearly show that only about 10 percent of businesses pursuing SCO have made it to Level III and beyond. In fact, so few organizations have moved their network to Level IV that many industries have no representative. The opportunity is to be the first value chain constellation in that level and thereby dominate an industry. Pharmaceutical and medical, banking, consumer goods in general, food and beverage, construction, and industrial equipment are examples of industries still trying to move out of an internal-only type of orientation and progress to Levels III and IV.

Several ingredients enable a nucleus firm to take a first mover position into these advanced levels. They begin with a dedication to apply SCO as a concept across organizations, accepting the need to combine resources with other constituents. With a network focus up and down the supply chain and partners interested in the same industry-dominant position, progress toward and through the advanced levels becomes possible. Application of e-commerce features across the breadth of that network will become the key enabler, as we now add a fifth level to the evolution we described in Exhibit 1.4.

A FRAMEWORK TO GUIDE UNDERSTANDING

Exhibit 1.5 is a framework that will be used throughout this book. It describes how a company moves its supply chain effort to a position in which e-commerce characteristics are introduced, assimilated, and used to advantage as a full network communication system is created. It will also show how the supply chain network

Progression / Business Application	Level I/II Internal Supply Chain Optimization *Stage 0*	Level III Network Formation *Stage 1*	Level IV Value Chain Constellation *Stage 2*	Level IV+ Full Network Connectivity *Stage 3*
Information technology	Point solutions - - - - - - Inform	Linked intranets - - - - - - Interact	Internet-based extranet - - - - - - Transact	Full network communication system - - - - - - Deliver
Design, development product/service introduction	Internal only	Selected external assistance	Collaborative design – enterprise integration and PIM	Business functional view – joint design and development
Purchase, procurement, sourcing	Leverage business unit volume	Leverage full network through aggregation	Key supplier assistance, web-based sourcing	Network sourcing through best constituent
Marketing, sales, customer service	Internally developed programs, promotions	Customer-focused, data-based initiatives	Collaborative development for focused consumer base	Consumer response system across the value chain
Engineering, planning, scheduling, manufacturing*	MRP MRPII DRP	ERP – internal connectivity	Collaborative network planning – best asset utilization	Full network business system optimization
Logistics**	Manufacturing push – inventory intensive	Pull system through internal/external providers	Best constituent provider – dual channel	Total network, dual-channel optimization
Customer care*	Customer service reaction	Focused service – call centers	Segmented response system, customer relationship management	Matched care – customer care automation
Human resources	Internal supply chain training	Provide network resources, training	Interenterprise resource utilization	Full network alignment and capability provision

*Includes order management.
**Includes inventory management.

EXHIBIT 1.5   E-business Development Framework

constituents get into a position to establish a functioning e-business model.

In the exhibit, we set the accomplishment of Levels I and II of the supply chain evolution as the starting position, the foundation for developing a collaborative e–supply chain effort and advancing to full network connectivity. That means a firm has to finish the first two levels, the internal portion, of the supply chain evolution before embarking on the e-commerce journey. The firm or business unit completing Levels I and II, because of the ongoing efforts to improve internal excellence, will be approaching internal optimization. A basic understanding and use of electronic communication for internal purposes will be in place through a functioning intranet. With better supply chain practices in place and internal cooperation at new high levels, the firm is in a position to begin an excursion into use of the Internet in combination with advanced supply chain techniques.

Along the vertical axis of the exhibit are the various business processes that will be impacted by the impending force of e-commerce activities. Each of these functions will be discussed in detail in separate chapters as we follow the framework to its logical conclusion. As each function is considered, we'll repeat the horizontal slice from the framework as a guide to progress from the Level I/II position to the most advanced, Level V capability. From the starting position in each function, the firm progresses through a three-level e-commerce evolution outlined on the horizontal axis. In essence, we are matching the final three levels of an advanced supply chain effort with the application of e-commerce to create what becomes an e–supply chain effort. The convergence of both efforts leads to the e-business models that will help a firm and its partners dominate an industry.

In Level III of the framework, the application of advanced supply chain management techniques is used to create the electronic network that will vie for the desired business customers and final consumers. In Level IV, the value chain constellation appears as network members begin sharing resources and utilizing joint assets to enhance the network. In Level V, full network connectivity is achieved as use of the Internet is pervasive and the network is prepared to do business in a digital economy. As mentioned, this is a position currently occupied by very few organizations. Across the e-commerce evolution, the use and application of the Internet increases as the linked constituents build together the extranet of communication so vital to success. As each business process is considered, we'll explain how the function and applications progress from a foundation position through each of the final three electronic levels.

Before proceeding, let's consider a firm that has moved beyond a Level II supply chain position by partnering with key constituents within its supply chain and applying Internet features to improve performance and delivery to its customers. Adaptec, Inc., clearly illustrates how to exploit an opportunity with the help of supply chain partners. This $700 million United States–based manufacturer (Milpitas, California) makes sophisticated computer subsystems, such as input-output (I/O) boards, to transfer information flowing through a PC from the hard drive. Central to these boards are application-specific, integrated circuits (ASIC) that embed proprietary software on silicon chips. Operating in a very competitive environment, the company is challenged by constant price pressures, rapid changes in the markets it supplies, and accelerating changes in the sophisticated components needed for its products. Adaptec met these challenges through the creation of a virtual factory and an Internet-based communication system, in partnership with Taiwan Semiconductor Manufacturing Corp. (TSMC), which makes the silicon wafer containing the chips. Their arrangement takes advantage of SCO and Web capabilities as illustrated in Exhibit 1.6.

Dolores Marciel, vice president of materials management, took an early step in the process when she began treating a select group of suppliers as partners. Using new computer software supplied by Extricity and the Internet, engineers from Adaptec and TSMC worked together electronically to design and integrate new components by combining their e-commerce intranets. Before the process

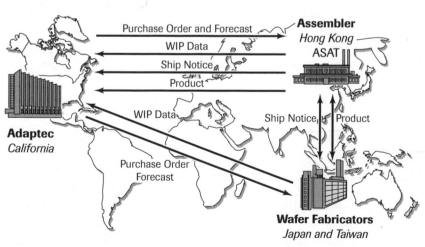

EXHIBIT 1.6 Adaptec's Virtual Company

improvements, at each stage in the supply chain, information was entered manually, most into different computer systems. Adaptec was using an SAP enterprise resource planning system, while TSMC's system was largely homemade. Moving all the necessary information through the interenterprise system via the Internet became the obvious solution.

By connecting their computer-aided manufacturing and design systems, the two firms were able to dramatically speed the data interchange and shrink typical cycle times. Orders and information now move over the Web with drawings attached. This linking of internal computers, using the Internet as the mode of connection, speeds the development process and provides the means to gain an advantage for Adaptec in its market. TSMC's manufacturing capability is made available direct to Adaptec product developers immediately, reducing the "art-to-part" cycle by as much as 50 percent. This improvement gives Adaptec a strategic advantage in development and introduction time and the cost of supplying its computer subsystems from a virtual factory across the Pacific.

Production of the Adaptec board starts at TSMC's plant in Hsin-Chu, Taiwan, moves to an assembler in Hong Kong or South Korea for chip packaging, and ends at an Adaptec plant in Singapore. There, the I/O boards are assembled and shipped—half to the United States and half to other countries. Other parts are shipped from Japan to the assembler or to Adaptec in California. With their new systems, the partners can track any of the inventory or semifinished product online in real time.

Starting with a delivery cycle of 110 days, the organizations worked collaboratively to apply optimization techniques (internal best practices) to their connected supply chain to reduce that time dramatically. By seamlessly integrating information flows critical to the process steps, the linked firms were able to reduce the cycle to fifty-five days, with a reduction of work-in-process inventory of 50 percent. Their experience points the way to the next evolution in partnering within supply chains—an external connectivity made possible through the use of the Internet.

As firms in Levels III and IV of the supply chain develop a dedication to use external resources, business alliances begin to form—directed by advanced supply chain management (ASCM) concepts (detailed in later chapters). These concepts effectively use joint resources to optimize the use of mutual assets, build profitable new revenues together, reduce costs to a feasible minimum, and surpass consumer expectations. Central to this realization is that ASCM cannot be accomplished without a communication system so far superior to competing networks that the e–supply chain system is the key mark of distinction that separates the network in the eyes of the consumer.

THE VITAL TECHNOLOGY CONNECTION

From automobiles and food products to pharmaceuticals and patient care, supply chain performance is the current business frontier, and firms are actively seeking the means to optimize the processes across their supply chain network. As progress has been made through a series of evolutionary stages, advanced technology and communication systems have emerged as the enabling features of the leading networks. Latent values were discovered through the mining of data (on sales, inventories, customer buying patterns, deliveries, etc.) that existed between organizations that would not normally share information valuable to defining customer and consumer needs and trends. Companies that have shared this vital data are forging ahead of those competitors still mired in the distrust of normal business relations.

Heineken USA offers a good example of this kind of progress. The situation for this importer of the well-known Dutch beer involved a complication with extended order cycle time and poor downstream communication. The old system used the traditional supply-side focus in which the Dutch factory sent beer to U.S. warehouses based on incoming orders. As much as sixty-five days of inventory were kept in the system because of the absence of more accurate data on how much was being consumed. The products were transferred from the warehouses to distributors who delivered the products to the customers. This practice left Heineken disconnected from the field knowledge of what happened to the beer after distribution. Furthermore, the cycle time was so long from manufacture of the beer until customer delivery, concern arose about the product's freshness and shelf life (White 1999).

The company decided in May 1996 to focus on the entire supply chain and began working with 450 distributors in the United States to improve the processes. Heineken had installed an enterprise resource planning (ERP) system in Europe (SAP R/3) and did have a functioning internal intranet. The first step was to work with representatives from the distributor base to determine how information transfer could be improved. With the help of a software provider and a lot of interactive discussions between the partners in the supply chain, an e-commerce pilot was started in September 1996, based on the downstream recommendations.

Heineken beer distributors, working with improved forecasting techniques, feed in actual depletion figures and replenishment orders through their now-linked Web pages. This interactive planning system then generates time-phased orders based on actual pull-through consumption, not anticipated demand. Distributors are able to modify plans based on local conditions or marketing changes. These adjusted plans are available on a real-time basis to the European brewery, which adjusts brewing and supply schedules accordingly. To complete the linkage between distributor and customer, the pilot involved five key customers who helped finish the supply chain linkage (White 1999).

The result is the development of a world-class extranet of communication, an Internet-based e-commerce system in which the distributors, Heineken USA and the Holland-based parent, are connected together and delivery is directly linked to customer demand. A unique feature is the self-regulating order planning that adjusts for inventory variance due to forecast error. Manual procedures were replaced with automatic processes, saving time and effort. Results included a more than 50 percent reduction in order cycle time, from twelve to five weeks; inventory was reduced from sixty-five days to forty, assuring fresher product in the stores; and the sales force was able to spend more time on trade cultivation, all the way to working with Heineken customers' sales representatives. *Information Week* magazine recognized the firm's achievement with its 1997 award for "innovative internet-based electronic commerce" (White 1999).

A mark of business change in the last half of the 1990s is how a few industry leaders transformed their focus from an exclusively internal excellence drive to looking at supply chain network structure. Within that structure, these leaders found the means to join independent companies into a value chain constellation to bring products and services to market more effectively than any competing network. Given all the competitive pressures that exert a downward force on profits, this combining of mutual resources for mutual benefit looms as a means of offsetting those pressures. It has become imperative for constituents of a supply chain system to explore the possibilities of further integrating their intercompany activities. E–supply chain, through full network connectivity, is the adhesive that will bind this cooperation together and lead to the coveted market advantage.

Future success no longer belongs to a single firm, no matter how massive or on what scale of global operations it functions. The future belongs to the networks of supply, of which those large firms are just one constituent. E–supply chain will be the approach that binds the constituents together and connects the value chain constellation to the designated end consumers. It is the model of success for the future. In the following chapters, we will elaborate on and bring alive this strategy through case studies and action initiatives taken by those companies jumping ahead of others just beginning to apply supply chain to their improvement efforts.

2

The Connection with Business Strategy

[handwritten:] Oper 564

Several perspectives must be accepted before embarking on a journey to connect electronic commerce and supply chain to a successful business strategy. First, the support people currently laboring in the "back offices" of the business world (behind the customer facing area, in nondirect support functions) will be critical to winning the future battle for dominance with e-commerce. These people, particularly those in information technology and systems, will have to step forward and take a place alongside those who create business strategy and infuse the technology ideas demanded of a new business orientation. Second, a company must understand the need is not for an e-commerce strategy to be added to the business plan; rather, a totally new e-business strategy is called for. Third, the Internet is going to transform business roles in virtually every function. As companies apply their new strategies, their people have to adopt these changed roles in spirit and action. Fourth, sharing information and business intent with key partners across a supply chain network is necessary before a firm is ready to cope with the current business-to-business-to-consumer commerce explosion.

THREE THEMES TO SET THE COURSE

With these perspectives as a guide, we will highlight three themes in describing the preparation and execution of e–supply chain. The first is that the future belongs to the business network (of which large multinational organizations might be one part) that satisfies specific consumer demands through a seamless (fully connected end-to-end) supply chain that establishes a sense of customization for those consumers. Within a few years, these "e-networks" will appear and begin to dominate industries. The alliance among Cisco, Ford Motor Company, and Oracle is one such e-network that is moving quickly in the automotive industry. Through their collective Internet exchange site, AutoXchange, this three-part network plans to handle Ford's $300 billion automotive supply chain with suppliers, dealers, and consumers. We will detail this arrangement and other automobile exchanges later in the book.

As the constituents of these networks come together, begin to share mutual resources for jointly beneficial initiatives, and collaboratively plan process improvements that enhance the deliverables to designated markets, the network can move to the third and fourth levels of supply chain progression. In these levels, market and channel strategies will change, reflecting the increased importance of segmentation and customization. Traditional business models will be replaced with new, dual-channel, Internet-enabled models as the network coalesces into a value chain constellation of suppliers, manufacturers, producers, distributors, and key customers, all jointly focused on the consumer segment of choice.

The second theme is a corollary to the first—the constituents' market value can be dramatically enhanced by jointly creating profitable revenue growth through integrated interenterprise solutions and responses. As the value chain constellation collaboratively develops business plans, they must have a central objective beyond satisfying the designated consumer base, an objective that rewards the owners of the constituent businesses. That superordinate purpose or compelling reason for the network alliances is to increase the market value of the member organizations via the consumer-centric supply network.

In the emerging global business environment, e-commerce is not just a tool of implementation, nor is it a minor part of business strategy. It has to be a centerpiece of business strategy. The third theme is that the value chain constellation and each of its constituent organizations will achieve the purposes and goals of the network by being supported with leading-edge technology, particularly electronic commerce. The use of Internet connections within a supply chain is an inevitable action as digital commerce is destined to be the medium of communication that binds the constituents together and connects the value chain constellation to the designated end consumers.

The number of success stories validating this contention grows at an amazing rate; a few illustrate our position. Cisco Systems is the world's largest e-commerce merchant, doing more than 80 percent of its sales over the Internet. This $12 billion firm, providing the connective systems that enable Internet communication, has used the strategy we'll describe to vault itself into the top echelon of *Fortune's* 500 in a matter of a few years. Cisco reported in November 1999 that the company was selling more than $37 million in products every day via the Internet.

Cisco's distinction is commendable, but it may be fleeting. Dell Computer has designs to sell more than $50 million per day over the Internet. This $20 billion Dell computer is the world's largest direct-selling PC company. As the firm has moved from its familiar 1-800-Buy-Dell number to a Web presence, it now logs over 40 percent of its business from the Internet. This firm is constantly in the business news as an example of the new strategy at work. In November 1999, it announced the company had reached $30 million per day in worldwide Internet revenues, with plans to reach $50 million in 2000.

Companies such as General Electric expect to save $500 million buying through the Web. Wells Fargo adds twenty thousand new electronic accounts per month. Frito-Lay knows by rack by store how much of each stock keeping unit (SKU) has been sold each day.

E–supply chain, a term we are using for the natural combining of supply chain and e-commerce, is the tsunami of change that will wash away the old models and transform business activity. It will be pervasive in those businesses that dominate markets and industries in the next decade. It will be at the heart of how to communicate, develop successful products and services desired by the consumers, improve process efficiency, and sustain low inventories with high fill rates and no returns. It will be the technique that greatly enhances the effectiveness of just-in-time (JIT) manufacturing practices. It will be the means that most positively impacts sales promotions and pricing, effectively sources materials and supplies, creates the most profitable demand (often in nontraditional areas), and uses assets most wisely across the network. Finally, it will be the means by which the value chain constellation firmly establishes market dominance.

These themes lead to one overwhelming conclusion: e–supply chain must be an integral part of any business strategy intended to take an organization forward in the next ten years. Moreover, this linkage with strategy has to evolve from advanced supply chain management (ASCM) techniques. As the network partners share best practices, it moves forward, eventually to integrate strategies across the collective business plans of the constituents of the value chain constellation being developed. Success won't come from one firm's intentions. It will come from the collaborative actions of linked organizations pursuing a common strategy that ends in market and industry dominance and greater profitability for all constituents. Moreover, those actions will take advantage of technology, particularly the Internet, for the development of electronic or Web-based solutions, as well as improved physical solutions to supply chain management.

A MODEL TO GUIDE THE EFFORT

In the new millennium, e-commerce and the response to consumer demand will have two dimensions. As supply chain partners come together to define these dimensions for a particular market, they must develop their own specific model to guide their actions. Exhibit 2.1 is a general illustration of these dimensions, demonstrating how a physical channel of distribution will be coupled with one that responds through a cyber-based channel. It is not intended to be the type of detailed drawing that will be used by a value chain constellation.

The traditional, physical channel of response entails factories, offices, and warehouses full of semifinished or finished goods, legacy computer systems for handling transactions, and lots of distribution equipment. This channel will be characterized by high friction between the links in the supply chain until e-network efforts smooth out the interactions. It contains brick-and-mortar buildings and inventories at multiple sites, so it will be capital-intensive. Logistics will be a core competency as the constituents work out the most effective means to deliver products and services.

In contrast, the cyber channel lacks capital-intensive facilities but employs a wide array of computers, workstations, and servers, operating with collaboratively developed integrated software. This channel is characterized by low friction due to the limited number of participants and the fact that most information is transmitted electronically. This system is dynamic, requiring the players to stay on the forefront of technology. Using an electronic medium is an important factor to the buyer in this channel, as is efficient delivery of

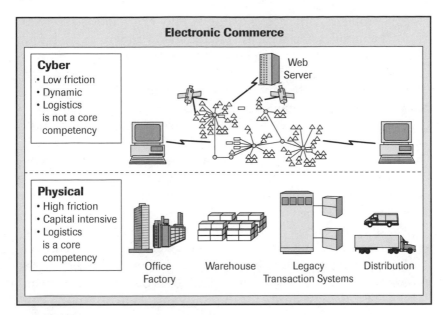

EXHIBIT 2.1   Two Distinct Dimensions of e-Commerce,
Cyber and Physical

the products ordered. Although the exhibit indicates logistics is not
a core competency in the sense that physical assets are not directly
involved in such a system, there is a logistics need to be satisfied.
Logistics remains a critical element, even when turned over to
third- and fourth-party companies, to assure the consumer gets
what is needed at the time of need. Efficient data handling and response to consumer choice are the unseen elements of this channel.

The changes implicit in this dual-channel model bring forth
challenges and new opportunities for the strategy planners. The
model provides an opportunity to redefine market assumptions,
value propositions, and delivery systems. New roles for all functions and constituents may be adopted. It is a time to redefine the
level of ambition and combine the best practices across the network.
It certainly is a time to challenge conventional thinking. An entirely
new business model based on these redefined propositions should
emerge. Other opportunities arise to optimize the customer points
of contact, reduce the distance between key customers and suppliers, and reorient the thinking toward a response system, rather than
the traditional push inventory to the customer concept. In this way,
e-commerce, as a feature of supply chain, has both strategic and tactical advantages.

The problem with most existing supply chain models, regardless of the number of channels, is that the flow moves in the wrong direction. Advocates now generally agree that the proper flow in supply chain optimization has to originate with a pull from consumer demand and then move upstream in the linkage toward the producer and its suppliers, and possibly beyond to the supplier's suppliers. It's time to sequence the flow correctly and build a proper model that connects e–supply chain and business strategy. This model should start with the options available to today's consumers and progress through where and how those options will be satisfied. One track will be the traditional physical delivery system; the second will be the emerging cyber-based track.

For the purposes of those firms emerging from Level II and beginning the development of a focused Level III supply chain network, a model will be very beneficial, but it must be specific to the industry and practices each firm faces. We encourage readers to use Exhibit 2.1 only as a guide for their advanced efforts and to construct an actual model, with the help of supply chain partners, to match the needs of their markets with the capabilities of emerging alliances. In Chapter 9, we will illustrate a four-channel model for a consumer products network.

INITIATING THE CHAIN OF REACTIONS

Let's follow the model on its journey of fulfillment. Beginning at the proper starting point, the consumer will decide to make some form of purchase. That purchase could be affected by advertising, impulse, media promotion, a coupon clipped from a newspaper, or an incentive received through the mail. In the new environment, it could also be more spontaneous or initiated by browsing the Web. In any event, the model should show there are two tracks or channels of distribution through which the demand can be satisfied— physical or cyber based. Integrated supply chain networks can satisfy demand through one or both of these channels, but a different combination of specific assets and resources will be utilized for each channel, and members of the value chain constellation must work together to find the right combination and deployment of those resources.

Through the physical track will come the more traditional system of response. The consumer proceeds to a retail outlet to buy the product or service. Many choices are possible, as an array of waiting inventory, on display and in some back storage area, awaits the consumer entering the store. This inventory will be the result of the typical push mentality that dictates moving products into the stores and hoping for sales. For years, that back area has been shrinking, but whatever remains is still a form of safety stock. In the future, this back area will be eliminated as firms move to the pull mentality using e-commerce features to link supply with actual demand into an e-network, with stocks far more in tune with consumption and replenishment based on online data.

Networks will focus on specific consumers while trying to optimize the use of collective assets and resources. When stores are reconfigured to meet the needs of these consumers, they will become a collection of segmented areas offering the precise products and services the designated consumers are seeking. Extra space with extra inventories that do not have a sufficient turnover will be minimized or eliminated. Superstores offer an ever-widening range of products and the chance for one-stop shopping, but as the networks become adept at gaining consumer loyalty in many of their focused areas, these large mega–shopping arenas will fall victim to the specialized offerings of the focused outlets.

As a portion of orders are drawn away from these physical stores by the growing number of consumers favoring the cyber channel, those who will order over the Web, the second channel blossoms. Early indications show the dominant Web users contain large percentages of the younger generation, dual-income families wanting to minimize time away from home, and older folks (who seem to like to buy for their grandchildren). As other Web buyers join these groups, the physical store is at risk to lose as much as one-third of current traffic and sales. This percentage is based on a reasonable five-year projection of the current growth rate of Web-based buying versus total consumption.

The advantage of the physical track is that the buyer takes the purchase home directly after the buy and has experienced a social event that might have some appeal. The store experience will not disappear for those who want to get out and see the array of inventory from which they can choose, try or try on what might be bought, and receive a feeling of freshness as when selecting produce in a grocery store. A Home Depot outlet may lure a consumer to its physical store because of the vast array of products available and the friendly service and advice of its skilled sales personnel. Another consumer may look for what is needed in a less confusing area by studying a virtual experience on the computer (or, in the near term, over the family television set), where he does not have to drive to the store and goes more directly to the sector of choice. The need for a large store is lessened. He can buy the products he wants, have them delivered to his house, and still receive the same friendly service over the Internet through a virtual experience.

With virtual reality a common experience now, the buying process can be made to simulate an actual store experience or be embellished with music, cartoons, animation, celebrity interface, and so forth. The difference is there is no need to spend the time and transportation cost to go to the store; engage a salesperson, if you can find one (and who may also intimidate the buyer); and wait for the purchase to be handled. With this cyber system, you must wait for delivery of the purchase, but that time continues to diminish and will eventually be a matter of hours in the best-designed e-networks. For those consumers who cherish the time available for family, this feature will become an inducement to choose the cyber track.

For an example of the cyber features, consider the case of Land's End and that company's response to one specific need within one targeted consumer group. Land's End found that some female consumers don't want to buy beachwear they can't try on. Responding to this need, the firm created a Web site called "Swimsuit Finder." Through this Internet interaction, the consumer can pick her body type and view suits likely to fit (see Exhibit 2.2). A "personal model," through virtual reality, helps the consumer size the suit, based on general measurements fed into the system. The result of this innovative approach to one particular consumer good was first-year sales of $61 million.

THE NEED TO ADAPT FOR DIFFERING CONSUMERS

We are considering two distinctly different types of buyers using two channels of response. Surely, overlap by consumers will result as they choose one or the other track, depending on the category of purchase, but one consumer group is changing preferences much faster than the other. The group attracted to the cyber track is growing geometrically and will continue to do so until parity is reached (perhaps in five years), when we predict the balance will be a 67/33 equilibrium between physical and cyber buying. We base this ratio on an extension of data supplied by Forrester, International Data Corporation (IDC),

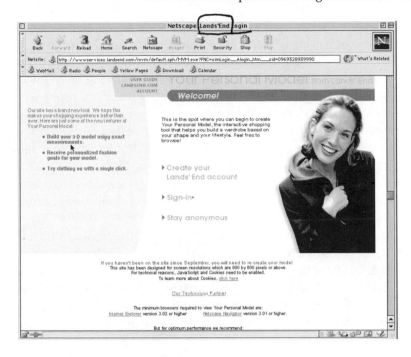

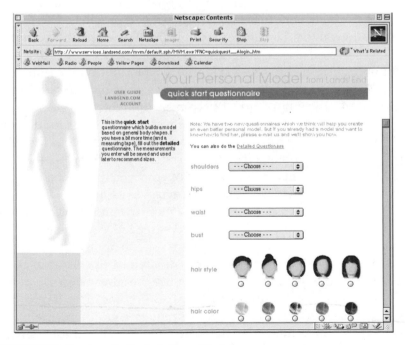

EXHIBIT 2.2   Land's End: A New Model

and the Gartner Group. Using their figures and projections for the percentage of business that will be conducted over the Internet, we developed best-case and worst-case scenarios to get a range for the eventual ratio. The ratio is for all business and will vary by industry.

Regardless of the exact ratio, undeniably there are times when virtually all shoppers want to get out and go to a physical store. There can also be no denying that an army of young and old buyers is emerging as consumers, and this army is hooked on using the computer (or at least a screen and some form of data entry) as the best means of acquiring what they need. Our view coalesces when there is a one-third/two-third balance between Web-based buying and traditional in-store shopping.

As we continue the satisfaction of the buy upstream in the supply chain, we move into the realm of business-to-business communications and see that there is a major divergence for those who are designing today's and tomorrow's supply chain networks. The e-networks being constructed have to be geared for both tracks, or they miss a potential one-third of future consumption. The physical track is steeped in tradition, but it must be modernized and has to settle the issue of how much of the products will be taken to the designated consumer by distributors. Since consumer satisfaction requires the e-network to bring the full array of products demanded by those consumers, sometimes small lots will have to be accommodated. There will also be geographic locations better suited to a distributor accustomed to breaking large loads into small shipments. As the lot size of the deliveries approaches one unit, the need for a new type of distributor-shipper becomes apparent.

Where some form of distribution is required, to take products either to the retail store from a distribution center or directly to the consumer, the next step involves transportation. In either case, there is outbound freight. This track now has inventory in the front and back of the store, in transit in the trailer, and in residence at the distribution center. The physical track clearly will be more inventory-intensive, requiring close coordination of demand satisfaction with supply in order for the network to come anywhere close to optimization.

On the cyber track, the Web has transferred the order back to the manufacturer who may or may not use the customer's stores for delivery. Most likely, the fulfillment will come directly to the buyer's house. In the case of high-technology equipment, there is a tendency to have the order delivered from an assembly center where a minimum quantity of component parts have been kept awaiting the final order so a customized product can be assembled

package delivery services

and shipped on short notice. In this case, the amount of inventory is truly minimized and approaches optimization as the need for semi-finished product is limited to the amount of lead time from order to shipment. The need for a fleet of trailers moving products from a large distribution center is changed to smaller vans, probably owned by a third-party transportation partner or express carrier. In many cases, the product will be taken from a manufacturing line or a packaging center with minimum stocks, packaged for local delivery, and sent on its way to the consumer.

Future storage facilities must be arranged to accommodate the 67 percent of finished goods that will continue to flow through normal retail outlets and the 33 percent that will go directly to the consumer (or whatever percentage emerges in a particular industry or market segment). The former storage will require bricks and mortar in the form of large, but now very centralized, warehouses and distribution centers, maintaining delivery to a geographic sector. Many SKUs will still be in residence in these locations, but the size of the inventories will be better matched with actual consumption data. In the latter situation, some inventory will be kept in the assembly and packaging facilities where final orders will be put together or kits will be made and sent directly to the consumer. The crucial point is that this is where the e-network takes a serious look at total assets devoted to inventory, final assembly, packaging, storage, and delivery. There is simply too much redundancy not to rationalize this area from a network and alliance perspective so use of total assets is optimized.

The physical track will continue to deliver two-thirds of the product flow but have far more physical handling, require more facilities and capital assets, and will still be measured in terms of months or weeks from start to finish. Some product will always languish in the stores and require a return shipment or simply accumulate more carrying cost until the inevitable below-cost sale that moves it away from the store. The cyber track will deliver the other third of the product flow but will function with minimum inventories, physical assets, and human handling. Carrying costs will be considerably less as the amount of supporting inventory will be dramatically lower.

CUSTOMIZATION VIA CONSUMER-SPECIFIC INFORMATION

Continuing the flow of orders to the upstream side of the supply chain, the physical track will move replenishment orders to the manufacturer and beyond. Some orders from the cyber channel may also go to these locations. In the e-network, the future solution will match standardization with customization. That means standard components will be available for shipping what the consumer perceives to be nondifferentiated products. It also means the most competent constituent, anywhere in the supply chain, will be performing the production process steps because of its better practices or lower cost. The network will diversify the process elements to enable assembly of finished goods matched with the orders, with customized features added to uniquely differentiate what comes out of the network in the eyes of the consumer. In the future, the shipping site could contain several firms in the network working together to fulfill orders.

The automobile industry offers an example of this transition. Cars are already coming from factories where external companies are on site doing the painting, supplying the maintenance and repair parts, and assembling some of the components. In Brazil, Volkswagen has its "Plant X" where suppliers are doing over half of the assembly. Our future view of a value chain constellation has the best partner doing the work required for total delivery of the finished products, possibly in jointly owned facilities.

To complete the chain, orders will be sent to suppliers so the necessary raw materials or subassemblies can be received in time for efficient completion of the orders. This supply base in the future will have to be inexorably linked directly to what is being consumed at the most downstream point in the chain so only the right amount of the right materials and supplies are sent forward. Waste and returns have to approach zero levels. Only through online use of a computer-to-computer extranet can such connectivity and accurate information transfer be established. In the cyber track, some suppliers could be directly filling orders for parts or components.

In the new format, variability is not an enemy to rigid schedules and seemingly optimized manufacturing processes. Rather, it becomes an opportunity to take advantage of changes in consumer demand. The secret will be the innovative use of automated technology and the Internet to make the process steps effective and efficient. As new generations appear, the variability that their changing demands create will not stymie supply chain networks. The integrated value chain constellation will quickly initiate the mechanisms for shifting productive processes to rapidly meet those demands before any other supply chain.

Long-term differentiation will be based on the network's ability to craft unique relationships with customers and consumers by agilely configuring tailored products and services that respond to actual demand. The transition from rigid to flexible response supply chains will be linked to e–supply chain systems that change from private, message-based architecture to network service-based architecture, from a data orientation to a process improvement orientation.

Overall, this two-track system will require a consumer-centric focus and attention so the designated consumer gets exactly what is wanted in the most convenient and rewarding manner possible. Implementation will require application of information technology to the consumer-to-business linkage as well as the business-to-business connections that make supply feasible. The extranet—an instant, platform-independent communication system among constituents—will be indispensable as the means by which all of the partners stay in touch with each other and through which tracking and expediting is accomplished. Features will include minimum network inventories, transportation costs, and fixed assets.

In addition, maximum consumer satisfaction and profitable new revenues for network constituents will be achieved. The cash-to-cash cycle (from cash outlay for raw materials to receipt of payment for finished goods consumption) will be the most rapid in the industry. Accurate predictions of what is needed where and when will replace speculation based on spurious forecasts because the network members are online, end-to-end with the swiftest speed to market of successful products and services.

Pericom Semiconductor is a firm intent on pursuing this type of future advantage. This San Jose, California, producer worked with J D Edwards to develop SCOREx, a supply chain software suite that will forecast chip demand and plan warehousing and distribution to PC manufacturers, including IBM and Compaq. First, e-mail orders from consumers come to Pericom. In the next step, manual entry is used to move these orders into manufacturing and on to order processing. The new and improved system has orders being piped directly into the manufacturing system via the Web (*Info World*, November 9, 1998, p. 78).

STRATEGY FORMATION CAN BEGIN WITH A NUCLEUS ORGANIZATION

The model to be developed by the eventual e-network members should contain two supply chain tracks for two types of consumer patterns. Because of our previous history, we now recommend the building of the desired supply chain network and eventual value chain constellation should begin with a nucleus company assuming a central role. The reason is a lesson in business relationship dynamics.

Throughout our experiences with building supply chain networks, we have encountered a serious problem selling the idea of using mutual resources for mutual benefit. As simple as that concept may seem, it has been a very difficult undertaking to get firms to trust any of their supply chain partners enough to share what they think is valuable internal information or data on best internal practices. When we clearly indicated that there were better external practices that a supplier, distributor, or customer could share with a manufacturer, for example, we were met with disbelief. They protested first that other organizations could not have exceeded their capabilities. Next, they told us that even if such conditions did exist, we would have to secure the better-practice information without the provision of equal sharing to the external company. When we explained that the concept of supply chain optimization requires finding best practices across a full network, the response was "We'll get there by extracting what better information we can, not by sharing our valuable insights." With that attitude more prevalent than not, we now prefer to position a nucleus company at the center of the network construction phase of the progression. This company should be capable of rallying supporters and driving full implementation beyond the preoccupation with improving internal excellence.

As firms come together to develop a mutual supply chain strategy, the effort will have the best chance of success when it is facilitated by such a nucleus company, probably a firm that has the largest scale or most recognized brand equity. This company would have the strongest position with the consumer and would probably be the most able to coordinate and direct the effort. A desire to construct an ASCM strategy that forces the new thinking and process innovations, with an extranet architecture supporting the network's uniqueness and matching it with continually changing consumer patterns and relationships, must be in place in this nucleus unit. Names such as Du Pont, Kraft Foods, Hewlett-Packard, Colgate-Palmolive, Wal-Mart, Procter & Gamble, Sara Lee, Tesco, General Electric, Unilever, and General Motors come quickly to mind as candidates for taking such a nucleus position.

The nucleus company invites a few key players from each appropriate constituent of the network to create an interenterprise team to initiate the collaboration by discussing such topics as the consumer, business customers, competition, and supply. The goal is to conduct a situation assessment and decide how to build a unified force to dominate particular market segments and consumers. The team analyzes demand, supply, competition, and enabling systems and works to agree on innovative features that will differentiate the network in the targeted market. It then progresses to defining the necessary implementations. That means building a joint plan for combining the best practices across the full network, practices that have led the constituents to higher levels of supply chain progress, particularly in the area of electronic communication. These practices and unifying plan come together into a series of strategic imperatives. An effective e-business model will be one of the final results.

With a strategic road map formed, the group then moves to suggesting integrated solutions to senior management. These solutions must be specific as to

- the differentiating processes that will be developed across the full network,
- the architecture for the enabling e–supply chain features,
- the sharing of physical assets,
- the use of mutual resources, and
- the people necessary for executing the most important changes.

Exhibit 2.3 details an outline for a team to follow in this next step of progression. This chart shows a supplier and customer in collaboration, which could be appropriate for a first attempt at network construction. The model can then be expanded to include a

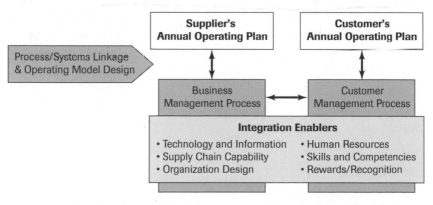

EXHIBIT 2.3 Teams Creating an Integrated, Process-Driven Operating Model

distributor and a manufacturer. In any event, a nucleus firm will initiate the process.

With the direction defined and agreement reached on how to apply resources, the group then moves to redesigning the processes and systems that link the constituents and introducing the elements of flexible customization that will bring the consumers the perception of personalization. (The elements of this redesign and customization will be discussed in succeeding chapters.) The end result is the desired unified strategy that binds the constituent companies together and an e-business model that makes sense for all participants.

The difference with this type of strategy development will be the global supply chain architecture that emerges and the application of best practices from many perspectives. The planning environment will include the total network, resulting in an irresistible distribution system for the targeted consumer base. Cycle times will become as critical as costs, so excess in-transit and storage inventories are not carried. International trade factors must be considered—duty, drawback, taxes, licensing, quotas, currency, and so forth. Multiple transportation modes can be feasible—ships, airplanes, trucks (full and partial), railroads, barges, and the like. The goal will be to achieve a consumer-driven global logistics network.

A radical information technology philosophy focused on managing visibility, speed, and flexibility across the interenterprise network will be necessary. Designs will be tested with various market groups. The concept of extended supply chains will emerge as a portfolio of assets, specially configured for the designated consumer base.

ASCM strategies have to move on a par with finance and marketing or, at the very least, become fused with both. Such a fusion leads to realistic target setting, resource allocation, and future time frames. Gaining this parity will be another obstacle to overcome. In summary, a pilot driven by a nucleus company is the best way to prove the validity of the concepts, build a collaborative model for the designated consumers of choice, integrate the information systems, and gain the executive support to achieve parity with financial expectations.

SUMMARY

E–supply chain is a natural enhancement for developing supply chain efforts. Without the accurate information transfer and data synchronization necessary for effective network construction and execution, existing systems will languish rather than blossom into a competitive advantage. ASCM and e-commerce come together to meet this need and establish the capability to move ahead on a variety of fronts crucial to future success. Enterprises that covet an advantaged position will apply Web-based extranet technologies to build robust delivery networks. The challenge is to select the correct consumer markets or business customers and then build the value chain constellation that will satisfy those consumers and customers better than any competing network. E–supply chain will be the functioning heart of such a constellation.

3

Supply Chain and the Need for Enabling E-commerce

13 pages

A global battle for consumers is raging in today's business world. In a military sense, armies always try to occupy the high ground to support their positions in battle. In a business sense, the high ground is use of the Internet—to enhance the capabilities of the conventional, physical channel of supply chain and define the emerging cyber channel. The not-so-secret weaponry is giving selected business customers and consumers what they want, with a rapid speed of response, through the distribution channel of their choice.

The twenty-first century is certain to bring more of the same conditions—brutal competition for the consumer. For the next two years, electronic commerce will be a necessity to sustain a competitive position. After that, it will no longer be a tool of defense; it will be the way to conduct business and gain new revenues, physically and through cyber space. It will be the necessary link between businesses in a supply chain network and between the network and its chosen consumers. In that sense, the future conflict becomes a technical battle among the best systems and networks.

Let's be clear on the premise we're espousing. Failure to participate in the emerging digital economy may not spell the demise of existing businesses. Large branded companies, for example, will continue to make, sell, and deliver their products. Our projections, however, indicate that up to one-third of future revenues could be at risk by not participating in the digital aspects of business—the emerging digital economy. An individual company can place whatever percentages they believe are appropriate to the amount of sales that will continue to move through the physical channel. They would be well advised also to anticipate a significant percentage moving to the cyber channel and prepare for that eventuality.

Before we describe how to develop the correct approach, an important caveat is in order. Business executives who become sold on the potential of e-business applications to help their performance must be cautious not to be oversold on a well-packaged and -presented formula that does not enhance their chances to defend existing market positions and secure the desired new revenues. Jim Shepherd, senior vice president of AMR Research, explained this concern in very specific terms when he stated:

> *The notion that a company can transform itself into an e-business by simply buying a piece of software and adding it to its existing infrastructure is wrong and dangerous. Companies need to carefully assess the impact of new e-applications and Internet Commerce on the IT environment and the overall business. A true e-business facilitates accurate delivery promises, enables overnight order fulfillment, and allows real-time, self-service information, all of which require very tightly integrated business systems.* (SHEPHERD 1999, P. 1.3)

The requirements cited in Shepherd's quote are the elements of a supply chain system with network capability. His warning fits our contention that future e-businesses will only be as strong as the collective supply chain infrastructure supporting the business and the capabilities of that network's constituent members. These points will be especially drawn out in Chapter 8, when we consider the impact of logistics on supply chain and e-business.

E-COMMERCE AND THE WORLD WIDE WEB

The intranet, Internet, and extranet have been discussed as enabling tools in the emerging digital economy. These three communication systems and most of the use of information technology are finding a way onto the public information highway, the World Wide Web (WWW). One message is clear: the nucleus firm (at the center of the developing network) and its allies that become the first e-commerce network in a market gain the high ground and the lion's share of that market. Dislodging those leaders becomes considerably harder than taking the high ground in the first place. So the imperative becomes to embrace what has become the global communication system and use it as quickly as possible.

Stories are pouring in about those in the vanguard of the change, but just a couple will help set the stage for our analysis of why the Internet is so important. MicroAge Inc. offers one example. This personal computer distributor realized that using the Web would make it easier for resellers of its equipment to bypass traditional distribution channels in its supply chain and get products to market faster. So the firm started transforming its business model in 1995 and became less of a manufacturer and more of a service company.

The idea was to help other companies looking for online installation and training services get to their solutions faster with more accuracy. Solutions become a key element in the value propositions offered by the new e-businesses. Using the Internet as the medium of communication, MicroAge put its inventory online in what is now called a "glass pipeline" for direct observation by its resellers. The firm went further, now offering data on rival inventories, as well as those in its network, to give browsers a full view of what can be found in stock. It then moves the desired products quickly through its delivery system to get the products to the point of need in shorter cycle times and with less safety stock. MicroAge has employed the Internet to protect its supply chain role and build a cadre of loyal consumers for the future.

Buy.com is an Aliso Viejo, California, reseller of computers and other products, bringing use of the Web to a traditional business purpose but with a significant twist. This firm uses the Web to sell equipment, admittedly below cost, in a drive to acquire a new consumer base. This is another technique often employed by the new entrepreneurs who worry more about building scale of operations before making a profit. Moving beyond the conventional model of selling its products through physical stores, such as Best Buy and Circuit City, Buy.com put availability of its products online. As a first mover in this aspect of Web-based selling, they are establishing contact and position with the desired consumer group, cyber buyers of computer products. In the words of a *Fortune* analyst, "Buy.com aims to build a large base of loyal customers who will return again and again to its Web site to buy products. The goods themselves become the bait. The profits will come from the sale of advertising and ancillary services like warranties and equipment leases" (Blum 1999, p. 120). This can be a successful game plan for a new e-based entrant to a traditional market. The company generated incredible first-year 1998 sales of $125 million.

THE EMERGENCE OF A NEW DIGITAL ECONOMY

The business world continues to move inexorably toward an economy in which more and more data are digitized for faster and easier transfer. In this emerging digital economy, fundamental rules and beliefs are being challenged. Traditional wisdom, for example, schools us to believe that the competitive landscape is relatively visible and stable. We know our competitors and what is happening in our markets, say the traditionalists. Not any more, says the digital believer. The digital wisdom counsels that you may know your conventional enemy (current competitors), but you may be totally unaware of new entrepreneurs who are planning to introduce a new model to take a portion of the total industry revenue. Barnes & Noble and Borders certainly realized they were not aware of all competitors when Amazon appeared, using digital information instead of hard copy of books to get consumers.

The traditionalists believe physical assets create barriers to entry because potential market entrants will have to raise capital to create similar assets. Their inventories represent opportunities to make sales that networks without those inventories will miss. The digital advocates think physical assets can be liabilities and barriers to change. Assets to them represent unnecessary costs tied up with slow turnover on the money. They also contain inventory with the possibility of becoming obsolete. Major airlines, in a traditional industry, were comfortable with their model that called for having assets tied up in airplanes and airplane slots at airports to secure market positions. A digital entrepreneur called Priceline.com concluded you don't need those expensive assets, just digital access to open seating and a means to offer the cyber buyer a deal.

Traditional wisdom says value is created in product features and lowest cost. While this approach appeals to the physical channel customer, it eludes the cyber buyer. The digital wisdom says value is created through products appearing to be customized with reasonable pricing that provide a solution to particular needs. Grocery stores offer products that constantly undergo innovative features at prices always touted as being the lowest possible. NetGrocer.com and Streamline.com offer a means to get your groceries at a time and place convenient to you.

As the new digital economy emerges, it does so in parallel to the traditional industry participants. The digital economy participants, however, typically optimize information flows, creating new relationships, customer values, and operational efficiencies. Many of these new entrepreneurs have no classical "assets" at all. They move quickly and threaten to take a portion of the total industry market share and profits with their new models. As firms begin to realize both threat and opportunity from this movement, new and old entrepreneurs are starting to redesign industry models.

The digital economy can threaten any existing industry landscape. On the physical side, companies moving to an e-business orientation question the flow and staging of products, and they insist each participant add value to justify its position in the supply chain. The new designers are always asking whether they can collapse the supply chain. They go further to question how many players are really needed, who has the core competence, and when should a process step occur. Existing supply chains, however, have been designed to take products to consumers through existing assets, so changes are hard to execute.

On the digital side, e-businesses question the real value any product has for the consumer and what solutions are being delivered. Their thinking is that everything has to be designed from the consumer back through the supply chain. They look less at enhanced physical systems and more at the flow of information, practices (e.g., promotions and pricing), and relationships between participants (e.g., brokers and distributors) to determine how a digitized solution can substitute for players and physical assets. The supply chain challenge, regardless of channel of choice, now becomes determining who and what is needed in the flow of response to consumption.

THE WEB'S OFFENSIVE AND DEFENSIVE CHARACTERISTICS

As one considers how best to employ a weapon as powerful as the Internet to enhance either channel of response, it must be viewed from a defensive as well as an offensive perspective. In the former sense, if a clever Web merchant found a way to displace a significant percentage of your profitable business, the loss could be ruinous. Such a condition is presented to those in the banking industry when a new software organization, such as Intuit, decides to go online as a financial services organization. Today, a similar group lurks around every corner, prepared to use the Web as a tool to gain share at the expense of established businesses. As soon as that new aggressor builds a 5 percent or larger share of the market, whether a profit is made or not, it can force changes in the market structure. A good defense demands preparation to meet such a challenge. But that defense is not just having a pretty Web page; it also has to include the means to do business over the Web.

Consider Exhibit 3.1, the Web page for retailing giant Home Depot. Notice that while information is available to the browser, little is offered that can be purchased, other than gift cards. With a dominant share of the physical distribution channel through its well-known and established home repair centers, this company is not in imminent danger of losing market share to cyber challengers. The company should consider, however, offensive and defensive features offered by the Web.

From a defensive aspect, if a new dot.com organization appears and can offer the same friendly service and expertise in specific areas of home improvement through a Web-based, virtual reality channel, a portion of sales are put at risk without a comparable response from Home Depot. If trends are any indication, some percentage of home improvement buffs will be drawn to the Web-based competitor offering a digital response. As the cyber

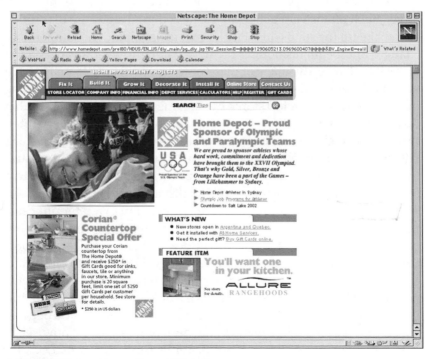

EXHIBIT 3.1   Home Depot Web Page

channel grows and adapts to its consumers, the percentage could reach double digits on an annual basis. Since Home Depot is the giant in the industry, a part of its market could be eroded. If the consumers lost are those willing to pay a bit more for the service, a measure of the most profitable revenues is lost as well. The good defensive posture requires building a transaction system into the cyber channel, or Web site, so customers who do not choose to visit the physical store can study the offerings, place orders, view inventories, track delivery, and find after-sale service digitally. The successful system will also have the supply chain infrastructure that can fulfill the orders placed as effectively as the best of the physical channels. These features will be discussed in ensuing chapters.

From an offensive perspective, the digital economy opens new opportunities to compete. The questions become how do we compete, and where should we focus our effort to have the most impact? Amazon.com exemplifies a firm that used a new model to go on the offensive against a well-entrenched and thriving traditional model. This company managed to change the model presented by Borders and Barnes & Noble with a system that had no internally sponsored supply chain. Amazon's model relied on the use of external assets through existing supply chains to move books directly to the cyber buyer. Such offensive practices in the new digital arena are disruptive and shake up the status quo. Firms have to anticipate such impending changes and begin fashioning the new value propositions needed to combat and take advantage of these new ways of going to market. If a Web marketer could garner sales from a group not currently shopping in the Home Depot retail stores by offering a virtual experience that results in the same satisfaction, new revenues would be generated through the Web site at the expense of the physical Home Depot store. Alternatively, Home Depot could find a way to get new revenues through a new channel by having a transactional Web site. Clearly, a feasible response is to develop both tracks of consumer response.

Pfizer Inc demonstrates the value of using the Web for offensive purposes by dramatically reducing the cycle time, from concept to commercial success, in the pharmaceutical industry. This large, global drug manufacturer encounters a constant problem with the introduction of new products in an industry where being first to market is crucial. By law, the firm must receive approval from the Food and Drug Administration (FDA) before introducing new products. To speed that part of its business-to-business process, Pfizer now sends electronic versions of its drug applications to Washington, D.C., for FDA approval. Formerly it had to "truck tons of paper to regulators and thumb through copies of all those pages manually whenever the feds had a question. By processing the material over the Web, Pfizer reduced the normal one-year approval time nearly in half" (Hamm and Stepanik 1999, p. EB14). The introduction of the successful product Viagra benefited greatly from this improvement.

After its experience with Viagra, Pfizer plans to move drugs through the process even more swiftly. The firm's researchers will use the Web to mine the technical data residing in its business-to-business network and collaborate with useful partners on new drug development. The plan is to link suppliers important to the development process more directly into the Pfizer R&D system. By sharing idea generation features, reviewing development online, and automating processes between partners, the members of Pfizer's supply chain network contribute to moving the new products at an accelerated pace. As Vice President for Research James Milson explains, "We've reengineered our business—digitally" (Hamm and Stepanik 1999, p. EB14). Obviously, the Web affords a business like Pfizer the opportunity to speed vital data and improve performance.

The Internet is enabling new players to assume new roles in traditional markets. It also affords the opportunity for existing players to develop new business models to defend current positions and build new revenues, often from a nontraditional base of consumers. Our points are basic. If you don't plan on using the Web for defensive purposes, expect a new intermediary to show up in your space and siphon off a percentage of your market share. If you don't plan on using the Internet for offensive purposes, then say good-bye to the new revenues that could have come through what is fast becoming the channel of choice for cyber-inclined buyers. Consider that beginning with a share of zero, 4 percent of cars in one year were bought sight unseen by cyber shoppers. Gartner Group, a respected analyst of the e-commerce phenomenon, predicts ten thousand new "iMarket" companies will form by the end of 2002. Expect this introduction to create turmoil, new opportunities to define new market roles, and the introduction of a host of new business models and value propositions.

GETTING RESULTS FROM ELECTRONIC COMMERCE

Use of the Web is not just putting in an e-mail system. It's beyond having an informational Web site or browser with reams of pretty pictures. It's more than offering an 800 number to order a catalog or provide a measure of customer service. It's about using the Web to allow a consumer, business or commercial, to buy something, have a problem resolved, receive satisfaction, and reduce the cycle time for order fulfillment. It's the emerging link of consequence with major business customers and end consumers of choice. The new game is about exploiting e-commerce for financial gain across a network of business interchange.

The correct orientation to make that exploitation is from consumer back to supply. One powerful executive is trying to bring just such an orientation to a very established industry. Jacques Nasser, CEO of Ford Motor Company, explained the needed perspective when he told employees, "To survive in a competitive market, auto makers must hear from the consumer." One way to listen is to make direct contact with consumers. Rather than rely on its car dealers to handle all consumer contacts, Ford has set up a Web site that lets consumers select and price cars of their choice.

The selections are then referred to dealers. Ford also routes the customer feedback from the Web site to its marketers and designers to help them plan new products. In the design process, the Web brings 4,500 Ford engineers from labs in the United States, Germany, and England together in cyber space to collaborate on development projects. The idea is to break down the barriers between regional operations so basic automobile components are designed once for use everywhere. When design plans conflict, the software automatically sends out an e-mail alert. Ford plans next to roll out a system for ordering parts from suppliers. "The ultimate objective is to enable the company to build cars to order rather than [based on] forecasts" (Hamm and Stepanik 1999, p. EB15).

In November 1999, Ford extended its use of the Internet as the company announced an alliance with Cisco and Oracle Corp. to further Web applications. The venture, called AutoXchange, will establish an online buying network where suppliers can directly access Ford requirements and submit pricing and delivery information. Jacques Nasser indicated the move would lead to saving billions of dollars through better sourcing and order fulfillment costs. General Motors (GM) announced a similar action when it introduced TradeXchange shortly after Ford. The two largest automotive companies are placing their future bet on use of the Internet as they both move forward with networks intended to assist in the acquisition of parts, assembly of cars, and delivery to consumers—all in one, integrated package.

Evidence of that intention and how fast concepts can change in the frenetic digital economy was delivered February 25, 2000, when GM, Ford, and Daimler-Chrysler announced their latest plans. These large corporations will form an integrated business-to-business supplier marketplace—through a common, global, Internet-based automotive trade exchange. Oracle (for the back-end ERP experience) and Commerce One (for the Internet-based, procurement side), which had previous relationships with Ford and GM, were to remain as technology partners in this new venture.

The potential for having one appealing marketplace site, for gaining lower transactions costs (through the automation of manual processes such as order entry, confirmation, payments, and shipping notices) and access to entire supply chains, had moved the big U.S. automakers to launch individual marketplace initiatives. Now the even more appealing possibility of reducing the higher costs to suppliers for participating in multiple marketplaces is changed to only having to enter one all-encompassing site. The reluctance some suppliers might have shown to dealing in separate marketplaces (for each automaker) is eliminated. From another perspective, the possible delay in seeing benefits develop has led the Big Three to abandon their individual efforts in favor of forming an alliance in the single marketplace. This move will be especially beneficial to smaller, resource-constrained, lower-tier suppliers, affording them direct access to an incredibly large volume of potential orders through the Internet. It could be a year before all the details are worked out (on standards, changing entrenched EDI systems, and agreement on strategy and execution procedures), but the move signals a trend that could be followed in many industries.

In the twenty-first century, the consumer, as well as member companies in the responding value network, will be in constant communication. The use of the Internet makes such communication so easy and so widespread that a firm cannot turn its back on what will be happening. Even those consumers using the physical channel for their purchases will be searching the Web for information on availability, price, and features. While consumers are online, the seller has an opportunity to influence their purchase decisions. Just as automakers must hear from the consumer to stay in business because of the large portion of buyers that might elect to use the Web in making their purchase decisions, so other industries must tune in those buyers inclined to taking a portion of future sales to the Internet.

This development means that there must be a feedback loop from those consumers back to the people designing and developing the new products. The procurement function must be equally linked so the right amount of raw materials and component parts are at the point of need at the right time. Shipping has to be accommodated for both the physical and cyber channel. Where distributors are involved, they have to be in the communication stream. Lastly, the consumer must be able to see what is in the system and have a means to stay in communication with the system.

The message is to reconsider the traditional channels of supply chain distribution before another network enters with a new business model containing innovative techniques or a new technology that could siphon off valuable revenues. Online businesses are rewriting the business model book by redefining and redesigning the way they deal with consumers. In the process, they jar traditional firms with a form of e-commerce innovation that often leaves the competition wondering what happened. The question for all those firms involved in supply chain is "Are you ready?"

To be ready and successful, starting a new market or developing new products and services may not be necessary. Current products and services are often viable for the changing marketplace; it may be that only the way of going to market has to be modified. The new market economy will be digitally oriented and collaborative across the supply chain. The companies entering value chain constellations determined to be the market leader need to balance consumer demands with the capabilities of the constituents to the network of response. That means having the appropriate e-commerce-enabled physical and digital channels of response.

OPPORTUNITIES IN THE BUSINESS-TO-BUSINESS ARENA

A wealth of intriguing opportunity areas exist in e-commerce and cyber space. An intranet is a *private* network where mainly corporate business-to-business information can be transferred. Beginning internally, these computer-to-computer linkages are established to improve communications among departments, functions, and business units. Benefits are found in more accurate and timely communication of vital information and the removal of physical obstacles to cooperative data interchange. It is, however, a fairly costly system to construct and maintain because of its need for direct linkage. The private network is generally enlarged so important external network constituents are granted access to privileged information.

Using the less expensive and pervasive Internet, the payoff increases dramatically as firms align themselves to network partners and link together an extranet presence. To gain the best return from an intranet, it is necessary to alter internal processes, linking the vital ones directly to the external opportunities enabled by the Internet. Today, a Level II leader has an intranet in place but has begun to expand its use as an element of communication in conjunction with the Internet.

If an intranet presence is becoming the norm and a valuable return on investment, then an extranet is the vehicle for moving to the competitive advantage needed in today's economy. Establishing an extranet with business partners becomes a logical next order of priority action. This move is not made for the sake of technology but for the collaboration benefits, cost savings, and market advantages it provides for the users.

An extranet is a *privileged* network linking companies together to address specific market opportunities. It can consist of suppliers, producers, distributors, and customers. Cisco Systems was mentioned earlier as a major user of the extranet to link directly from suppliers to customers. To further illustrate this point, consider the case of a company working through an intermediate step in an important consumer product area—tires. Michelin North America was an early adopter of extranet technology because it gave the firm a competitive advantage with its main customers—tire dealers.

Tire dealers not only sell tires; they recommend tires to consumers. Many ultimate buyers get their information and make their decision based on recommendations from these dealers. Michelin realized that helping tire dealers sell tires would enhance its revenues, but doing so would require more than providing information. The firm determined it would have to include sales presentations, evaluations, access to inventory, and assured delivery. Michelin had widespread brand recognition but wanted to be recognized as the easiest tire company with which to do business. The company knew that tire dealers were not accustomed to using sophisticated information technology. It also knew that the dealers worked off thin profit margins, and every investment had to pay back quickly. So Michelin used a collaborative approach. The firm worked with a group of dealers to describe their ideas and understand their needs. The concept was basic: let's find out what can help dealers rather than trying to ram an unfamiliar technology at them.

Michelin North America, Inc., started an electronic commerce project in 1995, well ahead of many companies studying such tools.

The goal was to strengthen the company's partnering with the thousands of independent dealers and distributors in the replacement tire market through improved customer service features. The name for what became Michelin's extranet linkage to those dealers is BIB NET. Named after the famous tire-man logo, BIB NET enables independent tire dealers across the United States to access corporate databases directly using Web-based technologies and running over UUNet's TCP/IP network. In this case, the business, customer, and consumer needs drove the technology solution. Talking directly to the customers before deciding on final features of the technology application became the critical differentiating factor in the design and development process. Web-based technology and a nucleus organization's extranet offered a seamless, low-cost connection that enabled online customer self-service solutions.

Although tires are a commodity product, Michelin sought to gain a competitive advantage in its market through outstanding customer service. Company executives wanted to make it as easy as possible for the distributors in their retail channel to access essential business information about Michelin tires, just when they needed data to service their consumers. In the process, they found the means to include buying recommendations from their product line. Dealers can check inventory status and receive up-to-date sales and marketing information, including recommended tire models for various vehicles, simply by using their Web browsers. The dealers can order tires or file claims for reimbursement online by completing basic HTML forms.

Michelin's quality of service has skyrocketed while its operating overhead costs have been reduced due in large part to the lower call center costs. A rule of thumb in this regard is that a Web-based transaction is approximately one-tenth the cost of that same transaction conducted in a call center, and there are no holds, no dealers abandoning calls, and no recommendation of a competitor's product. Internet technologies are not very expensive, do not require dealers to purchase special equipment, and do not demand deep technical training and expertise. Dealers have enthusiastically adopted the new environment, and Michelin has been able to reinforce relationships with its business partners in the replacement tire market. These partners are better able to satisfy their customers—the consumers needing to purchase tires.

The partnership with CompuServe allows the dealers to access Michelin's privileged extranet in the same manner as if they were at home browsing the public Internet. An inexpensive modem, a local telephone number, and the now ubiquitous Web browser enables the Michelin North America's distributor to find information on nights and weekends (the time when consumers generally shop). The key to Michelin's success was the involvement of a wide range of internal specialists working closely with and *listening to* the voice of its customers. Functions across Michelin were involved. Sales, customer service, and marketing worked with the dealers and distributors who knew about the need for changes in the Michelin processes and described what they could afford and would be willing to do. The application was developed with a business unit, Michelin North America, with dealers closely involved. The use of inexpensive Web-based technologies made it far less expensive than past efforts, and, finally, the collaborative mindset made it successful.

RESULTS WILL COME FROM AN ALTERED SERVICE MODEL

Making full use of the new technology tools and the application of e-commerce to enhance collaboration across a full supply chain network requires a shift in traditional business models. A company can use the power of its intranet to focus on recognized industry needs and seek a solution that would have market advantage. Over this network communication system, a firm or business unit can consider problems faced across an industry and apply intraenterprise resources (across many business units and functions) to develop solutions.

Constituents across an effective supply chain network collaborate on developing solutions. They do so by virtue of the expansion of the intranet into an extranet to bring products and services directly to the intended consumer base. Information on consumers and business customers establishes a sense of these constituents' strategies. With this awareness, the channel partners develop appropriate responses that draw on expertise created in distribution and order fulfillment. The strategic business units enter with market- and brand-specific responses that must be delivered by downstream partners. Corporate as well as business unit enablers are applied for the most appropriate customers and situations.

When the process progresses to the manufacturer, the amount of shared information increases. E-business will force companies into continually revising what information is shared and with which partner. As networked business processes are designed and deployed, more information will be shared in response to market changes and demands, including cost reduction, speed of product development, collaborative design, and further digitization of the supply chain.

New organizational models built around these concepts will be necessary in the future as companies take advantage of the power of e-business. Customers will expect a strong knowledge of their industry, an understanding of the issues facing the industry, and some awareness of best practices and solutions. A company will be able to use an intranet to link all its information, make it accessible to all stakeholders, and allow market leaders and account leaders to bring solutions to any customer.

This emerging model will become the dominant business strategy for networked organizations using the power of the Internet as a competitive advantage. The costs to purchase raw material, the costs to make and produce what consumers are demanding, and the costs to serve the desired consumers are all favorably impacted. Improvement comes from the application of what starts as an intranet and expands to include the value chain constellation partners and consumers. A progressive firm will reach them via an extranet over the public Internet. What will distinguish its interactions will be personalization. Customers will want to be part of a privileged constituency where their needs are met and each business transaction becomes a positive experience. A Web-enhanced supply chain model that focuses all assets, employees, capital, research, product and service development is what will shape the future.

SUMMARY

In conclusion, a war is being waged for consumer loyalty. Those firms who win the conquest will eventually be part of a value chain constellation that has optimized its processing and is focused directly in response to the demands of its intended consumer base. Application of e-commerce and its supporting technologies will be the weapon to fight that battle successfully.

4

Information Technology and Network Communications

Our thesis in this book is as follows: the World Wide Web and its incubator, the Internet, will have an enormous effect on every aspect of business. We'll also stress that the impact of this unstoppable force will change the roles and responsibilities of those within virtually every business discipline. We cannot sound the call too loudly. The IT department, for example, has to change its role swiftly. It must transition from a back-office support function to an integral planning mechanism for designing what must be the e–supply chain and e-business models that will assure future viability for the firm and its position in value chain constellations.

As this change is made, the CIO will encounter a dilemma. Faced with what is typically a lack of understanding of the ramifications of e-business across the organization, the CIO must become a driver behind a most difficult transition. In today's environment, new e-businesses with e-technology software appear virtually overnight and begin attacking traditional companies that have been late in developing a cyber channel of customer and consumer response. In the emerging e-business world, a new breed of entrepreneur is at work constructing interenterprise systems, with or without bricks and mortar, that use network communications to extract pieces of existing markets.

These entrepreneurs carve out their market shares by leveraging the use of information, collaborating with supply chain partners to design new business models, with great agility and ability to respond to consumer demand, and doing it all in cycle times unmatched by their traditional competitors. Helping a typical business executive understand such activity, how to construct a cyber model that complements the existing physical model and where to begin the beneficial application, is a new challenge to the IT professional. The challenge goes deeper, as the organization itself has to be taken through a phase in which "transformation planning" occurs. That means all functions and sectors of the business must align themselves with the new digital format. The necessary new roles and responsibilities have to be taught, understood, and applied as the firm transforms itself into an e-commerce-enabled organization.

In this chapter, we'll consider how to help companies determine the need for and how to begin development of an e-business model. This chapter takes the perspective of the CIO and the IT support group. We are not abandoning supply chain but will be looking more at the e-commerce aspects and the transformations required of a firm, as well as the rapid changes occurring in the business environment. We'll look at companies that have attempted to connect information technology with the needs of network communications to enhance the future viability of their firm and its supply chain partners. We'll also present guidelines and an architectural model to help with the e-business journey.

EXECUTIVE UNDERSTANDING AND SUPPORT: CRUCIAL ELEMENTS TO SUCCESS

Let's start our journey by determining how to secure the leadership understanding and endorsement that will be required to move into the brave new cyber world. This journey begins in Level I/II, as depicted in Exhibit 4.1, with what has become a typical management

Progression / Business Application	Level I/II	Level III	Level IV	Level IV+
	Internal Supply Chain Optimization	Network Formation	Value Chain Constellation	Full Network Connectivity
	Stage 0	*Stage 1*	*Stage 2*	*Stage 3*
Information technology	Point solutions ---------- Inform	Linked intranets ---------- Interact	Internet-based extranet ---------- Transact	Full network communication system ---------- Deliver

EXHIBIT 4.1   E-business Development Framework: Information Technology

axiom. In virtually every business endeavor, it is clear how important senior management support and involvement are to achieving the goals and objectives of the effort. In the areas of e–supply chain and e-business models, this need reaches a new dimension. Facing powerful and swift change, executives do not have the luxury of long time frames in which to gain knowledge and make deeply calculated decisions. This is a new arena, and it requires a transition to Level III of supply chain and e-commerce.

This need is compounded by the complication that very few senior executives at traditional companies have the technological grounding in what is necessary to make informed e-business decisions. They have access to their e-mail and executive information systems, but they use these tools typically to consider internal metrics, industry trends, and financial information. They understand the principles behind supply chain optimization and have probably helped guide the firm to significant Level I and II accomplishments. Most of these gains will be impacted by "point solutions," or software and data improvements that help between departments or at particular points of hand-off between processes within the supply chain. Many executives will not be grounded, however, in the technology needs to take the firm to an external environment or to utilize the advantages of e-commerce. We're considering the preliminary position of e–supply chain and characterize that level as "inform" since the intranet (internal communication system) will have improved cross-organizational communications.

Executives at this stage are just now planning e-commerce strategies or designing e-business models. They patiently watch what competitors do, but most are very wary of venturing into the cyber world until a nontraditional competitor opens up in their market via the Web and introduces a challenge to their business or a major customer insists on movement to the primary stage. Wise executives are beginning to at least surround themselves with astute advisers who counsel them on the coming tsunami of change. But their decision making is still slowed by a deference to traditional business models, most of which are being rendered obsolete by the coming e-business changes.

Therein lies the need for the CIO and his or her IT network—to educate, inspire, and help the executives forge the new business models demanded by the coming changes in electronic commerce. Before moving into how to deliver that assistance, let's consider a few definitions and messages that will help frame our discussion.

- E-business is the use of interenterprise or network technologies to connect the value chains of a nucleus company with its suppliers, distributors, business customers, and consumers—via the Internet, EDI, or other proprietary linkage—to achieve mutual business benefits.

- E-business derives benefits by applying technologies to enhance traditional business objectives such as increasing revenue, reducing costs, better utilizing assets, and improving customer and consumer service and satisfaction.

- E-business will transform roles in the marketplace for all companies. A determination of the most appropriate "market role" for the company to play in this new business model is necessary. As part of a value chain constellation, constituents must decide which partner has the competency to play which major role, particularly that of the nucleus position.

- Analysis of the interactions with trading partners and eventual customers allows for creation of a value proposition that makes sense to those customers, so each of the value chain constituents can design an appropriate system of response.

Transforming the concepts of supply chain and e-commerce into a viable e-business strategy and model becomes critical to future success. We thus must begin with one serious caveat: delaying a response can be fatal for CEOs and the CIOs who support them. The technology behind the Internet is of vital importance to a value proposition supporting an e-business model, and a CIO must facilitate bringing that technology to the firm. The growing need is for the CIO to be a vehicle for introducing the necessary knowledge into the minds of the company leaders. Moreover, the CIO must be an advocate for smart strategy as well as smart application of data management and information technology.

Stalling at the crossroads of the physical and cyber worlds can put corporate value and the future of the company at risk. On March 8, 2000, Procter & Gamble's market value dropped 31 percent, partially because of a disappointing earnings report and partially because the company was being viewed as "not being a tech" firm. Here is one of the leading Level III consumer groups being criticized for what amounted to stalling in the lead (Wall Street Journal, March 8, 2000, p. 1).

We have emphasized the incredible growth fueled by the Internet. The challenge is sorting out the technology and the business sense to produce a vision and strategy that secures the future.

As the hype is filtered, the CIO has to be actively working in this area, helping the CEO and senior officers understand what is important and pertinent, and providing direct assistance in making the appropriate decisions.

There is no blueprint for providing help in this area because the landscape is too new and complicated. Our advice is to bring some form of awareness training to the executive group as a first step. This training should be conducted by experts who can advise the group on the fundamentals of supply chain, e-commerce, the technology needs of the physical/cyber channel model of response, and the steps in building an e-business model and strategy. With an awareness of what the basic concepts entail, move to examples of what is being done in various industries. The key here is to stress examples from the company's industry as well as other industries. Since most business executives will want to cling to the old and comfortable business models, it takes a "wake-up call" that illustrates dramatic results to move them out of their own inertia.

The company cannot be timid in this regard. If the business model being used is over two years old, it is most likely obsolete. Most old models are broken in some aspect. Repairs are a temporary expediency. The need is not to patch the traditional way of going to market but to follow the advice of an expert, like noted author and lecturer Gary Hamel of the London School of Business, and "revolutionize" the effort. Don't risk the ranch. Try one business unit. Construct an e-business model and put it to the test. It helps during this period to hire a few mavericks to challenge the traditional thinking and help with the new design. Find some experienced people who have lived through the transformation from a physical channel world to a cyber world.

With better awareness and a feeling for what can be accomplished by studying other industries and models, the next step is to begin fashioning an e-business model for the chosen business unit. This construction requires moving the firm or, more likely, the business unit into Level III of e–supply chain. Now the unit begins its electronic network construction and starts to link its intranet with external constituents, so together the firms can "interact" and collaborate on building the network. The CIO has to enlist help in this construction phase from those who can turn the ideas being considered into a business vision that compels the executives to want to execute the new model. Done well, the effort of what becomes the pilot business unit moves management away from a feeling of immunity to a position demanding action. In the next chapter, we will describe a ten-step process for selecting the right partners and moving from initial idea construction to a full-fledge e-business model.

DETERMINING THE DEGREE OF WEB USAGE FOR A DIMENSION TO THE MODEL

Choosing the technology and deciding how much to rely on the Internet is more challenging than ever because of the rapidity with which new options appear. The sheer number of choices and the impact they can have on e-business models make decisions a difficult task. A look at the progression typically made will be useful in making those decisions.

The CIO has to determine, at a minimum, the starting point for moving onto the Web. Using the four levels of supply chain progression as a guide, we find a similar progression in technology application. Exhibit 4.2 diagrams the relationship between the level of complexity of Internet communication and time progression. Level II supply chain firms begin with some sort of Web presence to inform the visitor about the company. The result usually amounts to a form of "brochureware" in which a presentation is given, but only information about the organization is provided (locations, products, contact names, and addressees, etc.). In this stage technology is gen-

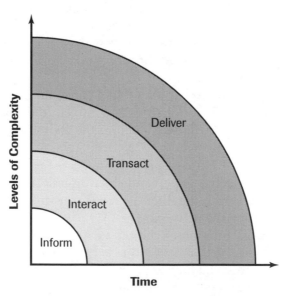

EXHIBIT 4.2   The Progression of Internet Action

erally focused on point solutions for specific problems and business enhancements, so the ability to do more with the Internet is typically limited. Basically, the company is using its communication system for internal purposes.

As the firm moves to Level III, the beginnings of an intranet appear, and the site should be prepared to interact with the viewer. Some form of enterprise resource-planning system is introduced in this level, and the intranet begins to expand to include suppliers and a few customers so the company is now able to enlarge its use of the Web. The intranet is a private network within the company, based on the technologies and models of the Internet, and users soon learn it does not have to be limited to internal issues. A few experimenters usually find a way to use this medium for external purposes.

Now the firm can progress into e-commerce and network formation with the help of a few external partners. This step requires expanding the implementation process to senior officers who must help decide which companies will be invited into the emerging network. Acting as a nucleus firm, a few key suppliers are invited as well as a distributor, if appropriate, and one or two key customers. (A usable procedure is described in the next chapter for completing this part of the process.) Connecting their computers via a linked set of intranets, these firms begin fashioning the communication system that makes the network viable. For a multi–business unit organization, the site will break down into sections describing the various units at this point.

No transactions can be carried out, but the basic function is to discuss what the company can do to help the viewer with its supply chain constituents. Specifications can be discussed, answers given to questions, locations and contact points given, and requests for help channeled to the right people. Inventory tracking can start in this stage, at least to the point of making clear to the viewer of the site exactly what stock of materials and finished goods are available. Progress through Level III can stall at this point if the intranet is not sufficiently integrated throughout the nucleus firm. That means the internal computer-to-computer system has to supply the cross-unit information necessary to determine, for example, exactly what is in inventory across the firm, where it is, and where it is headed. As an organization begins to realize the data are timely and accurate, inventory management finally becomes a real opportunity. Most early-stage Web sites get mired in extolling the virtues of departments or business units and not preparing to solve problems for customers. That's why we strongly advise that when the Web site development gets beyond the inform stage, it be done on a pilot basis for a single business unit. That way the bugs can be worked out before going corporate-wide.

With the linking of external computer systems, the firm progresses through Level III and interacts across what rapidly becomes the supply chain network. With experience and much testing and modification, the company and its network partners reach Level IV. This part of the process, however, can take up to a year or more, since the slowest of the constituents will delay the speed of implementation. The problems of handling information that comes through disparate software and protecting the proprietary data must be resolved. That requires adopting a common set of standards and building a platform for transferring information through the linked computers. A cross-organizational team will have to work out these details, often with the help of software advisers.

In Level IV, the nucleus firm and its allies move solidly to the Internet and begin developing the value chain extranet. The technology moves to decision support systems, including demand management, customer relationship management, and other advanced supply chain enablers. Now the key suppliers are definitely connected, as well as key distributors and customers. At this stage, the Web site is used to "transact" with the viewer. The Web presence can solve business problems for customers and their consumers. Later in the chapter we will describe an architectural model to help gauge the places where the technologies of the Internet can be used to augment or supplant a company's current technology portfolio.

As Level IV is being completed, the firm begins to understand that it isn't enough to have a Web site or extranet. The new technologies have to push out the old technology in favor of a new, technically based business model. In Level V, the Web site is used to deliver to the viewer and becomes a source of new revenues and a means to provide customer service. The technology has to move to a Web orientation in this level, as the capabilities of the extranet become the differentiating factor against other networks applying similar technical skills. Full network connectivity is the objective as the constituents work out the complications of completing the extranet across the value chain constellation. That means the cross-organizational teams will have progressed through the functional issues to be described in the ensuing chapters. They will have defined the order fulfillment process, worked out the logistical system for moving raw materials, semifinished and finished goods, developed a customer service system, linked manufacturing planning and scheduling via their ERP systems, and so forth.

INCLUDING THE RIGHT ELEMENTS TO MAKE THE MODEL VIABLE

As the e-business model is constructed, making certain it contains elements that will appeal to intended customers and consumers is crucial to good execution. In the process, companies that have pursued a particular business model for many years will need advice on how to keep the central elements that have been successful in the past, and what new e–supply chain features they will need to make the model viable in the cyber world. Currently some of the companies from the most traditional businesses are reexamining their business models and applying leading-edge technology to redefine their offerings to customers.

An example is Tokheim Corporation (www.tokheim.com), a Fort Wayne, Indiana–based manufacturer of gasoline-dispensing pumps. Tokheim is the world's largest producer of these pumps and has been in business for a hundred years. The company has embarked on a project with some technology partners to define the gas pump of the future, and they intend to change our view on how we interact with these machines. Let's take a look at their new, experimental model. Imagine a gasoline pump with a computer screen, similar to what you use on a daily basis, with an LCD display panel such as is found on your laptop computer. Through this equipment, Tokheim will unveil its Apex system, the gas pump of the twenty-first century.

Families stand in front of a gas pump, on the average, thirty to sixty minutes per month, equivalent to watching a network television show. As with the TV show, this experience offers attendant opportunities for sales, marketing, and entertainment. "Less than half of the fuel customers visiting convenience stores ever venture into the store, rendering in-store merchandising efforts ineffectual for the majority of a store's customers," said Douglas K. Pinner, chairman and CEO of Tokheim Corporation. It is not beyond imagination to picture a family on a cross-country trip relying on one provider for services and fuel, because of the content of the gas pumps and the conveniences it provides. Games, serial stories, maps, coupons, fast-food orders, and so forth can be offered. The services, including advertising commentary and instant demographic analysis, are on the near horizon. Pilots of this technology have already developed the prototype models.

Now imagine pulling up to your favorite gasoline station, ordering food and having the order delivered to your car. Now picture yourself in the Dallas, Texas, area where Chevron and McDonald's are implementing the new business model. Other pilots have allowed consumers to order groceries from a convenience store while at the gas pump, have the groceries delivered to the car, and pay for everything in one transaction. "The millennium [gasoline] dispenser is a truly revolutionary development in our market," Pinner concluded.

The impact this new model will have on supply chain is equally dramatic. The Apex system will allow communications from the pump to anywhere in the world over a TCP/IP network. Changing prices, diagnosing problems, and giving real-time sales and demographics information are included features. Changes in taxes, tariffs, and services can be managed from a central location, eliminating waste, errors, and duplicate efforts. Doing a better job of managing inventory will be a bonus feature. Direct link to the refinery will allow production scheduling to be accomplished with a far greater accuracy, lowering safety stocks, and improving forecasting (perhaps to the point of obsolescence). Of course, one of the central intentions is to make the consumer experience more personal and valuable.

While this example shows one possibility that can be derived from an innovative use of the Internet, as the CIO directs the firm, he or she will benefit from an understanding of what is working and what is still in the hype stage. Some of the guidelines we found to be most useful in choosing the right information technologies include the following:

1. Choose technologies based on the Internet or World Wide Web. Generally, these technologies will be in wide use and will have the stamp of the Internet. Find out when they were conceived, how they work in the Internet community, and determine whether they support standards and policies of the Internet. They will be designed for a network economy and planned from the ground up for connectivity (to be readily available and inexpensive). An example would include an electronic mail package based on Internet standards such as POP 3 and IMAP. A network protocol such as TCP/IP, the backbone of the Internet, will be included.

2. The next tier will be those applications that have been reengineered to work with the Internet and the World Wide Web. They will have extensive modifications to their inner workings, interfaces, and file formats—to coexist in the world of the Internet and WWW. They could be office suites that can read and write the standard format used by a Web browser or a database that has been modified to include XML (extensible mark-up language).

3. The last tier to consider are those applications and systems that have not been modified or have only a thin layer of a Web interface put on top of them. These systems should be the last choice. They are not designed for connectivity outside the organization. The key to success is external connectivity, linking across the value chain constellation. This tier is not suitable for that application.

In general, use the rule of displacement. Internal-only technology is expensive to create and install. In contrast, use of the Internet is inexpensive. As you install new applications on an external basis, take some of the old applications out. As a higher level of advancement is achieved, the Internet technologies should have forced many of the old systems out of the company. A few guidelines include these:

- *Avoid proprietary systems when possible.* Remember that the technology provider's job is to lock you into using a single line of products. That is to their advantage, not to yours. Think connectivity and the sharing of information over the supply chain network.
- *Think about speed.* Some components have a long life and can be safely purchased in advance and used for a long time. These components are typically lower level, part of the physical infrastructure.

Exhibit 4.3 shows a life cycle for some common components of technology vision considerations. The network infrastructure should be designed for a reasonably long life cycle. The physical system and media employed will have a term of up to ten years. As the computing platforms (or servers) are designed, the hardware, storage, and routers should have a life of up to six to seven years. As the core applications and operating systems are chosen, the life cycles are going to be more limited. The ERP databases and operating systems may only have a life of three to four years. When the

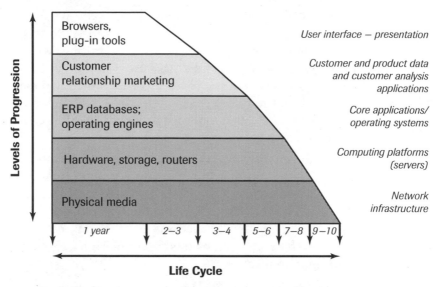

EXHIBIT 4.3   Technology Vision Considerations

network moves the customer and product data interchange and customer analysis applications, the cycle shortens again. Finally, near the top of the component considerations, the user interfaces with browsers, plug-ins and tools, and the cycle time could be down to one year or less.

As the components are considered and selected, the life cycle must enter the decision process. If the life of a given component is measured in months rather than years, the user has to expect rapid change and a flexible approach. If the time is years, a more traditional approach can apply. The question in making the choice is how to pick the right pieces and have them all work together and meet the business needs. Today's dynamic environment is such that some change is inevitable, and therefore periods of transition have to be accepted. Technology will not stay static, so the CIO must be prepared to deal first with the business needs, help construct a flexible model, and bring the enabling technology in as a support function.

CONSIDERING THE INTERNET STRATA AS THE MODEL IS CONSTRUCTED

Before choosing the technologies to keep up with changes and bet the business on, it is important to understand the Internet economy. Exhibit 4.4 uses research from the University of Texas at Austin's

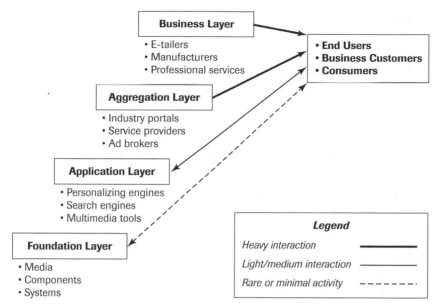

EXHIBIT 4.4   The Layers of the Internet Economy

Center for Research in Electronic Commerce (http://crec.bus.utexas.edu/). The study was sponsored by Cisco Systems.

An appreciation for the strata of the Internet and its four layers will lead to the understanding of the trends, players, and the economic model of the Internet. When making strategic decisions, purchasing selections, and installation and operation choices, it helps to have a format for guiding the process. As you calibrate your e-business position, these strata come into play.

The physical *foundation layer* of the Internet consists of the following:

- Actual media used—the fiber optic cable, copper wires, and radio waves that transmit signals

- Network components—routers, bridges, and telephone switches that connect the media across constituents

- The computer systems and operating systems that process the information

- Middleware that provides the conduit between applications

- Systems management—security and the tools and operating procedures that make the technology operate

Companies providing products and services in this area tend to be either household words or virtual unknowns. They include America

Online, AT&T, Checkpoint, Cisco, Corning, Nortel, Redhat, Sun Microsystems, and Tellabs. This first layer supports activities of the WWW and the Internet. It is the same in the public Internet, the internal intranet and the extranet you construct with value chain partners. The makeup of the technology only changes by application, and the connection to the business customers and end consumers is minimal. This layer offers opportunities to leverage purchases as components that are most often in use are selected. By collaborating with network partners on the extranet construction, further opportunities will develop if an agreement is made on standardization.

The *application layer* of the Internet is composed of the following elements:

- Personalization engines—software that gives a Web site or application a unique flavor for an individual consumer or business customer
- Commerce applications—catalogs and back-end financial tools
- Search engines—tools that help find specific information
- Broadcast and multimedia techniques—tools that package information in forms normally found in entertainment
- Development tools—specific tools to create applications and content delivered via the Web
- Training—education via the Web

Companies providing this layer include Art Technology Group, Asymetrix, Broadvision, Inktomi, Microsoft, Netscape, and RealAudio. The connection with business customers and consumers increases in this layer and moves to a form of light to medium interaction. Now selectivity has to be more careful, and the leverage generally comes with a consortium buy by members of the developing network.

The third, *aggregation layer* consists of the content aggregators, agents, and intermediaries. They may or may not have their own technology, but they will package and deliver to you. The following elements comprise this layer:

- Industry portals—companies or associations that deliver services or provide outlets for an industry segment
- Portals—companies that aggregate content, provide search capabilities, and sell services or give services supported by advertising
- Service providers
- Advertisement agencies and ad brokers

Companies in this layer include ANX (the Automotive Network eXchange), Charles Schwab, Doubleclick, E*Trade, Expedia, Lycos, PC Order, Travelocity, VerticalNet, and Yahoo! Now the connection to the customer base becomes serious as the interaction enters the heavy area. Costs increase dramatically in this layer, and a consortium of development, selection, and purchase is recommended.

The fourth level is the *business layer*. This is where you will find companies offering to sell you a specialized product or service—e-tailers, entertainment companies, professional services companies, and manufacturers and service providers that augment existing channels with an online presence. The firms include such well-known companies as Amazon.com, American Airlines, Dell Computer, and IBM, and less recognized organizations such as cdnow, ibaby, netflex, and Red Rocket.

In this area, the products and services are designed for specific applications that have been thoroughly worked out and are focused on particular markets and consumers. A special feature can be included in these offerings. For example, when publishing company Encyclopedia Britannica Inc. decided to make its famous encyclopedia available online for free, the unexpected surge of Internet traffic was so large that it slowed response to such an extent that the site had to be closed. The problem was solved with a technique known as *network caching*. Caching relieves the pressure of active Web sites by storing frequently accessed information in RAM or disk memory, eliminating the need to process requests repeatedly for that data. CacheFlow, Inktomi Inc., and Novell sell such high-end software to Internet services providers, and Cisco Systems is expected to include caching and other performance-enhancing functions in its switches and routers.

ARCHITECTURE AND TRANSFORMATION PLANNING

When asked to put together a plan for a business strategy and e-business model, technology professionals start with architecture. This element is a necessary e–supply chain device when developing strategic information support systems. Contrary to popular belief, architectures do not have to be engineering diagrams. They are a means to describe the components, the style of construction, *and the functions to be performed. For our purposes, we'll call the overall model enterprise* architecture.

Architecture should have three components:

- The applications architecture—how applications are developed and the tools and processes used to develop them
- The technical architecture—the physical and logical components used
- The information architecture—what data is needed and how it is found and presented to users

Business needs may dictate the development priorities for the three components. For example, a company's technology policy might dictate that the preference is to buy packaged applications for speed of deployment. In that case, the technology architecture should be developed first. Another company might have a view based on e-business. This firm would develop their applications architecture first. Companies in the entertainment industry (those providing entertainment over the Web) might develop their information architecture first. The three components, when finally put together, become the enterprise architecture—the way systems are first combined and integrated within the company and later throughout the network. This total architecture will go from the actual wiring and connectivity to the way someone navigates through the network systems.

As the firm and its network construct the architecture of choice, an increasingly popular trend is to use an applications service provider (ASP). Companies that want to rent applications can turn to this option. Access is given via an extranet, and a company rents and uses particular applications. This technique is popular with smaller companies that have neither the desire nor the serious funds needed to invest in information technology. Application outsourcing offers the promise of using just what is needed and paying as you go.

Planning for the future is critical, hard work but often not as difficult as getting the plan into action. The element needed at this point is called *transformation planning*. Moving the company into the world of e-business is going to be a major undertaking. Changing the systems generally proves to be an easier task than changing the business model under which your organization will operate. Transformation planning has, at a minimum, the following steps:

1. Conduct a gap analysis.
   - Do you possess the skills and time to proceed with implementation?

- Does the functionality meet the necessary new business model?
- Is the current implementation consistent with your new architecture?
- What are the operational impacts going to be?

2. Analyze the dependencies.
   - Identify the application components.
   - Which components or modules will be changed?
   - Determine the ripple effect (i.e., will a change in one application or module affect many other applications or the entire system?).

3. Define your approaches.
   - Install a new application.
   - Rewrite an application.
   - Transfer the application (use porting tools to move or modify it).
   - Utilize the old environment temporarily, while other changes occur.
   - Add new functionality with modern tools and processes, and eventually change the old application entirely.
   - Change some portion and add new functionality with the new tools.

Each system will have to be analyzed separately and in depth. The amount of work required to make a complex change system work will be greatly influenced by several factors:

- The business situation the company faces, the health of the organization, and industry trends
- The focused customers and key suppliers and the level of technical sophistication they possess
- The installed base capability and the age of existing systems
- The amount and skills of the technical staff

First, the new implementation assumes the company can apply e-business tools to create a competitive advantage through significant improvements over current performance. The immediate savings are also expected to cover the cost of the transformation and implementation. An example of a firm that successfully applied this alternative is an aerospace and defense company located in California, where it manufactures rocket engines. The aerospace industry is highly competitive, and advantages derive from factors such as time to market with innovations and efficiency of total performance. Companies tend to work together on large, complex projects. The company needed to develop imaginative new designs for rocket combustion chambers. At the same time, it had to reduce development time and manufacturing costs. The company decided to use the power of advanced supply chain management and the Internet, with astounding results:

- Decreased manufacturing costs by 97 percent
- Cut the development cycle by 50 percent, from two years to one
- Reduced manufacturing cycle by 63 percent, from two years to nine months
- Reduced the number of parts from hundreds to *six*!
- Created a knowledge repository for reuse on subsequent projects

This accomplishment was the result of using an extranet with approximately one hundred other value chain members and a software product called ipTeam from Nexprise Inc. (www.nexprise.com) of Santa Clara, California. Theirs is a classic story of how to create business-to-business value across the supply chain. Breaking down traditional barriers and using a collaborative approach to find the benefits were necessary ingredients for creating that value.

For starters, the internal team had to do things differently. Many were physically located in distant locations at different facilities. They had to use the intranet to have it appear they were all in the same location. This feature not only facilitated interaction but greatly reduced travel costs and time. As the project expanded and eventually covered people in California, Texas, Alabama, and Michigan, the intranet became an extranet. Everything from initial brainstorming to final design and approval and manufacturing plans was done over the virtual network.

The external companies involved did not have to change their normal systems, but they had to link into the extranet. One other aerospace company used their computer-aided design (CAD) software from Texas. Team members could view the drawings and mark them up for amplification and questions. Another company in Huntsville, Alabama, provided launch vehicle requirements working from the same business requirements. When these requirements were changed, everyone on the team knew it simultaneously (no more ripple effects from changes). A firm in Whitehall, Michigan, was responsible for figuring out how to make the complex castings.

They not only had the business requirements and drawings but also added the thermal and combustion analysis to the conceptual design by the primer contractor. Team members all used their CAD packages, word processors, spreadsheets, imaging, and more. They could work across the public Internet or inside a secure firewall set up especially for this purpose.

An example of one facet helps demonstrate the collaborative system developed—a necessary change to a design after specifications had been finalized. Instead of meeting in person, the team conducted one to two multimedia teleconferences each week, talking on the telephone while viewing the worksheets or notebooks in "real time." This process of sharing best practices and discussing innovative ideas accelerated consensus building on design modifications, shortening design iterations from days to hours.

In another example, when the stress analysis showed a problem with the center column of the original model, the designer, manufacturing analyst, and CAD modeler conducted a "virtual meeting" to resolve the issue. Using video conferencing capabilities, the involved parties were linked together with visual ability to study diagrams, blueprints, and specifications as though they were together in a single room. They were able to view the same documents and notations in the "system notebook" that provided details of the design to each constituent, and then they could mark them up in real time. The result was that the designer suggested a thicker column, the stress analyst verified its suitability on the spot, and the manufacturing analyst confirmed the change would not increase costs—all in real time.

In addition, all of the data generated during the meeting, including the analysis result, was captured in a highly searchable format. That means any necessity for a later review or analysis could be facilitated by easy access to what had been discussed and concluded. Therefore, this company will be able to leverage information discovered during the design process for subsequent projects. Doing this required a new business model applied across supply chain constituents in a trusting atmosphere. Those are the elements of e–supply chain at work. The results can be replicated, not just in a manufacturing setting but in every environment where teams learn to collaborate across distance, time, and cultures, using the new technology tools available. Reducing costs and cycle times using more efficient methods and systems brings the promise of advanced supply chains and e-business to realization.

SUMMARY

To summarize the view on building an e-business model that will enhance the firm's ability to capitalize on the use of the Internet, you start first to set a direction for the technology and then develop policies to support the necessary changes. Next, you develop the architecture and framework to work within. Then you migrate to the use of this architecture with a transformation plan.

Our advice is to select the most likely to succeed business partners with the strongest e-business advocates and begin a pilot program. Look at your supply chain network, and find a few willing and able suppliers who want to make the test with you. Select a distributor to help where that sector is necessary for success. Find a business customer that wants to see e-business work as much as you do. Collaboratively, build a process map of where the network is heading. From the supply chain needs that you develop, begin creating the e-business architecture that will enhance the transactions across that network. This effort starts with connecting the collective intranets. It extends to the selection of a programming system and the means to build the required extranet. It must include finding the talent necessary to do the building and installation that will come from architecture.

Eventually, this group effort will lead to the introduction of an appropriate Web site, including processes from informing all the way to transacting and delivering to the consumers who come to the Web site for satisfaction. When the results meet the minimum requirements for a successful venture, review the effort, modify it for better performance, and try it again. When the traffic meets or exceeds expectations and you think you can shift the burden of customer support and order tracking to a Web-based system, then you are ready to proceed.

5

Constructing the Future Roadway

With the CIO and his or her people energized to take an active role in designing the e-business model that will complement the supply chain effort and result in a competitive advantage, the organization can turn its attention toward the external environment. Now the firm begins a serious effort to select and work with suppliers, distributors, and key customers to form a supply chain network. As the alliances coalesce and collaboration becomes critical, the partners can advance to a value chain constellation. To accomplish such a position, the internal attitude that schools "We are the best at everything" must move to one in which carefully selected and willing partners join the firm and begin constructing the necessary new e-business model. In this chapter, we'll outline and describe a collaborative methodology that results in such formation—the alliances and purposes that will guide network formation and result in a value chain constellation.

CONSTRUCTING THE MODEL: INITIAL ACTIONS

Whether or not you accept the analogy of a tsunami, one inescapable conclusion results: the Internet and digital economy it is creating are revolutionizing the way in which consumer-based interactions are being conducted around the world. The degree of penetration may vary by business sector, but the use of the Web is going to impact your business, if not now, certainly some time in the near future. An ever-increasing number of transactions are being transformed from physical purchasing of inventory held in storage to a cyber-based relationship between a 'Net-wise buyer and an electronic system of response. The business-to-business system of communications and delivery supporting those transactions will be critical to a successful endeavor. Again, whether you accept the 67/33 ratio we predict for the physical/cyber balance is not of great importance. Select your own ratio, and you'll see that the time is now to begin building your model to prepare for the future state of equilibrium.

Every day, the World Wide Web grows by roughly a million pages. As this proliferation is studied, companies are deciding which business and consumer channel of response can be an opportunity for building new revenues and which might risk losing a portion of current, profitable business. Making the right decision secures the desired new revenues and profits. But with the right decision comes the requirement to form a superior business-to-business-to-consumer network of response. The best way to create what will become that system of network response is to have a model showing the way to the future. Constructing that model proceeds through these steps:

1. **Determine which company will play the role of the nucleus organization around which the network system that will satisfy the intended consumer audience will be constructed.**

This step simply means that one organization has to assume the position of prime mover. A firm with a stable of branded products fits this bill, as does a large industrial products company, a major bank, a health care organization, or a utility. This company will draw in the necessary external constituents to help develop the model, plan the strategy, and prepare the model for testing.

This firm will make the initial contacts, arrange the first discussions, outline the concepts and principles to be considered, define a tentative target market and consumer group, and host the first meetings. Essentially, this first step is intended to initiate a serious discussion of how a group of linked constituents can begin to draw on each other's strengths to build a superior business model. The key ingredients, of course, will be trust and mutual respect. Bringing together companies that share those attributes will define the level of success from the effort.

2. **Form a focus group of supply chain constituents from among the most trusted and reliable suppliers, distributors, and customers to begin constructing the model.**

The nucleus firm has to prepare a process map for one business unit, product line, or service before the group assembles. This exercise can be performed with the help of some of the expected attendees. The purpose is to orient the discussion so it does not wander into generalizations but, rather, a specific direction for the group effort is developed. The map may be amended many times and discarded later, but it directs the initial discussion to meaningful progress more quickly. With this map, the focus group members can orient their thinking and begin to consider how, where, and why concepts could be shared for the benefit of all companies represented. The idea is to search for optimization through the sharing of best practices across the total dimension covered (i.e., across the full supply chain network described by the map).

The goal in the first interaction is to try to bring the thinking together so what each firm has learned about supply chain optimization can be used to create a network performance closer to optimized results. The actual business unit, product line, or service used for the first focus effort is less important than the gathering of people willing to share improvement information. Each time we've conducted such group interactions, we've found a significant number of good practices not being applied by other firms in the network. Identifying areas of need and then bringing best practices to those areas can only benefit the total system of response the group is trying to create.

Since a lot of future support depends on the results of the first focus group, it is critical that solid progress is made. Carefully, a list is prepared of the possible suppliers, distributors, and key customers to invite to the effort. From among the list of a few trusted suppliers, for example, will come a shorter list of those with e-commerce capability—companies that can play a realistic role in e-model development. The list is then further refined to include those with a willingness to make an investment in what should be a mutually rewarding, controlled-risk effort to build in a new e-business model. One or two of those companies should be invited to participate in the focus group meetings.

In a similar manner, the list of distributors should be searched for firms with the necessary level of technical capability, willingness to participate, and preparedness to make a calculated investment. Again, one is selected to participate in the initial discussions. Finally, the customers are scanned to find the appropriate partner that represents the movement of the products and services to the focused consumer group. The most difficult problem in this part of the exercise is finding firms where you can overcome the traditional adversarial relationship that focuses any discussion on how to cut costs for only one party. Only when you have an environment of determining how to apply mutual resources for mutual benefits will you have the forum for making progress with an e-business model and strategy effort.

3. **Thoroughly analyze the current situation to determine where the network is versus potentially more advanced groups or leading practitioners in any industry.**

This step requires each member of the discussion group to come prepared to talk about their e–supply chain strategy in a frank and constructive atmosphere. They must be ready to share best practices in key areas of important process steps and be equally prepared to discuss where they are leading and where they have information that others are in the lead. Each attendee company should be represented by those knowledgeable in supply chain, logistics, and distribution. People familiar with the targeted consumer group and the interenterprise relationships between constituents should be present. Most important, an IT expert should attend from each company (i.e., a person who can help construct the absolutely necessary communication network that will evolve from the effort). The subsequent analysis this group will make has to proceed with some fundamental understandings.

Accept one certainty: the world is becoming digitized. There is no turning back, so whatever actions come out of the focused discussion, they must include how to reach the desired consumers through the dual channels of contact. There must be a cyber response as well as a physical response to consumer demand.

The recognition has to be that supply chain relations are changing from the order-to-invoice process to a portfolio of collaborative initiatives that enhance the total customer-centric network performance. Remember that the consumer has won the revolution. New strategies and models have to be focused on end consumption and how the supply chain network responds in an efficient and seamless manner.

The understanding should also include knowing that the Web has enabled the generation of new capital and business on a global scale. Barriers to entry are reaching new lows, so whatever model prevails, it should be global in scope and assume that a rash of competitors will challenge the model.

Network communications are needed to replace traditional hierarchical communications. Real-time access to needed data has to be available without errors across the total supply chain network.

CONSTRUCTING THE MAP: INTERMEDIATE ACTIONS

With an environment of trust and sharing permeating the group, the members are now ready to begin construction of the desired future state e-business model and the map for getting there. The next steps require intense effort, cooperation, and considerably more time allocation. As the intermediate phase of the interaction goes forward, the participants' sponsors must make a nearly full-time commitment. The following steps are then accomplished:

4. **Collaboratively develop a vision and value proposition for the alliance, and secure senior management endorsement and enthusiastic sponsorship.**

Together, the members of the network move from sharing best practices to getting very serious about discarding traditional business models in favor of an e-business approach that secures the future for the value chain constellation. This is a time for innovative thinking. There can be no ties to the past. Best practices that served an organization well previously can be brought into play as a segment of the new strategy, but only if it makes sense in light of the consumption patterns being considered. Novel thinking has to be encouraged as the group is invited to put up totally radical designs and concepts, all focused on how to go to market in a more successful manner given the future imperatives.

Patience must be exercised in this step to secure the thinking of every member of the focus group. Typical nominal group techniques can be applied, but the focus has to be on the construction of a more powerful business model that will withstand the attack of the new cyber mercenaries. Several visions will and should appear. The group must be encouraged to develop new, often conflicting, views of how to capitalize on future conditions. Now there is fuel to really energize the group and get concepts out in the open that would otherwise be kept private.

Modifying the possibilities to fit the intended future position and adopting the best vision come next as the group moves toward preparing something of value for management presentation and review. The model selected will most likely not be the final version, but it has to reflect collective input across the network and, at the least, challenge current thinking. Again, certain parameters should guide this part of the interaction:

■ Partners in a value chain need to reconcile their advanced supply chain and e-commerce plans in terms of the inter-enterprise objectives, infrastructure needs, technology requirements, and use of resources with the goal of developing a viable business strategy and implementation model that has benefits for all constituents.

■ Partners need to understand that, in the future, the issue for consumers will be visibility—they want to see where the goods are. Networks will need to show inventory wherever it sits in the delivery pipeline. The ability to monitor and analyze information and forecast demand throughout the value chain from original source to consumption and back will be a distinctive network feature.

Exhibit 5.1 is a diagram of how a focus group moves to the advanced supply chain levels through three phases of e-modeling. The steps are coordinated to match levels of progress across the supply chain evolution and the building of a collaborative e–supply chain effort. Let's consider each of the three phases in more detail.

Phase 1

In the first phase, companies with Level I and II supply chain experience come together in the recommended focus group to consider how to share best practices and begin construction of the future e-business model. There is no real network at this point; it is just being created. As a result, it appears as a nodule on the interaction circle representing the sharing of concepts between constituents. These concepts will have meaning for the individual companies but will initially not be very clear to the group. The interactions we have seen will be on how internal excellence has been achieved by the separate organizations. The arrow points on the outside of the circle are intended to indicate there is much

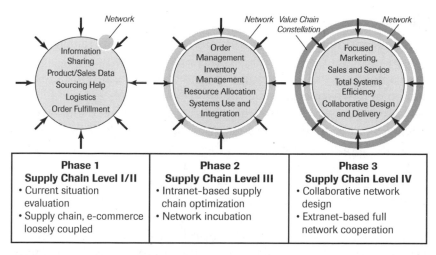

EXHIBIT 5.1   Collaborative E-business Modeling

learning to share, but it will come at first in the form of point solutions, not network collaboration.

Information sharing will occur along with product data and improved practices related to sourcing and logistics. It is important to consider the order fulfillment process in this step, as network strength will come from having a seamless system that appears to the consumer as being flawless across the total supply system. What will become a state-of-the-art order management process must begin with analyzing how each constituent goes about securing, entering, and processing orders. The IT group will be particularly active at this time, sharing ideas about how to construct a network order management system and how to use the best applications to make it efficient and user friendly.

The current situation for all participants is laid out across the process map in this first phase, so a meaningful discussion can occur regarding how one or another firm has made significant progress in specific process steps. One firm, for example, may have a particularly good order fulfillment process that can help other constituents. Another may have special strength in purchasing certain mutually used items or categories of procurement. A third could have a logistics system that merits copying. Sharing across these constituents brings the level of performance for the group up to higher levels and begins to engender the kind of cooperative attitude to continue the effort.

Phase 2

In the second phase, the network has taken on importance, as the group considers Level III actions. In the exhibit, the network moves from a nodule to a band around the interaction, signifying the formation of a network focus. Group discussion moves beyond telling each other how good a constituent company is to how the best competencies can be used to gain a network advantage. Symbolically, the arrow points are now more inside the circle of interaction, indicating that the level of knowledge being shared has greatly increased.

Now the groups move into analyzing how to gain access to and satisfying the targeted consumer group. This effort necessitates intently discussing order management, inventory control, delivery techniques, and how resources are applied for maximum benefit. A customer-centric attitude takes hold of the group as they proceed into Phase 2, sharing their latest systems and technologies and the means to focus applications on satisfying the targeted customers and consumers. The sharing becomes very serious as the group has to come to grips with how to build an interactive system that brings the critical data to the point of need in a very usable and friendly manner.

Phase 3

In the third phase, the value chain constellation comes into focus as the outer circle integrating the full effort. The network and how it will differentiate itself in the market are established in the minds of the design group. All intranets have been expanded and special parts combined into the communication extranet that binds the constituents together. The members are now hard at work in Phase 3, collaboratively designing the marketing and delivery systems of the future, and bringing specific definition to the new roles that have to be played. Product and service development is done together in record cycle times from idea to commercialization. Total costs are approaching optimization as full network connectivity and best practices will be bringing efficiencies to each process step. The width of the arrows in the exhibit opens up to indicate the degree of sharing that is taking place at the key points of interchange. The vision is now clear in the designers' minds and hearts.

This step calls for presenting the group thinking to management for receiving critique, advice, and endorsement and gaining future support. The group arranges a time and place with the important senior executives from all companies to present a preliminary report on progress and recommendations. This interenterprise executive group will listen, advise, modify, and either endorse forward movement or call for more work on the preliminary work. The usual result is for the executives to gain a better awareness of the conditions that have been considered and what the potential results can be. They start to see more clearly what an amazing transformation could transpire and how the changes will benefit all participating constituents.

This part of the action really becomes an ongoing step in the process. When the vision is far enough along that it merits review with senior executives for acceptance and advice, the group has to arrange a review session. In a similar manner, as progress continues through other steps toward completion of the model and map, executive reviews should be conducted with at least an oversight committee or leadership committee. The worst thing that can come out of this effort is for the group to dedicate enormous effort to a vision, model, plan of action, and execution recommendations that are turned down by management. To assure success, the review process and endorsements have to be continuous, spaced to meet the availability of the reviewers and the progress of the designers.

5. **Determine the gap between current and desired future conditions, and begin developing a list of initiatives that will close that gap and establish the desired future advantage.**

Each member of the focus group will bring information to the discussion regarding some initiatives that have delivered discernible advantage for their company or for any leading firm or network. The idea now is to share this information so the network will develop a feel for what can be accomplished if the full network design is executed. What the group wants to have happen is to bring each link in the value chain to a point of excellence so there are no weak links, and the constituent whole is the desired best capable network of response.

The action in this step is oriented around documenting the best applications that will come from the network design, and then comparing expected results against other networks (if there is comparative data) and a predetermined future state that would certainly secure a competitive advantage. In either case, the gap between current and desired future conditions should be detailed and order-of-magnitude benefits for closing the gap determined.

Exhibit 5.2 illustrates one way to orient the analysis for the group. Across the top of the chart are the levels of supply chain progression. Down the left-hand side are the important factors that must evolve to an advanced stage for the network to be effective. This list can be modified by the focus group to include more or

	Level I/II	Level III	Level IV+	
	Stage 0	Stage 1	Stage 2/3	
Technology	Core applications; operation system	Linked intranets	Network infrastructure	Internet-based interenterprise communication and assistance
Product development	Company specific	Customer focused	Network collaboration	Design or redevelopment of products/services to match consumer needs in shortest cycle
Marketing	Static	Best customer product promotion	Joint	Targeted consumers, markets, customers, products, pricing
Sales	Adversarial	Cooperative	Advocate	Opportunity development and closure
Customer service	Disassociated; reactive	Pro-active linked	Full network; self-service	Problem resolution: process assistance
Order management	Semi-manual	Electronic	Automated	Online, error-free prioritized fulfillment
Production planning	MRP, DRP	ERP	Linked network	Replenishment-based through extranet connectivity
Inventory management	Adversarial	Visible; cooperative	Advanced, least-cost capability	Available-to-promise global, end-to-end visibility; joint management
Logistics	Manufacturing push	Dual-channel consumption response	Network distribution	Product/service to end consumer through optimized network
Payment	Invoice	EDI	Debit-credit EFT	Funds remitted to producer upon withdrawal; automated payables and receivables

EXHIBIT 5.2   E-Business Model Evolution

fewer categories and to change the designations, but it has to contain the most important factors for their future state vision.

Notice that each category progresses from what is the best that can come out of the first two levels of supply chain evolution to what can be accomplished as Levels III and IV are reached. Sales activities, for example, move from being typically adversarial and focused primarily on pricing, to a cooperative environment in which suppliers work to help buyers find hidden savings in a relationship that benefits both parties. The evolution continues to the point where the sales rep is an advocate for the best customers, often working on site to bring opportunities into the open and finding solutions that close the issues. Other factors progress in a similar manner across the stages. If the focus group takes exception to the terms we have employed, they should alter the matrix to fit their thinking. It then becomes their guide to the desired future conditions.

With this list of conditions, the group can apply order-of-magnitude measures to derive the benefits that will accrue to the network. Now comes the desire to close the gap and begin reaping those rewards. The group begins preparing the list of initiatives that will produce the intended results, concentrating on prioritizing those actions. The intention is to have a document that summarizes the group's thinking and elicits support from their management because of the compelling case created by the potential payback.

6. **Select some actions from the list to begin creating short-term improvements that will provide the funding for the balance of the effort.**

Now the group pulls together its best thinking to develop a list of specific initiatives that will become the foundation for immediate network action. The concept is to find actions that will require cooperative application of resources to implement some of the initiatives having the best and shortest-term payback. These "low-fruit" actions are carefully selected, with an eye to a high probability of success. The constituent companies dedicate people to each of these initiatives to carry out the prescribed implementation. Typical examples are a new inventory management system, a full network transportation model, increasing revenues in a test market with specific consumers, design of a network Web site, an aggregated purchasing effort, and an enhanced order fulfillment system.

A team sponsor is selected, and each initiative is completely fleshed out with necessary resources, scope and charter, action steps, timetable for each step, measurement system to validate results, reviews with management, and future state deliverables. Care should be taken not to select too many initial actions. This is a time for proving the validity of the vision, map, and model. The group does best to select one or two initiatives and work diligently to make certain they are successful exercises.

CONSTRUCTING THE MAP: FINAL ACTIONS

With a vision to guide the effort, management endorsement to go forward, and a list of short-term actions that will prove the concept and provide enough payback to fund further efforts, the group is ready for the pilot. In the final phase of the modeling effort, a specific business unit has to be selected for the implementation of recommendations.

7. **Complete the map to the future through construction of an e-business model that contains the necessary two-channel distribution system.**

At this point, the original process map will have been marked up, changed to reflect new concepts, and look pretty much like a scarred battle plan. With a targeted business unit in mind, the map is now redrawn to reflect the best practices accepted by the group. From original supplies through consumption and postsale service, the idea is to bring the design to a form that can draw on the mutual network resources to come as close to optimization as possible.

To guide the map construction, Exhibit 5.3 is useful. From the purchase of raw materials to end consumption, everything should be moving in a collaborative manner. Through the production or manufacturing phase (Process, Make, Produce), mutual resources will be applied, particularly from the IT functions, to make certain the necessary information is available to enhance the new techniques that will be tested.

As the process moves toward consumers, all of the design efforts will reach fruition. Now the group puts the redesigned process steps on the map on a two-channel basis. These "immediate impact areas" are where the emerging model will be different and better

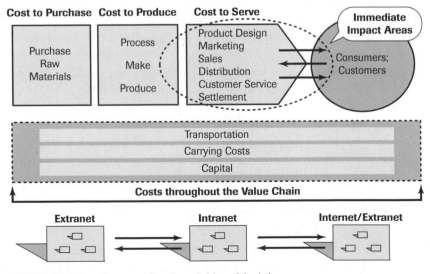

EXHIBIT 5.3   Cost-to-Service: A New Model

than the competition or not. Each important process step will be enhanced through the collaborative thinking and idea exchange that has preceded this step. Costs throughout the entire value chain will be present, as the group will have shared enough activity-based costing data that reasonably accurate estimates will be placed beside each process step. The cost to purchase (done collaboratively), cost to produce (enhanced by shared best practices), and cost to serve the customers and consumers (enhanced through the new marketing, selling and servicing roles) will be understood—as current state and targeted levels. Each of these functions and how they can be improved will be discussed in the ensuing chapters.

From this map and the information it contains, the group now fulfills its central mission: to design a new e-business model that will guide the network's efforts on a pilot basis. This model will be a dual-channel system of response focused on specific customers and consumers. It will include how best to service through a physical channel and a cyber channel. It will contain elements of supply chain optimization, advanced supply chain techniques, and application of e-commerce across the physical and cyber channels to the consumer. Keep in mind there is a need to define the new roles that will be required of all the players as they act out their parts in the model. Selling on the Web, for example, must be accompanied by helping the focused consumer solve problems. That takes more than getting an order and may include offering competitive pricing information before consummating the transaction.

8. Select a business unit for piloting the actions determined necessary by the focus group.

With the process map designed for optimization and the model for serving the consumers through two channels completed, the group approaches its management to select the nucleus business unit for initiating the pilot. Much as a nucleus firm was selected in the beginning to lead the effort, now necessary is a central unit around which the constituents mobilize actions. Do not be concerned about the completeness of the map or the details of action at this point. There has to be an element of the Michael Dell model in this step—to get started and adjust as progress is made, because specific actions will have to be guided by the needs of the business unit and its market conditions. The best advice is to look for a visionary business unit leader who wants to take the unit forward into the e-business world and will put forth the necessary resources to develop a meaningful pilot.

The parameters are basic. The unit has to be large enough to operate as the nucleus unit driving the pilot. There must be some perceived value from developing an e-business model and some immediate benefits for the actions. The leader has to be willing to devote the personal time to see the pilot through, from beginning to end. This leader should be made aware of the other constituents participating and spend time developing high-level relationships with senior people within those organizations. Around this nucleus test site, the suppliers, distributors, and customers array themselves with the plan to provide people, techniques, and systems to flesh out the model and put it into actual business conditions.

9. **Establish a time frame for the pilot implementation, and develop a list of specific actions to be taken, the necessary resources to execute the plan, the expected deliverables from those actions, and the metrics that will validate the results.**

A pilot of the type recommended here generally requires a reasonable time frame to be allocated, particularly so results can be authenticated. The time chosen will vary by situation, from six to eight months for a reasonable, simple, and midsize business unit to twelve to eighteen months for a large, complex business network. The concept is to move the model into a geographic sector, across a product or service line or across a full business unit's offerings. Be wary, however, of trying to accomplish too much, too fast. This is a time for testing what will become the guiding template for other business units and the means to capture above-industry results. A work plan detailing the actions to be taken, with names, times, and expected deliverables, is absolutely essential in this step. The group may modify the model and the process steps as the pilot proceeds, but the initial effort has to be guided by this work plan.

10. **Review results, amend the map, plan, and model, and then begin replication across the full value chain constellation and other business units. Reward the designers.**

Once the results have been documented, they should be reviewed with the senior managers from each constituent company participating in the pilot. During this final step, the concepts are either validated or amended to meet the test conditions. The model will be refined many times to reflect the results on each of the constituents. Best practices will become even better as the individual teams modify their recommended process steps. The value chain constellation will move from concept to reality as the new revenues and higher profits make the effort seem worthwhile. Finally, after the effort is declared successful and concluded, some form of reward should be given to the group participants who will have made the ideas and concepts into a viable e-business model.

SUMMARY

The outline described in this chapter can be amended as the group moves forward. It is an example of what we have found to be the most effective, straightforward way to bring constituents together and design a network first, and then progress to a value chain constellation—with an e-business model for the future. When the participants are satisfied that they have created a value chain constellation that will have meaning, purpose, and success in the targeted marketplace, the group does not disband. A smaller focus group now turns its attention to Level V and creating the full network connectivity that binds the value chain together and really differentiates its actions in the eyes of the business customers and consumers, from whom the expected new revenues will flow. Subsequent chapters will describe how this most advanced effort proceeds through applications for each of the major business functions.

6

Changing the Face of Purchasing from Tactics to Strategic Sourcing and E-Procurement

As supply chain processes mature, improved buy-sell conditions are emerging. Under these conditions, more total-system approaches with deeper trading partner relationships that take advantage of mutual capabilities in a stronger collaborative spirit are being developed. A few organizations that have progressed into Level III and IV of supply chain have discovered that improved relationships lead to superior business conditions in which the continuous mutual savings exceed the cost reductions that once would have been temporarily wrung out of compliant suppliers. These *network* savings can derive from a set of win-win conditions, and the purchasing function can lead the way to that development.

The traditional roles under these new conditions change, requiring both parties to work for strategic solutions that benefit both companies and further the advantages sought by the supply chain network. The pathfinders show there is a way to an advanced level of purchasing technique. They do so through a system in which the buyers move to a more active role in developing supply chain strategy with the help of some of their most important and trusted suppliers. They use new processes developed with the help of the information officers and technologists in the new relationship, particularly taking advantage of features of e-commerce. These features, including electronic network buying, aggregation of cross-business and cross-industry purchases, and a host of Internet procurement options, are developing so rapidly that buyers and sellers become confused as to which options best suit their applications. In this chapter, we'll consider the new strategic sourcing role and sort through the e-commerce options to bring some clarity to what is becoming one of the hottest areas in supply chain improvement efforts. We'll pay particular attention to the phenomenal growth of network buying through the ubiquitous online trading exchanges, or "Netmarkets."

The explosive growth of trading exchanges has impacted nearly every industry. Some estimates put the current number of exchanges at five thousand, serving nearly seven hundred industry segments. From the recently announced auto industry exchange, Covisint (www.covisint.com), to bliquid.com (www.bliquid.com), a self-listing equipment exchange, the online marketplace is booming. What is yet to be determined is whether these Netmarkets are the last gasp of the old purchasing model that intends to aggregate volume to drive down prices, or the beginning of the move to Level III and IV and collaboration to form value chain constellations. In either event, one facet of the movement is clear: the Netmarket phenomenon has changed the movement in the last twenty years from dealing with fewer suppliers with predictable quality (a legacy of the W. Edwards Deming dogma) to becoming indifferent to the number of potential suppliers, as long as they meet purchase specifications.

A second facet is that the sheer size of transactions going over these exchanges will have to impact nearly every industry in some manner. AMR Research (AMR), in its June 2000 report, forecasts that some $3 trillion will flow through online exchanges by 2005. At a minimum, participation in these exchanges has to be investigated to determine whether they should be a part of the sourcing and selling strategy. Later in the chapter, we'll analyze most of the features of these Netmarkets. For now, a brief review will help establish a framework for understanding their potential impact on a business.

Exhibit 6.1 is presented courtesy of Larry Lapide, vice president and service director at AMR Research, and depicts four types of trading exchanges. Along the vertical axis, the exchanges have been divided by ownership into (1) those in which the owners facilitate the trades that take place and (2) those in which the owners are major traders. Along the horizontal axis, the exchanges are divided into (1) those that intend to make the designated market more efficient and (2) those intended to enhance core business processes.

Beginning in the upper left-hand quadrant, we see the *independent trading exchanges* (ITEs). In these exchanges, the independent owner creates liquidity and manages interactions and collaboration among the exchange participants. The structure is company-neutral (any firm meeting the membership criteria can

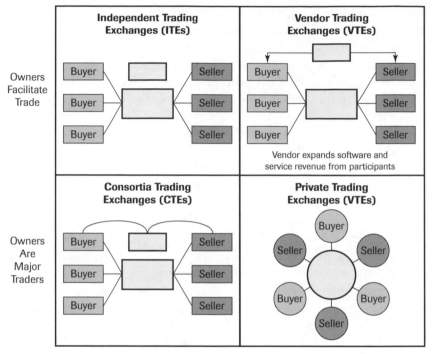

Source: AMR research.

EXHIBIT 6.1   Business Models for Trading Exchanges

participate) and operates for a profit. The concept is to unite many buyers with many sellers. The exchange is technology-neutral, and buyers and sellers must be certified by the owner. ITE examples include Chemconnect, e-Chemicals, PlasticsNet, e-Steel, and MetalSite.

In the upper right-hand quadrant, we see the *vendor trading exchanges* (VTEs). Here the technology vendor is the owner and again creates liquidity. The owner manages interactions and collaboration among the exchange participants, expanding the software usage and deriving service revenues from participants. Industry- or market-based efficiencies are intended to drive cost reductions and asset optimization. The structure is that of a hosted industry or service exchange, usually with anchor tenants (large-scale, central-role firms) in particular categories of buying. The transactions can be among many buyers and sellers or between one buyer and one seller. It is obviously a technology-biased marketplace since the owner wants participants to use its software. Certification of the buyers and sellers is required, along with credit verification.

Examples include SoftgoodsMatrix.com and USA istar Exchange (sponsored by i2 Technologies), ORMS (Ariba), MarketSite and Logistics.com (Commerce One), and IPlanet (Andersen Consulting).

In the lower left-hand quadrant, we find the *consortia trading exchanges* (CTEs). Here membership is select and based on supply chain participation. Industry members create the liquidity and participate because of the opportunity to focus on industry efficiencies that drive cost reductions and asset optimization. The structure is independent—company-neutral but with industry affiliation. Many buyers deal with many sellers over a technology-neutral medium. Terms and conditions are generally predetermined, and buyers, sellers, and credit are certified. This type of exchange tends to focus on value chain partnering. Examples include HighTech.com (ten high-technology companies), Covisint (five automobile firms), and e-Chemicals (thirteen global chemical companies).

Finally, in the lower right-hand quadrant are the *private trading exchanges* (PTEs). Here the membership is select and based on relationship to the sponsor who creates the liquidity. The purpose is to manage interactions and collaboration with the sponsor's community of participants. The structure is generally branded with one to many interactions through a hub hosted by the supply chain sponsor, who eventually takes ownership of the PTE. It is technology-neutral with preestablished relationships between known suppliers and buyers. Examples include Ford's AutoXchange, GM's TradeXchange, and Sun Microsystems' Microelectronics Division.

Many of these exchanges are in the formative stages, as several large corporations have announced their intent to join or form an online marketplace. In some cases, companies have announced participation, but little has been done to prepare them for using the exchange. This chapter will help you formulate the appropriate strategy for your company as you consider these new Netmarkets.

THE CONTINUAL EVOLUTION OF THE SOURCING FUNCTION

So much of the cost of running any business is tied up in purchased goods and services that management will always look to this function for help in reducing costs. Generating $100 million of new sales might be an exciting accomplishment, but generating $100 million in procurement savings has a much greater impact on earnings. Clearly, the sourcing function must continue through a supply chain progression to reap the most benefit from its relationships with key suppliers. Based on our research, these benefits can include cutting transactions costs (ordering, paying) by as much as 90 percent, gaining additional price discounts up to 10 percent, reducing cycle time (from order to delivery) by 75 percent, and improving compliance to agreement (eliminating maverick buying) by as much as 30 percent. The movement has to be from viewing purchasing as an operational focus to thinking of the function as strategic sourcing. In the advanced stages, that means moving from internal automation of purchasing process steps to external supply chain collaboration and using e-procurement techniques (see Exhibit 6.2).

Level I/II involves little cross-organizational cooperation, as most companies prefer to let each business unit perform its own purchasing function. The challenge is to help the internal customers of those business units (e.g., engineering, manufacturing, and logistics) find what they need at reasonable prices, quality, and delivery and not interfere with smooth operations. As progress is made, purchasing becomes recognized as an important aspect of supply chain improvement, and the effort accelerates, particularly to leverage business unit volume for further improvements. Unfortunately, this effort does not take advantage of the firm's total volume, and savings are limited to the leverage of the individual business unit volume. A built-in constraint exists in this starting position.

Eventually, the supply base is narrowed, quality issues are resolved, and buyers begin to develop extra savings. Working with those sources representing a significant portion (70 percent or more) of the total buy, purchasing reduces costs through improved working relations with this core group, which eventually becomes strategic suppliers. It is with this group that further enhancements that directly affect costs and operations are sought and developed.

Progression Business Application	Level I/II Internal Supply Chain Optimization *Stage 0*	Level III Network Formation *Stage 1*	Level IV Value Chain Constellation *Stage 2*	Level IV+ Full Network Connectivity *Stage 3*
Purchase, procurement, sourcing	Leverage business unit volume	Leverage full network through aggregation	Key supplier assistance, web-based sourcing	Network sourcing through best constituent

EXHIBIT 6.2   E-business Development Framework: Purchasing, Procurement, and Sourcing

Relationships grow with this smaller, strategic supply group, through focus group sessions and meetings directed to specific problems within the supply chain interactions. Joint teams are formed to work on finding solutions that would not develop through the normal negotiation process. With experience and encouragement, these teams move to areas that start to have mutual benefit. Soon, the discovery is made of how much valuable information (particularly on internal best practices) is residing within each company. Most of this data are never fully utilized because both companies think it is proprietary and contains information that should be shared with no one.

As the focus groups/teams experiment with sharing information and practices that help the interactions and do not destroy either firm, information hidden in the databases comes into play. A team focused on moving the order fulfillment interaction to a more automated process, for example, will discover that one of the firms is much further along. Sharing how the better practice was developed and installed does not give away secrets that hurt the firm. Rather, it enhances the cycle times and cuts costs across the interaction. That type of sharing leads to opening up more data on special services being provided to other customers by the sellers and better fulfillment techniques by the buyer. Cycle times begin to shrink, safety stocks go down in size, utilization of mutual assets (e.g., trucks and warehouses) occurs, and the parties find ways to enhance the purchasing and delivery processes.

From this position, the sourcing group moves to Level III of the framework, beginning to look at electronic network formation and how to use advanced supply chain management techniques. In a preliminary move, internal buying is consolidated. Realizing that the best values come from leveraging the largest possible volume position, the buying firm moves first to consolidating purchase categories that have a nondifferentiating effect on business units under a form of central control for the whole company. Typically, that effort starts in areas of nondirect materials and services, such as office supplies, computers, software, travel, furniture, MRO supplies, guard services, cafeteria help, and temporary personnel. With this internal aggregation, enhanced pricing and features will derive to the firm. As this effort reaches its full potential, the purchasing function turns its attention to how to aggregate volume with external sources, usually beginning with the core group of suppliers, and possibly some key customers who want to take advantage of the better pricing secured by the internal aggregator.

As the firms reach the peak of Level III, joint teams are focusing on redesigning the interactive processes. Further savings then generally await some type of computer-to-computer automation of processes between the firms through the extranet we have been considering. The idea is to seek savings that can come from a greater network aggregation of purchasing power, which can also be automated. Web-based buying has become a sophisticated art for the Level III companies as pooled purchasing and aggregated buying are developed by organizations wishing to consolidate the buying of materials and services to gain extended purchasing leverage. An ever-growing number of firms offering software for catalog searching and order placement can be canvassed to determine where there is a fit for specific purchase categories, and automation begins. With success, the effort can be expanded to more direct areas and possibly into capital spending. As an example, Chevron, the large oil and gas company, plans to move its procurement system for a $3 billion annual buy onto the Web. This move will give the company buyers access to manufacturers of oil and refineries, drilling and exploration components, as well as to service providers of oil and refinery components. The company ultimately plans to expand online procurement to its entire global purchasing budget of $10 billion.

THE MOVEMENT TO STRATEGIC SOURCING ACTIVITIES

The challenge is to improve strategic buying activities while automating transactional activities. The traditional buying track includes identifying the product or service, making the buy decision, placing the order, receiving the order, and paying the supplier. Most firms have dramatically improved these fundamental processes through team-focused improvement efforts that automated labor-intensive process steps. Now the opportunity presents itself to move to the more advanced techniques in Level IV of our framework, taking advantage of electronic systems and techniques to develop e-procurement techniques.

This movement requires taking the buying organization into a new, technology-rich environment with other members of the value chain constellation using Web-based techniques. With the first wave of digital business marketplaces becoming operational and the number of offerings escalating, the new options proliferate.

Competition among these new marketplace entities is intensifying as new players and alliances emerge, offering a means to secure many traditional purchase categories electronically. This situation can be both beneficial and threatening. Before taking what could be perceived as a major risk with established relationships, a buying group is best advised to start with a safer approach. They can study an indirect category or one on which the manufacturing process does not depend for sustaining current operations (office supplies, automobile leasing, fax machines, copiers, etc.).

The suppliers (who may not be among the current key sources) can be assessed and reduced to a small number that have the electronic capability and compatibility of culture to try building an electronic interface. The buying group makes sure the total company volumes have been consolidated for each category. They may also pull in a larger aggregation by working with other suppliers and customers that make purchases in the same category. With this larger volume, they approach the selling group, and joint teams are established to work out the electronic communication systems. By staying in the indirect area, the firm minimizes risk but learns a lot about how to build larger-scale volumes that lend themselves to an e-procurement system. It is strongly advised that the senior purchasing officers design these experiments with the direct involvement of the chief information officer.

Next, the activities include finding and qualifying key strategic suppliers; establishing regional, national, and global buying and supplying arrangements; having suppliers track their own performance in terms beneficial to the network; and defining and managing the enabling information technology (extranet) systems. The idea is to create an e-business purchasing system that handles the purchase of indirect operating resources initially and then progress to more direct materials. A good beginning is to select from a menu of indirect categories and start developing an electronic system of ordering, receiving, tracking, and making payment. An arrangement with one of the catalog software providers could be tested at this point. As experience grows, the number of categories can be enlarged and a movement made to more direct materials with the more strategic suppliers, particularly of capital goods. With the use of Web-based enabling technology and a new strategic sourcing paradigm, the results can be very significant.

Advancing the art of strategic purchasing by using e-procurement enhancements requires conducting a search for where the current purchasing money is going. Consider a large global business that has total revenues of $8 billion, $4.8 billion of which is consumed by cost categories. Of this subtotal, we'll assume $3.64 billion is in foreign, regional, and corporate accounts payable, and an additional $910 million is spent on capital expenditures and corporate purchases, bringing the total sourcing disbursements to $4.55 billion. If it is further assumed that the firm has already made significant savings in purchasing, it is within this area that the hunt for additional savings proceeds.

Exhibit 6.3 delineates the potential by breaking out the $4.55 billion into categories with high leverage for improvement. The dollar totals and the number of suppliers by category are isolated, narrowing the hunt. A focus team will go through the matrix and circle those categories offering the best chances for further savings. The decision process will be based on the amount of dollars, the number of suppliers, the chance to make significant improvements, and the speed of the impact on savings. If the number of suppliers per category seems large, it is consistent with our research and shows that the tendency persists to avoid lowering the number of suppliers in nondirect categories. One factor that points to the opportunity for improvement is the large number of people we find doing the purchasing in these areas, many of whom do not work within the purchasing function.

Commodity	Annual Disbursements (in millions)					$ Totals	# of Suppliers
Advertising/marketing	$3	$8	$12		$14	$37	45
Advisory services	2	5	6		8	21	123
Benefits	26	93	113		30	262	345
Freight	6	32	53			91	1,023
Fuel	56	125	165			346	713
Insurance	6	34	47		50	37	61
Labor	125	470	615		195	1,405	
Leased equipment	12	45	70		11	138	767
Legal services	1	2	3		5	11	102
MRO	110	368	521	370		1,369	3,459
Packaging	16	23	43			82	892
Software, Hardware	7	20	45	50	15	137	652
Taxes and licenses	5	26	44		50	125	52
Telecom	13	56	46	60	12	187	27
Tires	10	45	87			142	1,123
Travel	2	8	10		40	60	102
Totals	$400	$1,360	$1,880	$480	$430	$4,450	9,486

High Leverage

EXHIBIT 6.3   Pick Your Targets

In this example, the high-leverage areas are selected as freight, fuel, MRO, leased equipment, packaging, and tires. With this information, teams can now be formed to begin a deeper investigation and develop specific improvement ideas. Now the exercise proceeds to establishing new types of relationships with a smaller group of key suppliers in each category. That means procurement strategies are created for working out the details of new relations that can benefit both parties. Sharing of best practices occurs, as the teams look, for example, at which firm has the best software and systems for executing orders and making payments. The team can look through some historical data to find best on-time delivery practices, most consistent accuracy in delivery and fill rates, and highest-quality service. With each group investigation, the ability to process through an electronic system is a major factor in decision making. A basic need will be for a third- or fourth-level organization to be dealing with suppliers that are at the same level of capability. Anything less increases the cycle time for completing an order.

With the direction determined, the team now moves to developing the actual working relationships and action plans. Depending on the level of sophistication and the importance of the category to both parties, the relations move along four stages. Beginning in the traditional stage where the mutual benefit is not clear, there is no long-term continuity expected, and the relationship is project focused. It can progress to the basic, transitional stage where the partners determine the other party's needs in advance or work with each other to clarify and achieve those needs. The issue in this stage is that both parties must benefit in the long term from the new relationship; that is, solutions have to bring ongoing, continuous improvements for both parties.

The defined scope is collaborative in nature and execution, and a sense of established, ongoing "give and take" prevails between the parties. Trust emerges in this stage as joint groups from both parties collaboratively design the solutions. Activities start to span functional and organizational boundaries. There is a true sharing of resources and benefits, and the drive is for innovations that give the network an appeal in the eyes of the business customers and end consumers. The relationship is process driven, and problem solving is cross-organizational in nature. There is continuous operational and strategic renewal occurring.

In summary, the process proceeds through these steps:

1. Category buying teams are formed to search the highest-priority categories with the help of selected suppliers.

2. Joint data warehouses are mined to find the most useful information to enhance the purchasing and delivery processes and to build the future extranets of data interchange that overcome the barriers in the existing disparate legacy systems.

3. Procurement processes are redesigned, often as part of an ERP implementation, to develop improved techniques and to define the necessary electronic data systems.

4. Preliminary e-procurement solutions are tested and implemented.

5. The improved systems are applied internally and externally to reap the greatest benefit from the changes—internally to shorten cycle times, reduce inventories, and gain best pricing; externally to optimize the buy processes to gain the greatest leverage by category.

ADDITIONAL SAVINGS CAN BE SIGNIFICANT

For purchasing groups that have progressed into a Level IV position, the savings through the development of a core group of key suppliers working through an electronic network can be significant. Our research finds price reductions of 2 to 15 percent, overall purchasing process cost reductions of 50 to 90 percent, cycle time reductions of 30 to 60 percent, and inventory reductions (primarily through lower safety stocks) of 30 to 75 percent. The next wave of procurement opportunities has to come from supply chain advancement—the building of network strength on an interenterprise basis.

Exhibit 6.4 shows what we are considering. In the early stages of development, the purchasing group typically makes some impressive gains as the supply base is consolidated and price reductions are achieved. As the effort approaches the end of Level II, we generally see diminishing returns on the effort, as suppliers simply refuse to give any more concessions without reciprocal benefits (beyond keeping the business).

As the procurement effort moves to Level III, the elements of electronic procurement, networkwide (consortium) purchasing and procurement portals take on significance. It is in this area that electronic network formation occurs and procurement excellence becomes a more meaningful objective. In Levels IV and V network sourcing is accomplished through the best network constituent. We have discussed some of the elements of networkwide purchasing and e-procurement, but a short overview will position the discus-

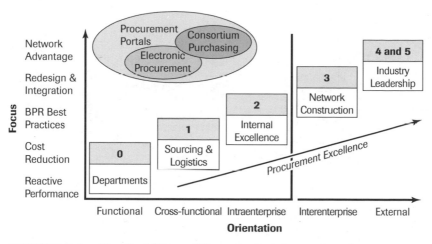

EXHIBIT 6.4 The Next Wave of Opportunity Is Interenterprise

sion for a consideration of how portals become the new tools for achieving further procurement savings.

Electronic Procurement

E-procurement begins with the automation of the requisitioning, approval purchase order management, and accounting processes through an Internet-based protocol. The key elements of this automation include the following:

- A Web browser user interface
- Utilization of standard Internet communication and security protocols
- Software supporting the requisitioning process, including approval and work flow, and product catalog maintenance

The conceptual architecture appears in Exhibit 6.5. We can see that the buyer has a new electronic system at his or her disposal. Communications from key internal customers and external suppliers, coming over an Internet access system, are linked together in the new procurement network. Through this access, the buyer can select from product catalogs the items needed to meet manufacturing or delivery demands. The approval is accomplished online, significantly cutting the cycle time, and the work flow proceeds through the network. The purchase ordering process is automated and feeds directly into the firm's ERP system for retention, payables, and any reconciliation that is necessary. Financial services (for credit and payment) and logistics services (for pooled shipments and cross-docking) can be accessed

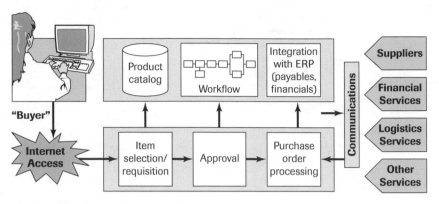

EXHIBIT 6.5   Conceptual Architecture

online, speeding those processes. The primary benefits from this new architecture are improved compliance and better pricing for purchases of indirect goods and services. From our results with many companies, the initial savings fall into three areas:

- Better purchasing information for improved contract negotiation and management results in a 7 to 27 percent reduction in cost.

- Improved transaction handling results in a cost reduction from greater than $100 per transaction to less than $4 per transaction.

- The cycle time for completing transactions is reduced from 30 to 50 percent, order to delivery.

Networkwide Purchasing

As the procurement function moves to negotiating contracts for multiple enterprises, additional values are found. By better utilizing the expertise and advantages gained in buying across the network, categories can be analyzed and the procurement passed to the best capable network partner. Now the pooled leverage increases, and infrastructure and techniques are shared to get the best arrangement for suppliers and network buyers.

What typically happens is that one firm and one or two key suppliers work together to supply a larger base of business, using Internet techniques to reduce buying and selling costs. Inventory and transportation remain as member responsibilities, but deliveries are typically made through a pooled transportation system. Inventories are spread over a larger base, and safety stocks are held

Category	Price Differential (%)
• PC	10–30
• Laser printers	10
• Copiers	15
• Fleet (auto leases)	11–17
• Computer hardware maintenance	30
• Packaged software	20
• Servers	10
• Office suppliers	25
• MRO (nonproduction equipment)	25

Source: CSC Analysis.

EXHIBIT 6.6 Benchmarks Suggesting Significant Savings

at central locations that make sense to the network. It is a win-win set of conditions that results in better savings for all participants.

Again from experience, we have listed in Exhibit 6.6 the potential price differences we find between nonaggregated and aggregated purchasing for selected nondirect categories. When applied across a pooled arrangement with e-procurement features, these savings lead to the next round of improvement opportunity.

The Procurement Portal

The next movement is to consider a procurement portal. A *procurement portal* is a business entity (software provider, pooled purchasing group, network exchange site, industry-specific buying aggregator, etc.) that provides an infrastructure and buying/selling services in support of the management and operations of procurement. It takes cyber-based practices one step further and provides a gateway to a subject area that can lead to buying communities and new iMarkets. The portal scope may be narrow and vertical (plastics, steel, chemicals), broad and general (MRO supplies), or hybrid (MRO supplies to electronics engineers). Generally, portals operate under a "Metcalfe" effect that draws increasing numbers of participants to the portal once it has been introduced. (Metcalfe's law states that the power of a network is proportional to the square of the number of participants.)

A conceptual diagram is presented in Exhibit 6.7. In the portal (in the center of the illustration), information from all of the network constituents flows in and out as the extranet is used to link the system across the enterprises. Procurement acts as the controller, guiding the system. Contracting and contracts management are facilitated through the entity that has responsibility for the category sourcing. Logistics are connected so the inventory is visible, moving as directly as possible to the point of need and with minimal safety

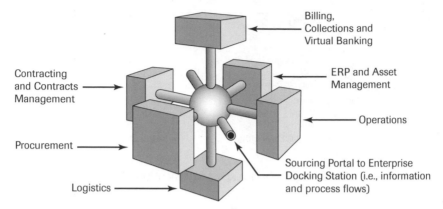

EXHIBIT 6.7   The Procurement Portal

stock. The ERP systems are linked so that planning is more accurate and bottlenecks are minimized. Operations receive what is needed at the time of need. Billing, collections, and virtual banking are also online and handled electronically.

Connections to the portal are built in a standard manner, much like hardware components for a docking station. Procurement transaction information is linked with ERP transaction data and logistics transaction information. Spaces are reserved for any additional data the network members think are important, but the critical aspect is that the entire system is visible to the participants. The infrastructure, which is now shared among enterprise constituents, can be further developed with rich functionality that would be cost-ineffective for the companies to develop individually on an internal basis. That means the portals can become marketplaces where companies go to do additional business, attracted by the low transaction costs that the portal provides. (This is the evolutionary step.) Purchasing information between the enterprises is now captured and exchanged in a common format. This means the buying communities now linked together can leverage spending across more enterprises, developing more consortium opportunities with relatively low development costs. Protocols and standards are further refined and controlled. External partners can now "plug in" and add services, creating even richer functionality. Leading examples include logistical and financial services. The benefits include all of those listed for e-procurement, plus these:

- Shared infrastructure and efficiency in operation
- Elimination of the risk associated with a significant capital investment

- Participation in marketplace advantages
- Transaction costs are lowered for member companies
- An affinity group created by the portal—buyers become sellers

BEYOND PORTALS TO ONLINE AUCTIONING

Eventually, online auctions will have a major impact on the way e-procurement is conducted. Two forms of interaction are becoming common in this area of business transaction: auctions and exchanges. In an auction, a seller considers bids from multiple buyers (individuals or companies) and controls the process. Exchanges involve a neutral party that operates an exchange and sets ground rules for many buyers and sellers who use the exchange for transactions and pay a fee for each transaction conducted. E-steel is a typical exchange site. Auctions and exchanges can yield significant revenue for excess supplies and inventories that were previously sold through liquidators paying a few cents on the dollar value. TradeOut.com is one of the new breed of Internet intermediaries allowing companies to post their lots of excess inventory onto its Web site for viewing by potential buyers. IBM and PartMiner have formed an alliance to develop an e-procurement service that helps electronics companies locate and procure supplies.

Some of the most exciting areas of e-procurement are the online auctions that have developed and the emerging Internet procurement business models that include some form of marketplace activity for acquiring materials and products. The idea, generally attributed to Glen Meakam, founder of FreeMarkets, Inc., is simple but radical. His concept was "to make suppliers compete for manufacturers' orders in live, open, electronic auctions" (Tully 2000, p. 132). FreeMarkets, built for $50 million, now has a market cap of $7 billion and has led to the introduction of many similar auction sites. General Motors, Raytheon, United Technologies, and Quaker Oats are some of the users. Joining other early promoters of Web-based buying, such as Ariba and Commerce One, FreeMarkets is saving companies money by exposing the possibilities online for finding better pricing and cutting transactional costs. With an automated system, the costs of ordering, paying, securing product information, and dealing with the typically large amount of paperwork connected with buying and selling is dramatically reduced.

Followers are quick to appear in this business environment, and the options are proliferating and taking on industry focuses.

On March 25, 1999, America Online Inc. announced an arrangement to feature online auction leader eBay on its service. On March 30, 1999, Amazon.com gave the phenomenon its blessing by launching Amazon.com Auctions. The same day, Priceline.com launched its initial public offering (IPO), and auctions have taken off like a rocket. Even traditional retailers like Sharper Image are adding sites. According to Forrester Research analyst Kate Delhagen, "It's only a matter of time before every retailer has an online auction." San Francisco Internet market observer Keenan Vision Inc. predicts consumer and business auctions will account for 29 percent of all e-commerce by 2002 (Hof 1999, p. 30).

Today, we see marketplaces (i.e., Web-based trading sites) offering a variety of choices. There are those that only offer to service targeted markets such as e-steel, paperexchange.com, e-plastics, and e-scrap (catering to buyers seeking scrap paper supplies). There are software vendors teaming with service providers to create industry portals, such as Rightworks and Commerce One for financial services. And there are proprietary software companies combining their search engines with service offerings that permanently lock in specific buyers, such as Ariba Technologies moving to offer Corp.Ariba.com. The range is expected to grow as we see a second wave of more focused offerings starting to appear, such as the recently announced marketplaces for automobile and food manufacturers.

The implications of this phenomenon are enormous. These cyber auctions could push aside a significant portion of current business-to-business-to-consumer techniques and bring on an era of online, dynamic pricing in which market pricing will rule the transactions. Thanks to the Internet, buyers and sellers around the globe can conduct instant bargaining at very little cost to those doing the transaction. Industrial auctions such as FreeMarkets' Online Inc. now sell coal and printed circuit boards to companies across the globe. The advantage is the Internet's ability to make pricing information available anywhere, to anyone online, at any time of the day. Thus, a dynamic marketplace has been created, replete with the necessary market makers that spawn the concept and seek a profit for being the intermediaries in the transactions. Variable pricing is destined to become a new business art form over this emerging purchasing network. Consider these examples:

> *PNC Bank Corp. in Pittsburgh began accepting bids last month to determine what interest rate some consumers will receive on a limited number of certificates of deposit. Deere & Co. is auctioning used farm equipment to customers on behalf of its dealers. And Visteon, the*

$18 billion parts subsidiary of Ford Motor Co., this summer held a "reverse auction" to source $150 million in circuit boards and other automotive components. By year's end, Visteon wants to solicit bids from its suppliers for another $350 million in multiyear contracts. (Dalton 1999, p. 45)

Consider another example of how far and fast the phenomenon can extend. On March 16, 2000, Reuters reporter Simon Hirschfeld announced that

fifty food, beverage and consumer product manufacturers are planning an open, electronic marketplace to link all participants in the industry supply chain. Leaders of an exploratory committee include executives of Kraft Foods, Procter & Gamble, General Mills, Nestle SA, Unilever Plc, and Best Foods. Other participants in the initiative include Coca-Cola Co., Gillette Co., Johnson & Johnson and others. The plan was conceived less than two weeks ago at a meeting of e-Commerce executives of the various companies. (FROM A CSC INTERCOMPANY MEMO)

A brief analysis of the various techniques being applied will reveal the scope and depth of what is transpiring.

Auction Markets

Electronic auctions are one of the new options that should be considered in developing a commodity sourcing strategy. These auctions should be evaluated in terms of the necessary attributes that must be exhibited in a particular commodity market to make this technique an appropriate alternative. Moreover, there are various kinds of auctions, and each should be categorized so it is matched with the particular commodity being considered. For an auction market to develop and make sense, three attributes are necessary:

1. *Indifference between buyer and seller must exist;* that is, it should be a situation where the buyer is truly indifferent as to the source, so long as the commodity meets required specifications. At the same time, the seller should not have a preference among buyers based on a previous segmentation analysis. All purchasers of the commodity come to the auction with equal desirability, so long as they can accept delivery and make payments within the prescribed time frame.

2. *The price of the commodity should be the only variable left unspecified.* If nonprice elements (quality, delivery lead time, freight costs) are important, then partnering methods are

more appropriate. Commodities do not need to be homogenous, but they should be classified so that qualitative differences can be readily discerned.

3. *The auction has to produce some profit for the market maker.* It must in some way improve the efficiency of the market, producing value for both buyers and sellers so a portion of the added value can be extracted as earnings for the market maker.

With these conditions as a guide, we'll illustrate five categories of auctions:

1. *Classical auction.* One seller and multiple buyers characterize this auction. The auction is for a specific lot, possibly followed by many subsequent offerings of similar commodities, but only one buyer can be successful. Because this type of auction is for individual lots sold to a specific buyer, homogeneity between the lots is not required. This method can be used when the requirement for indifference to sellers is not necessary as the seller will be known. These auctions are often used to dispose of excess inventory, aged inventory, off-specification product that is still useable (e.g., paper or steel coils with damaged edges) and product that is soon to be replaced by newer offerings. The classical auction may be conducted as a real-time auction where bidding continues until no more bids are forthcoming, or as a "candle" auction in which bidding is allowed for a predefined time period. The leading bid at the time of expiration wins the lot.

2. *Reverse auction.* One buyer and multiple sellers characterize this auction. It is the classical auction in reverse, with specific buyers bringing their specific requirements to the site and using an auction to secure prices from multiple sellers competing to secure the contract. This is an alternative to the traditional "request-for-proposal" (RFP) methodology through which buyers normally solicit bids on their requirements. It is appropriate when the buyer is genuinely indifferent as to the seller's identity and credentials and is prepared to accept the lowest bid. Other, nonprice factors may not be unimportant, but these factors must be explicit in the lot requirement so price is the only variable to be determined. Under these circumstances, the seller who wins the bid will be committing to a delivery contract that specifies performance criteria. At the same time, the buyer is committed to the purchase at the agreed price. This technique is often used for one-time,

high-value purchases in which the requirements can be accurately and completely described in the "lot."

ChannelPoint Commerce exchange, for example, provides a site where insurance brokers, consumers, and underwriters can gather to research, buy, and sell insurance policies. Recruit Dynamics uses online auctions to recruit contractors and consultants. Flashline.com has a reverse auction service for outsourcing development of software components (Dalton 1999b, p. 48).

3. *Dutch auction.* This auction is characterized by one seller and multiple buyers, but with multiple lots available. In a classical auction, the procedure is for one lot—only one buyer can win. In a Dutch auction, the seller has a finite number of homogeneous lots available and wishes to dispose of them all at the conclusion of one auction. Under these conditions, the lowest successful bid sets the price for the entire collection. An example is the auctioning of an IPO of stock by Witt Capital. In a typical IPO, the company decides the amount of capital it wishes to receive from the offering and the number of shares to be issued. For example, Company A might wish to raise $20 million from its IPO and has twenty million shares available. It offers the shares at an opening of one dollar. In this situation, if the company undervalues its shares, the issue will be oversubscribed, and speculators will profit from the difference between the IPO price and the market price. This is money that could have gone to Company A.

Conversely, if the company overvalues its shares, it will not realize its required capital and will have unsold shares remaining. The company, therefore, loses out if its estimates of market demand are incorrect either way. Witt's solution is to offer the shares through a Dutch auction, with each investor bidding for his or her preferred amount of shares at a price he or she is willing to pay. The IPO price for the entire issue is then set by the winning price for the marginal twenty-millionth share. This method can be compared to the yield management model discussed in the fourth option later, and it is used where there are regulatory or other factors that prohibit setting differential prices for the same items. In the example cited, it is illegal to offer IPO stock at different prices—all investors must pay the same price.

This model could be applied where there is a known, finite supply and the likelihood of demand competition. The existence of a secondary market could be an indication where this auction is applicable. Another application might be for selling computer chips where the new processor has great demand and insufficient supply when it is first introduced. It could also apply to any product that is similarly subject to supply shortages or great demand fluctuations. A necessary characteristic is obviously that sellers are indifferent among various buyers.

4. *"Demand management" auction.* We place this category in quotation marks because Priceline.com has applied for a patent on the use of the term *demand management.* This technique differs from the previous models in two ways: there are multiple buyers and multiple sellers, and the market maker plays an active, rather than passive, role as the intermediary. This model is applicable for markets in which the chief attributes are perishable inventory, inconsistent or unpredictable demand, and great differences of price elasticity among buyers. Priceline currently deals with airline tickets, hotel reservations, groceries, and rental car reservations—commodities that fit the application. The firm has announced it plans to extend its purchasing system to businesses. It's targeting business services such as advertising and telecommunications, and procurement of office supplies and IT equipment (*Information Week,* March 6, 2000, p. 44). An example from their current area of auction illustrates the technique used.

   Let's say your grandmother, who lives in Pittsburgh, wants to book an airline reservation three months out, to visit you and her grandchildren in Boston. The travel agent will quote a best advance price; in this case, assume it's $250 round-trip. She might decide to try to better this deal by going to Priceline.com. This effort involves specifying the day she wishes to travel and from which airports she will consider flying. She may also specify how many connections she would be willing to make, but she cannot specify carrier preference or time preference during the day. At the Web site, she enters how much she is willing to pay for the ticket (let's say you advise her to put in $100).

   Priceline receives the request and polls every airline that has scheduled flights that fit her preferences. Each airline responds back indicating it will accept or reject the offer. If one airline accepts her price, she has bought a nonrefundable ticket charged to the appropriate credit card. Priceline responds to your grandmother, either saying that the offer was rejected or providing the itinerary for the trip. If she fails to get acceptance, she can try again with a higher bid.

In the area in which Priceline has concentrated, yield management pricing is the practice being applied. Sellers benefit by at least covering marginal costs associated with the product or service, considering that this price is better than receiving nothing for what becomes perishable inventory (empty seats in the airline example). For this type of model to work, there must be multiple sellers (as distinct from classical and Dutch auctions) as well as multiple buyers and mutual indifference among those buyers and sellers. Anonymity of buyers and sellers is present in this model and guaranteed by the intermediary, a feature that is probably necessary to ensure fair operation of the market.

5. *Stock market model*. This market is characterized by multiple sellers, multiple buyers, homogeneity of commodity, and mutual indifference. The market may be mediated (e.g., the New York Stock Exchange, which uses market makers to set the bid/ask spread) or not (e.g., Instinet, which merely matches bids and asks and executes the trades). The real difference is that a mediated market guarantees you can make a trade—the market maker *must* make a market, whereas with Instinet, if there are no buyers, you cannot sell the stock. This type of market is limited to genuine commodities. An example would be "neutral spirits," which are a commodity ingredient for whiskey and other alcoholic liquors. The market in this area is small, in terms of both buyers and sellers, so there is little demand for a futures market. The type of market represented here is likely to be a private market (like the energy market, which is not open to speculators) offering a different method of selling and procuring specific commodities in place of contracting between specific buyers and sellers. Markets could be established to sell capacity, both spot and future, for process industries, for example.

In addition to these specialized auction and exchange models, there is an increasing number of automated buying agents. This term refers to the technology that automatically scours the Internet for companies pricing on a specific requirement and makes the procurement from the lowest-priced vendor. In a business-to-business context, this requires price to be the most important factor in the sourcing decision. It also requires that the intelligent agent can, in fact, carry out the task. The suppliers whom the agent polls must all refer to the particular item required in the same way, meaning they must conform to the same catalog standards in reflecting their products and pricing. There is still some time needed for all participants to catch up to this standards requirement.

Online procurement systems are streamlining purchasing operations, saving time and costs, and altering the traditional purchasing function. As ERP systems mature, we expect that the percentage of transactions conducted over these media will only accelerate. Beyond the initial savings, there will be new free time for the buyers to assume the role being advocated, that of a proactive adviser to management. The role becomes showing how to use the remaining face-to-face supplier relationships to help mold the new e-business models so much in need for the twenty-first century.

As the hype surrounding these new options increases and purchasing groups seem drawn toward the vortex of action, other alternatives are appearing. There is a trend emerging for repackaging software applications for service purposes, moving the pricing for the software from a one-time payment to a leasing arrangement. Application service providers (ASPs) now rent software packages for a fixed monthly rate, delivering access through a wide-area network (WAN), virtual private network, or the Internet. Other organizations are now offering to "host" procurement services sites on a fee basis, which is attractive for smaller companies and those not wanting to make a large investment in a full software application or to be locked into a proprietary arrangement.

SUMMARY

The next wave of procurement improvement will focus on how to further the leveraging of purchasing power, expertise, and infrastructure across companies in a supply chain network. As former adversaries learn to work together to move their supply chains to advanced levels, Web-based e-procurement systems will offer a tremendous opportunity to promote better-managed, indirect spending. Companies that have mutually attained a level of internal excellence will now look to some form of network-based buying, conducted over the Internet, for additional opportunities. Procurement portals will serve as a basis for bringing these complementary opportunities together in a powerful way. As the portals are being constructed, buyers can turn to a variety of auctions and exchanges for both buying and selling. In all of these new efforts, new roles must be adopted as procurement is ushered into the electronic era.

7

Building an Interactive Engineering, Planning, Scheduling, and Manufacturing Capability

During the last two decades of the twentieth century, manufacturing firms worked diligently at improving operating costs, particularly in the areas of direct labor, direct materials, and inventories. Service organizations also struggled with how to effectively provide superior customer satisfaction with the fewest people. Quality, purchasing, and logistics were prime areas of attention as team efforts were typically required to create beneficial infrastructure changes. Reengineering entire processes became a driving force behind most of these efforts as redundant process steps were eliminated and redesigned steps were set in place.

As organizations began reaching the point of diminishing returns on what were essentially cost reduction efforts, while still facing pressures on profit margins, they turned to alternative means to survive and prosper. Many firms realized that cost improvement is finite and new business would account for future gains. In the past, these revenues were often gained by using the fruits of the improvements, by reducing prices in step with lower operating costs. This technique did little to sustain the previously enhanced operating profits. The pressure on cost reduction also never really subsided, and the search intensified.

Toward the end of the last decade, supply chain was discovered and initiatives appeared that brought an end-to-end focus on improvement. Now profit seekers turned their attention to indirect labor and materials and services, as well as better use of network assets to satisfy customers. They looked to supply chains to bring the next wave of improvement and return on effort. Some notable advances were made, but most of the truly large benefits eluded many of the seekers because they refused to share any of their previous learning with external partners. Caught in the flawed perception that only those improvements that they had made internally bore any value, most companies overlooked the benefits that could have been gained by collaborating with key suppliers, distributors, and customers.

THE VALUE IN NETWORK COOPERATION

The emphasis on business improvement is shifting. Companies are moving fast to work with external partners to find the next levels of savings. They are making alliances with high-technology firms to find system savings and better access and use of the Internet. They are setting up network communication systems with business partners to determine how to satisfy designated end consumers in a total supply chain network. The leading companies are looking outside their boundaries for help with sales growth as well as savings. Work is being focused on the demand side to find new consumers with more enduring characteristics. The dominant business models of the future will be more responsive to these new consumers, and the successful networks will embrace these external partnering models in an interenterprise system that will become a value chain constellation. The winning groups will fuse high efficiency, high productivity, and high value to deliver high consumer appeal. That requires a new level of interenterprise connectivity

This chapter describes how to integrate the vital information flows across all of the important members of a full supply chain network. It explains how to collaborate across the network, using features of e-commerce, to create value for the targeted consumer base that will provide new revenues. An advanced supply chain effort will include an integrated enterprise-wide resource planning (I-ERP) system with connectivity at each of its important links. Through this linkage, best applications will be shared with appropriate trading partners.

Referring to Exhibit 7.1, at the start, most companies looking at engineering, planning, scheduling and manufacturing rely on previously developed systems, such as material resource planning (MRP and MRP II) and distribution resource planning (DRP). These systems are time proven and can be very effective at raising the level of manufacturing efficiency within the organization. With a

Progression Business Application	Level I/II	Level III	Level IV	Level IV+
	Internal Supply Chain Optimization	Network Formation	Value Chain Constellation	Full Network Connectivity
	Stage 0	*Stage 1*	*Stage 2*	*Stage 3*
Engineering, planning, scheduling, manufacturing*	MRP MRPII DRP	ERP – internal connectivity	Collaborative network planning – best asset utilization	Full network business system optimization

EXHIBIT 7.1   E-business Development Framework: Engineering, Planning, Scheduling, and Manufacturing

desire to move toward network formation, the firm finds that something else is necessary—building network alliances requires sharing information on planning and scheduling with external partners. The next move has to be toward linking computers and data systems across the supply chain network.

As mentioned, this sharing does not come easy, and it is inhibited by problems inherent in the resource planning initiatives. Having watched the progress of many firms as they installed enterprise-wide resource planning (ERP) systems, we can report that most are characterized by overspending and underaccomplishment. Stories abound of how firms decided to integrate disparate legacy systems into one planning and delivery system. While some of the perceived benefits were realized, most efforts took far longer to accomplish than predicted and were accompanied by many cost overruns.

The good news is that once installed and operating, the ERP system offers an opportunity to reap unexpected benefits. With ERP in place, the company is prepared for the vital upstream and downstream linkage of systems that enable network planning and execution. This is an essential move, since any link in the value chain that does not have this connectivity puts the total chain at risk, because it introduces longer cycle times for response and higher costs.

We are talking here of direct linkage, over the Internet, of computers within the supply chain network. An extranet must be established among the various key suppliers, distributors, and business customers so the necessary information on design, engineering, manufacturing, scheduling, and shipment that impacts supply is put in a form to be shared. At the same time, information on the actual demand that needs to be fulfilled has to move equally easily through the network so the response system can efficiently match the correct supply with the correct demand. In the current digital economy, each of these flows of information has to be electronic and available across the value chain being created. We're considering the means to establish synchronization of engineering, planning, scheduling, manufacturing, and delivery of products and services to specific business customers and end consumers. Forecasting becomes less critical in this environment as the customer information on actual consumption is used for interactive planning through Web-enabled members of the value chain.

Brochure Ware

At the beginning level of the effort, when the Internet is first used and we characterize the results as "brochure ware," firms turn to the Web (independently) as a static marketing device, generally for a single, public audience. This is the necessary learning segment of progress when data are transmitted over the Internet and traditional companies achieve some efficiency with better information distribution, usually on an internal basis. The changes impacted by the Web usage are not major, but the probing is valuable in the lessons learned about Web-based reactions and depth of penetration with messages. This is the "inform" level of implementation.

Publish and Subscribe

At the next level, "publish and subscribe," the company uses the Web to facilitate necessary communications with different audiences. Sales in nontraditional markets may be sought, for example, as the firm extends its learning and curiosity into how further gains can be made. E-commerce is better understood across the company in this phase, and experimentation becomes more sophisticated. Many firms begin to realize there is a role for e-commerce and that an external viewpoint can have beneficial payback. Dun & Bradstreet, a leading provider of business-to-business services, for example, is planning to deliver more than half of its products through the Internet in the twenty-first century.

Ordering

As the company progresses to the third level, termed "ordering," the Web is used to enable transactions with diverse audiences. Now there is a decided move to use external help. The number of business entities included is expanded in this stage, as Web-based buying and selling becomes a reality. Examples have been given and will continue to be discussed as we see the proliferation of organizations introducing new ways to buy and sell products and services. Quicken Mortgage, for example, qualifies users for a loan online and offers a choice of mortgages from a variety of network lenders. American Finance & Investment sells mortgages directly to consumers. This start-up operation has eliminated branches and brokers in its business model.

These nonmanufacturing examples show how the same techniques are finding their way into service organizations. From a manufacturing perspective, this stage brings the need for online accessibility to planning and scheduling so an efficient network response can be created. The emphasis moves from making point optimizations (at a particular process step in the supply chain) that may do nothing for the overall system of delivery, to establishing a totally effective system of response. That means, across the network, unnecessary steps are eliminated and product movement is placed in the hands of the most capable partner. Across this more effective system, the customer stays in direct contact with what is occurring in the manufacturing and delivering processes. This step is enabled because the partners are using their extranet to transfer the vital data online for visible inspection, analysis, and changes to the manufacturing and delivering systems.

Deliver

In the next level, called "deliver," online services appear as the experimentation is turned into a mechanism for improving manufacturing and delivery efficiency and building new revenues with customers attracted by the better system of response. Now the Web is used to connect and work with the other network members to further enhance the ability to deliver or directly provide the products and services the business customer and end consumers are choosing. A virtual business community begins to form as the network coalesces and the constituents share information on how to progress via the Internet. This cooperation becomes a force in generating the full network connectivity, which will be used by all the key players in the eventual value chain constellation.

Boeing Aircraft, for example, uses the Internet to establish new channels for its after-market sales. Results have been very rewarding. Ten months after the launch of its Parts Analysis and Requirement Tracking (PART) Web site in October 1996, Boeing transacted more than $40 million worth of business. PART is an extranet that allows Boeing's commercial customers to place and track spare parts orders over the Internet, many of which have not been manufactured by Boeing. Because Boeing's parts page links to major shipping companies' Web sites and tracking systems, they can modify orders right up to the time of shipment and then track the orders en route. This response is enabled through the cooperation of Boeing's external supply chain partners and their connection to the PART system.

Toshiba launched its Internet parts replenishment system in conjunction with its Memphis, Tennessee–based distribution and warehouse facility. Since that location is next to Federal Express's major hub, 98 percent of the company's parts orders are shipped by overnight delivery. Toshiba's dealers save money because of leaner inventories and are more responsive to customer demands, both in time and support features.

Community

At the final level, the "community" stage, the network fully utilizes the Web for marketing, partner interaction, personalization for specific consumers, and the building of the business community that becomes the value chain from beginning supply to final consumption. The value chain constellation coalesces, and collaborative planning is conducted. With this full network connectivity, the manufacturer does not guess at what is being consumed and does not push highly efficient productivity into inventory (for sale at whatever prices are necessary to create consumption). Rather, the new objective is to replace what has been consumed by virtue of knowing, on an hourly basis, what is going through the sellers' cash registers or Web pages.

Few enterprises have in place the requisite communications architecture to enable data velocity and accuracy across their supply chain networks. They rely on batch EDI and manual processes, which inherently introduce delays. Collaboration becomes the e–supply chain solution as current computer-aided systems and software are linked from end to end of the value chain and become focused on meeting the actual demands of end consumers.

ERP: THE TOOL OF ADVANCEMENT

ERP is a set of applications that have been designed to bring disparate manufacturing and business functions into balance. Companies either take the best of their legacy systems and merge them with "best of breed" software into a uniform planning package, or they adopt a totally new packaged system so resource planning and manufacturing execution is brought close to optimized conditions. Companies such as Baan, J. D. Edwards, Oracle, Peoplesoft, and SAP have been in the forefront of this movement.

We have discussed how these installations have been plagued with difficulties and extra costs, but the value and payback are now becoming clear. At the enterprise level, all modules have impact and contribute some improvement. For example, computer-aided design and manufacturing, already in place in most manufacturing environments, can be linked to enhance product development cycle times and greatly improve product data management efforts. In an advanced system, software from Trilogy Company allows customers to go online to configure their own products and get complex pricing information. These product configuration systems can be made available directly to manufacturers' ERP systems. The customer knows immediately whether the selected products are in or out of stock and when they can be obtained. Manufacturers of computers, networking equipment, and furniture are pioneers with this type of interactive software.

At a call center or customer service location, access to newly available and valuable information from the planning, scheduling, and manufacturing modules helps provide the answers and solutions supply chain customers and consumers are seeking, often on a real-time basis. Within a manufacturing cell, all of the necessary data for efficient processing is at the operator's fingertips. At the level where a device is being created, new data are also available (from customers describing what they want and possible alternative designs from R&D) that enhance what will be delivered to the final customer.

Because of the advances made in ERP software, businesses have improved their engineering and manufacturing operations while enhancing their accounting and financial practices as access and attention are given to actual costs. Now the users are turning their attention to customers, suppliers, and business partners. The future of ERP is all about improving the supply chain process steps by fostering greater collaboration across multiple business functions and enterprises and taking advantage of the investments made in a total resource planning system.

According to Tom Stein, a prolific writer on e-business, an integrated set of applications that link together such back-office operations as manufacturing, financials, and distribution "will become a subclass of a much bigger and broader enterprise business system." He predicts ERP will extend into transportation, warehousing, sales force automation, and engineering with computer-aided design and product data management systems (Stein 1998, p. 20SS).

Software providers are hard at work trying to respond to this next level of evolution. To meet the challenge for more extensive use of ERP, leaders such as SAP and Oracle are now developing their own supply chain, sales force automation, and data repository links to existing manufacturing and financial applications. In November 1999, Baan Company released version 2.0 of its Supply Chain Planner, as well as an application called "Supply Chain Order Promising" designed to maximize customer order fulfillment capabilities across multiple production sites. SAP previously introduced mySAP.com, an open, collaborative business system that integrates SAP and non-SAP software. This company also offers SAP APO, which supports supply chain and demand planning, forecasting, distribution requirements planning, scheduling, and product and factory planning (Baron 1999, p. 110).

Mike Schmitt, senior VP of open systems solutions at ERP vendor J. D. Edwards & Co., envisions a world in which companies use a single, integrated system to manage the entire customer life cycle. This means tying together in one package many disparate applications, including order entry and manufacturing, supply chain management for transportation and warehousing, and sales force automation for customer service. Manufacturers should be able to configure an order, assemble it, ship it to the customer, and service that customer all on one integrated ERP system, says Schmitt (Stein 1998, p. 21SS).

Some examples show what early pioneers have been accomplishing. The U.S. unit of Taiwan Semiconductor lets customers such as Intel, Motorola, and Adaptec access its order management system through their ERP systems to help them monitor the manufacture of integrated circuits at TSMC's plants. The company selected software from CrossRoute at its San Jose, California, operation, an application integration suite from CrossRoute Software, Inc., to connect TSMC's order management system directly to their clients' ERP systems. It took nine months to link its system to Adaptec's SAP R/3 system, but the result was faster data transmission and shorter production cycle times in a suitable format for access by Adaptec's staff (Adhikari 1998, p. 12SS).

A range of technologies exists today that promote faster and more accurate information flow between network partners. Many are low-cost, Internet-based solutions suitable for business-to-business-to-consumer integration. These more powerful solutions use a combination of Web-based infrastructure and cooperatively developed systemic applications. Extranets can be leveraged to create a communication infrastructure with a secure environment and transfer an enriched offering of data crucial to business success. By applying application logic across a network, the partners can also participate in simulation trials that test novel approaches without the typical risk in roll-out programs. These extranet applications are well beyond EDI and show the way to a strategic set of capabilities.

One area of capability being improved is that of inventory management. Uncertainty breeds higher inventory and safety stock. The use of a mutually developed linkage for making the inventories visible online and tracking movements can erase most of the uncertainty and reduce the amount of extra stock in the total system. Interactive links built into the interenterprise connections can also focus attention on constraints that inhibit meeting delivery schedules. Software from i2 Technologies, for example, offers a particularly strong suite of programs to pinpoint these constraints and eliminate the bottlenecks they cause in manufacturing processes. Exceptions to planned schedules can also be exposed to improve total network visibility and find solutions. Software tools now exist that allow businesses to link their ERP systems, regardless of type, with those of their trading partners to transfer critical information and speed delivery of goods and services. Through industry-sponsored moves, high-technology firms, telecommunications companies, banks, and some industrial groups (automobile, steel, plastic, and chemicals) have formed strategic consortia to provide standards and specifications for secure electronic transacting. These networks enable consumers and businesses to perform a wide range of traditional functions securely over the Internet.

With so many issues to consider as firms build the necessary data linkage in a supply chain network, the process developers must be aware of what makes the most sense for the network being enhanced. Most e-business projects go astray when they do not adequately address all areas of important business change. Exhibit 7.2 lists such critical implementation points. As the e-business program is created, the players can array the elements of importance to their network and then make their own list of important applications. The idea is to not overlook a matter of importance to the joint effort, which limits the network's enhanced capability.

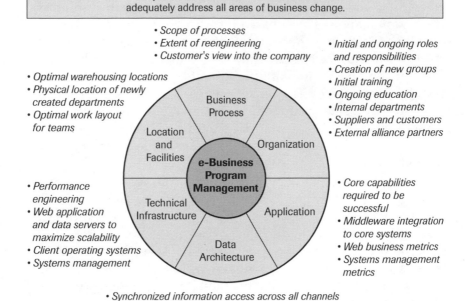

Projects that fail are often those that do not adequately address all areas of business change.

• Scope of processes
• Extent of reengineering
• Customer's view into the company

• Initial and ongoing roles and responsibilities
• Creation of new groups
• Initial training
• Ongoing education
• Internal departments
• Suppliers and customers
• External alliance partners

• Optimal warehousing locations
• Physical location of newly created departments
• Optimal work layout for teams

Business Process

Location and Facilities

e-Business Program Management

Organization

• Performance engineering
• Web application and data servers to maximize scalability
• Client operating systems
• Systems management

Technical Infrastructure

Application

Data Architecture

• Core capabilities required to be successful
• Middleware integration to core systems
• Web business metrics
• Systems management metrics

• Synchronized information access across all channels
• Distributed, replicated vs. real-time pass-through transactions

EXHIBIT 7.2 Implementation Points for Consideration

ERP-TO-ERP CONNECTIVITY

Extending ERP into advanced supply chain management has become the ingredient that allows for the higher-level actions that differentiate the network. It enables a network to become efficient in that the constituents can coordinate everything from raw material and engineering design to parts components and final assembly. It enhances the flow to distribution and on to retail outlets and the final delivery to consumers. The result is better forecasting, tighter delivery schedules, reduced inventory requirements, and streamlined communications. The operation is moving to what Forrester Research calls "dynamic trade"—the ability to satisfy current demand with customized response (McCullough 1999, p. 10). On the demand side of that ability, collaborative demand planning is accomplished by allowing order and market information to flow upstream continuously from the point of sale, while data on product availability and inventory levels flow downstream. This continuous data loop eliminates or substantially reduces the type of incremental distortion that occurs when each link responds to their own interpretation of supply and demand data. It also greatly enhances

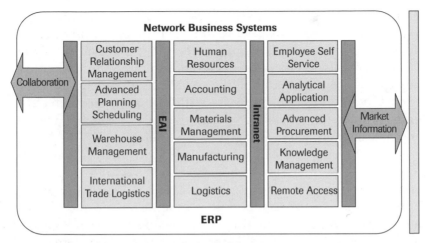

Source: AMR Research Enterprise Applications Conference, June 1999.

EXHIBIT 7.3   Extended ERP Evolves to Network Business Systems (NBS)

the planning and scheduling system's ability to meet actual needs and not waste asset utilization and use extra safety stocks.

On the response side, collaborative order fulfillment goes further. It is characterized by making negotiated or joint decisions, such as order size and frequency, and by facilitating the transfer of management and ownership of inventory. One result is less distortion of demand. The greater the synchronization, the greater the value added to the supply chain network performance. The most highly synchronized order fulfillment approaches let customer demand data directly drive orders, instead of basing orders on forecasts.

Exhibit 7.3, created by AMR Research and presented at their Enterprise Applications Conference in June 1999, shows the evolution we are considering. Using collaboration as the binding ingredient, firms in a Stage 2 value chain work together to combine useful data from their intranets in the areas described. Enterprise application integration (EAI) also occurs, as the linked internal systems are used to develop joint efforts on customer relationship management, advanced planning and scheduling, warehouse management, and international trade logistics. This latter collaboration is conducted over the Internet. At the same time, market information flows from the retailers and final business customers back into the network so data from the end consumers are available for all constituents.

ERP systems integrate all manufacturing applications at the back end, from manufacturing scheduling to billing and ordering. Tools that let companies establish ERP-to-ERP links are application integration suites, e-commerce systems, and middleware. Some ERP suppliers will create custom links between their product and others, or users can use development tools to create their own links. Ariba Technologies Inc., for example, offers an Order Request Management System to communicate information about orders between buyers and sellers. It works with EDI and e-commerce systems. Employees can place orders over the Web that will be automatically fulfilled by designated suppliers.

Cisco Systems uses Ariba Technology software to automate its purchasing ERP system, which is based on Oracle 10.x. For high-value items, employees send purchase requisitions over the Web through Ariba's system to supervisors for approval, instead of filling out a paper form and going through a manual cycle. On approval, purchase requests are imported into the Oracle ERP system where the process is completed and the system either prints out a purchase order or sends it to suppliers through EDI. Lower-value items are ordered directly through the online catalog set up in Ariba. Cisco buys about $500 million worth of products a year, and automating the process has saved a considerable amount of time and money.

Mapics Inc., which offers Mapics XA, an ERP application for discrete and batch process manufacturers, works with its customers to create custom interfaces to link ERP systems to those of suppliers. Mapics XA has forty-six modules and provides predefined translation maps to communicate over EDI with various corporations such as Kmart, Wal-Mart, and J. C. Penney.

These actions and those of many others are paving the way for serious integration of multiple business applications across a total supply chain network. Exhibit 7.4 illustrates where the trend is leading—to an integrated ERP (I-ERP) network system that links trading partners together so best practices emerge and the total effort is enhanced. Arrayed around the nucleus ERP network are the types of collaborative work that can improve a value chain constellation. From Web order processing and fulfillment through planning, forecasting, distribution, and customer service, companies are integrating their resource planning systems in a way that improves overall performance.

BUSINESS EXAMPLES PROVING THE VALUE OF ERP LINKAGE

As firms select from the menu of applications of the ERP linkage, they find improvements could exceed the results of previous cost

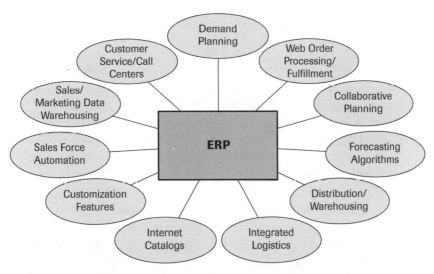

EXHIBIT 7.4   I-ERP Capabilities That Enhance Supply Chain Interactions

reduction efforts and better enable their supply chain response system. Colgate-Palmolive Company, the consumer product giant, in an effort to continue the automation of its supply chain, is moving forward to connect key suppliers at plants around the world to its electronic supply chain network. The firm has already used an SAP planning system for accurate and flexible shared planning and delivery and for lower inventory costs. Ed Tobin, VP of global IT at Colgate-Palmolive, explains, "Electronic business-to-business integration is a logical extension of the way we work with our partners." The company had to react quickly when data from downstream customers were introduced. "When we started getting point-of-sale data from customers, there was no function here to receive it. We had to create it," says Tobin. This is not an unusual situation. The complication is the impact automation generally has on the business process, since e–supply chain brings major changes in the companies that must deal with each other. "Business change is the issue," Tobin adds, explaining that Colgate isn't ready to force such jarring changes on its suppliers (Cone 1998, p. 2SS).

When some of its large customers, such as Compaq and IBM, demanded that Pericom Semiconductor Corp., of San Jose, California, a $50 million manufacturer of electronic components, automate or lose their business, the first reaction was negative. But realizing they had no choice, the company faced its challenge and found it had to remake its business processes, down to the level of lot sizing and bar coding. "Your channel master will tell you how to do business," says Mike Schmitt, senior VP at J. D. Edwards, which implemented an ERP system for Pericom (Cone 1998, p. 4SS). The system, fed by weekly EDI runs from customers, generates new manufacturing orders and manages inventory at third-party warehouses.

Miller SQA, a Holland, Michigan, division of Herman Miller that builds make-to-order office furniture, buys used cubicle dividers, hanging components, and work surfaces and reworks them to create new products for sale. Part of its business strategy is to compress the information and manufacturing cycles as much as possible. That means Miller SQA has worked hard at its supply chain, eliminating process steps and reducing the cycle times from order entry to order fulfillment, while taking out as much of the paperwork flow as possible. Going further, the company linked its planning systems with key suppliers and business customers, so they now work together as part of a fully integrated supply chain. The company uses Symix SyteLine from Symix Systems Inc. as its ERP package and stores data in Progress databases running under SyteLine. Miller SQA has several hundred suppliers, so creating interfaces with all of their ERP systems was unthinkable, according to Jim Von Ins, director of information services (Adhikari 1998, p. 18 SS).

The company decided to create a supplier extranet. As soon as an order is accepted, the material requirements are immediately made visible to its key suppliers. The company has created real-time integration between its sales configurator and its scheduling system. Miller SQA opted to use a combined Web-EDI solution and set up a Web site using Lotus Development's Domino, and it developed SupplyNet, an application to extract customers' orders from its Progress databases and publish them on its site. This integration, combined with improved supply chain planning and sales configuration tools, has enabled Miller SQA to reduce order fulfillment cycle times from twenty-one days to fewer than five days (Adhikari 1998, p. 18SS).

COLLABORATIVE PLANNING, FORECASTING, AND REPLENISHMENT

Concurrently, different resources within a supply chain network spend time devoted to interpreting demand data and matching it with supply information. Often, these groups do not effectively communicate with each other in the manner being advocated in this chapter, much less collaborate on supply chain decisions. Traditional trading partner initiatives such as aggregate forecasting and replenishment (AFR), vendor-managed inventory (VMI), and jointly managed inventory (JMI) have achieved only partial success, primarily because of poor information, disconnected systems, limited scalability, and a lack of interenterprise cooperation.

Collaborative planning, forecasting, and replenishment (CPFR) is an early development (Level III) effort, which requires creating a new business model designed to overcome many of these obstacles. CPFR takes a holistic approach to supply chain management among a set of value chain constellation partners. Approved as industry guidelines by the Voluntary Inter-Industry Commerce Standards (VICS) organization and the Uniform Code Council (UCC), CPFR has the potential to deliver increased sales, interorganizational streamlining and alignment, administrative and operating efficiency, improved cash flow, and greater return on asset performance.

The effort developed from a trial plan with the Retail Working Group by Benchmarking Partners and an initial pilot program between Warner-Lambert and Wal-Mart. Twenty-six companies served as a subcommittee to the VICS Merchants Issues Committee. These companies contributed to the guidelines of what has become the application model. The process begins with an agreement among trading partners to develop a collaborative business relationship based on exchanging information to support the synchronization of activities to deliver products in response to market demands. Using CPFR, partners minimize inventories that buffer interactions between processes and focus on improving the accuracy of plans to support the flow of supply to consumers. Participants discover bottlenecks in the system and find mutual solutions.

An extension of this effort is collaborative supply chain planning (CSCP). CSCP is made especially viable by Internet technology. It is designed to increase collaborative decision making between those firms responsible for providing supply, pertaining to what, where, when, and how many products will be sold. CSCP guides the development of Internet-enabled, collaborative processes across trading partners' value chain constellations, thereby helping link suppliers and customers in the creation of mutual business plans through full network connectivity. These plans can include supply chain strategies, partnering agreements, promotion plans, product and service development, forecasting improvement efforts, and replenishment plans.

By leveraging Internet technology through an extranet, CSCP provides a low-cost medium for exchanging information in a real-time, platform-independent environment. It is scalable to large numbers of trading partners, products, and users, which is important as some firms will be a part of multiple value chains. CSCP can drive, for example, improvements to category management, shelf sets, SKU rationalization, and new product introductions. The result is improved revenue, better ROI, and higher profit margins. The procedure moves through two phases:

Phase 1: Strategy begins with the arrangement of collaborative workshops at which a vision is developed for creating a collaborative business model that addresses readiness and impact in the areas of business process, organizational structure, technology, skills, culture, metrics, and partnering strategies. These strategies identify those partners, categories, and products that should be involved in a collaborative planning effort. At the completion of this phase, the companies involved will have a clearer understanding of what supply chain cooperation means to the business, its financial impact, and competitive implications. Then a road map can be developed that specifies how to ready an organization for collaborative partnering and how to roll the program out to trading partners.

Phase 2: Pilot and implementation is a work session designed to establish specific agreements between the selected trading partners. These agreements address the goals and deliverables such as development of joint performance measures and establishment of communication procedures and business process flows. With agreements in place, a pilot is developed for implementing the new business model and enabling technology. The purpose is to prove the value of the strategy, test novel business techniques, and begin preliminary implementation of the highest potential concepts. Under test conditions, focus on operational excellence changes from reactive execution to proactive joint business execution, the type of external network linkages, and activities of advanced network relationships. Stronger cooperation between network members yields higher consumer satisfaction, better revenues, and profits. A typical result of the workshops is the determination of which software is most appropriate. With so much from which to choose, this is an important aspect of the effort.

A number of additional aids are available. In an advanced effort (Stages 2 and 3), a few leaders in cooperative software development use a technique known as *collaborative filtering software*. This software has features that enable the partners to make decisions and perform joint tasks important to consumer response. One example of this technology is provided by net Perceptions, a company offering software called GroupLens. This software researches consumers' preferences and matches them with products they are most likely to purchase. It is a concept similar to a country store in which the software recommends products to a customer in the same way a small store manager did in days gone past. As consumers spend more time and money at the Web site, the software learns more about individual preferences and offers better-targeted options.

VALUE CHAINS PROSPERING WITH INTERACTIVE CAPABILITIES

As manufacturing organizations come together with their key suppliers, distributors, and business customers to create I-ERP cooperation, the potential for further improvement becomes enormous. Exhibit 7.5 depicts the kinds of joint actions being pursued by Level III and IV supply chain firms. In the center of the diagram, a nucleus company typically sets the stage for the interactions and, with its partners' help, sets out the areas for concentrated effort. In the bubbles outside this area are the opportunities to which teams can be assigned for creating action plans. Nine of the more popular efforts are listed, but more can be added, depending on the circumstances of the network effort being pursued. Service organizations can create a similar diagram with their partners.

It's a little too soon to predict the ultimate results that will come from building an interactive engineering, planning, scheduling, and manufacturing system. The leaders are hard at work fashioning what will become a new way of cooperating across a value chain constellation. In one case, Toyota Motors announced plans to build Camry Solaras only five days after they receive a custom order from dealers. This custom order will include specifications for an exact color, trim, and options. To do this, the company had to overhaul its parts procurement system, which had been geared to a thirty-day lead time. Using its Cambridge, Ontario, plant to test the system, the company will begin building vehicles on five days' notice from Toyota dealers. Applying their "logistics kaizen" with suppliers, to make sure the right colors and combinations of parts arrive at the plant exactly when needed, the firm can save money and become more responsive to consumers.

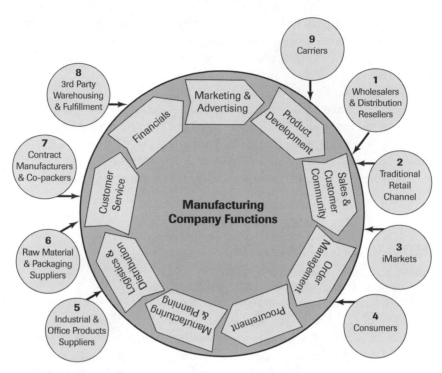

EXHIBIT 7.5   The Opportunities in Value Chain Interactions

At the heart of Toyota's new system is sophisticated software that allows planners to create a virtual production line fifteen days in advance of actual production. The system calculates exactly how many of which parts are needed at what time at each point on the production line to assemble the custom car. The calculations provide provisional orders to the plant's three hundred suppliers by hour and minute. To speed delivery and take advantage of transportation opportunities, Toyota has worked out a delivery system for the full network, so trucks (on a programmed schedule) make deliveries and pickups, much like a postal route. Parts are moved between suppliers and to the assembly plant in the most efficient manner, with only the inventories needed to sustain productivity.

SUMMARY

Exhibit 7.6 summarizes what can result from a collaborative effort to link partners across a value chain constellation and plan the future together, not just in better engineering and manufacturing ef-

Increase Revenue	Deepen Existing Relationships to Gain Competitive Advantage
• Enable existing channels • Extend reach in existing channels • Open new channels • Web-based cross-selling and up-selling • Targeting campaign planning and execution • Cross-channel marketing and promotion	• Web surveys and focus groups for product development • Implement team-based customer service • Personalized experiences on the Web for both reps and consumers • Interactive 1:1 marketing
Improve Efficiency and Effectiveness of Processes	**Improve Service and Responsiveness**
• Reengineer and automate business processes of channel participants • Automate consumer self-service and product purchasing • Electronic supply chain linkages (EDI, extranets with suppliers and third-party distributors, etc.) • Automate information distribution on new products, pricing, promotions, and so forth	• Interactive customer service • Multimedia queuing and skills-based routing integrated with the Web (e-mail, interactive chat, etc.)

EXHIBIT 7.6   E-business Opportunity Summary

ficiency but across the full supply chain network. These results will vary by network and the amount of resources applied to the joint actions. The important factor to consider is that these new levels of improvement can be the logical extension of current initiatives that have been effective but are slowing in terms of potential return on effort.

During the early part of the twenty-first century, current communication systems will be found lacking in the basic ingredients needed to make an effective business-to-business-to-consumer value chain constellation. The need for a high-velocity, error-free system that functions with real-time architecture is too important for organizations not to investigate the ingredients of full network collaboration. The solution comes with a cooperative effort to share best technology practices, select the most appropriate software and systems, and create an extranet that is unequaled in a particular industry or market segment. All enterprises that compete in such a dynamic environment must invest in the type of collaborative effort described in this chapter so the future is enhanced through the most effective data transfer and utilization known.

8

The Logistics Impact

As companies progress with their business allies to advanced supply chain management, they accept the tenet that no single firm can optimally perform all of the functions required for procurement, manufacture, and delivery. They recognize the need to build a network of response all the way to the consumers. These companies also accept the reality that, in the future, their systems must be prepared to service business customers and consumers through both physical and cyber channels that have been e-commerce enabled. Of central importance to this understanding is the need to determine which partners in the supply chain are most competent to perform each process step.

In no area is this partner determination more critical than logistics, where a myriad of process steps occur, where demands placed on manufacturers accelerate at a dizzy pace, and where supply chain competency via e-commerce can be the difference between profit and loss. As business organizations continue to chase further improvement opportunities, make no mistake—supply chain networks will only be as good as their collective logistics systems.

BUILDING THE LOGISTICS NETWORK OF THE TWENTY-FIRST CENTURY

It is through a redesign of the logistics steps, from supply to manufacturing and beyond, that the linkages between demand chain (needs expressed by the customers and consumers) and supply

Progression / Business Application	Level I/II	Level III	Level IV	Level IV+
	Internal Supply Chain Optimization	Network Formation	Value Chain Constellation	Full Network Connectivity
	Stage 0	*Stage 1*	*Stage 2*	*Stage 3*
Logistics*	Manufacturing push – inventory intensive	Pull system through internal/external providers	Best constituent provider – dual channel	Total network, dual-channel optimization

*Includes inventory management.

EXHIBIT 8.1   E-business Development Framework: Logistics

chain (responses from the suppliers and manufacturers) can be integrated to result in an effective supply chain network. Beginning in Level I/II, as depicted in Exhibit 8.1, companies have to abandon the typical manufacturing push mentality that says, "Make the products at high efficiency, and then push them toward the customer." This stage cannot reach optimization because it is too full of safety stocks and extra inventory to cover possible shortages of product.

As the constituents begin embarking on the electronic network formation stage, they must do so with an understanding that the system will be designed so customers and consumers will pull products and services through the combination of internal and external providers. As they do, the partners must determine which supply chain partner should perform which function and how technology can be applied to facilitate each of those steps. As the network then shares logistics expertise and uses technology to provide information and systems that dramatically improve cycle time, cut inventory, reduce total costs, and delight the consumer, a long-term advantage is created.

Competence in locating, acquiring, and coordinating the delivery of raw materials—components and services, for example—can be a key to competitiveness if value is added at each process step and the products in demand reach the consumer in time of need. Relying on best suppliers for sourcing the most critical materials (most of which are ordered and scheduled for shipment electronically) is one feasible solution in this area. It allows the nucleus firm to then concentrate on internal skills at the key process points in manufacturing and delivery. Turning over the downstream distribution function to reliable partners further helps the drive for optimization while keeping the nucleus organization's attention on core competencies. This downstream partner can be a network member, if the firm has the core competency, or it can be one of the third-party providers, or a lead logistics provider, both of which we'll be considering. The selected partner can assume the responsibility for aggregating loads from many SKUs, packaging, making delivery, handling domestic and foreign paperwork, and transporting the goods to business customers or directly to consumers. Eventually, the total distribution system could be placed in the hands of an aggregator that handles the total shipments from end to end of the network.

Care must be exercised here, as a factor that can inhibit a well-conceived operating plan, designed to include Web-based buying and selling features, will be a poorly executed logistics system supporting the plan. Logistics chaos that results in nonfulfillment of orders, late deliveries, excessive back orders, and an overabundance of safety stock will sound the death knell for those plans and the designers. Today's business customers and consumers are simply too short on patience with supply chain systems to accept anything less than logistics excellence. This excellence demands the development of a value chain constellation in which the best provider at each process step is in charge, over the dual channels of response, and enabled electronically.

Many of the existing distribution networks are being managed by systems designed for much simpler operations, systems that are being strained to keep up with customer and consumer expectations. Consider the logistics implications from a manufacturer, using a multichannel strategy, which wants to optimize selling in both the physical and cyber channels. This manufacturer might sell its factory outlet (end-of-life) products through company stores or directly online. It may sell premium products through its best retailers, online through those retailers, or via a wholesale online channel. The firm will also sell through the traditional channel partners requiring goods to be sent through distribution centers to stores and awaiting shelves.

Such a company needs a multifaceted logistics program involving many partners that can do most of the shipping from a single or a few distribution centers. Typically, these centers are not equipped to handle such variety. When we investigate emerging supply chain network logistics systems, we find few that are well equipped technologically to efficiently handle a variety of products and volumes. We find a larger number where the warehouse management system (WMS) and transportation management system (TMS) in the distribution centers are products of systems designed for a simpler era.

These systems cannot handle the growing complexity of merchandising efforts splitting into two channels of response. We generally advise these companies to start by designing and developing a network system with the help of supply chain partners.

To understand the pitfalls that can be avoided, consider the case of many of the successful online sellers that have been mentioned throughout this book. Most of these companies get off to a good start and begin to feel very satisfied about their performance, only to find that their success breeds other problems. As sales build, the consequential fulfillment requirements create a challenge as well as a blessing. As SKUs proliferate and geographic dispersion increases, the demand for short cycle times and accurate fulfillment only accelerates, placing enormous pressure on outdated systems. Web-based players find their future is inextricably linked to service capability. Central to that capability is logistics performance. The successful online sellers that seek to avoid brick-and-mortar sites by utilizing cyber selling direct to consumers have found that they still need a supply chain to fulfill their orders. And not just a traditional supply chain—they need one that has been technologically enabled to respond at Internet speed and be efficient at what can become lot sizes of one.

Most online sellers avoid some of the complications by keeping SKU levels manageable and supporting fulfillment from single facilities, but their own growth prevents maintaining such a system for long. Forrester Research, Inc., states that less than half of the respondents to its *1999 Logistical Report* "make a profit on each packaged shipment, and most fail to accurately measure the total cost of fulfillment" (McCullough 1999, p. 3). Clearly, a solution is necessary that handles current demands as well as greatly increased single-lot shipments to consumers buying over the Internet.

In Exhibit 8.2, Forrester predicts that residential package shipments will go over 2.1 billion per year by 2003. When this phenomenal growth is coupled with seasonal variation and demand peaks, the requirements foisted on a traditional logistics response system compound. As consumers continue to demand short order-to-receipt cycle times, the pressure will increase on distribution systems to move cyber-based orders quickly, often in less than twelve hours. Companies responding to this requirement will have to establish distribution capabilities that focus on servicing individuals, not just large business customers. Shipments in the future are going to be by packages, not pallet loads, and those packages are as likely to go to Timbuktu as Topeka.

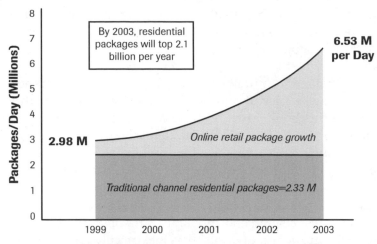

EXHIBIT 8.2 Online Retail Package Growth Booms

With global expansion, the problems compound again. The Forrester report also indicates that "85 percent of firms can't fill international orders because of the complexities of shipping across borders. Of the 15 percent that can handle global orders, most are shipping to only a few customers in Europe and Asia where they can fill orders out of local warehouses" (McCullough 1999, p.3). One respondent to the survey indicated that the firm did not ship globally because it did not have logistics systems in place allowing such shipments. When it comes to order entry, for example, some logistics systems only allow shipment to five-digit ZIP codes, thereby eliminating international service.

As supply chains lengthen and become more complex, additional tools and relationships are needed to plan and coordinate activities. We now turn our attention to how e–supply chain best practices can be formulated and applied to manage and execute the logistics component. The first question is which component activities should be handled internally and which are better performed externally.

The next set of questions deals with how the various best practices and logistics strengths across the network can be leveraged in a mutual fashion to create a logistically excellent value chain constellation. This leverage must include the best application of e-commerce and be tied directly to the overall supply chain operational plan. With careful collaborative planning and execution, the emerging constellation can optimize its total performance and walk away

Network Optimization		
Freight cost and service management	**Fleet management**	**Load planning**
• Inbound/outbound rationalization	• Total cost analysis	• Mode selection
• Carrier management systems	• Equipment utilization	• Load building
• Total transportation cost and service	• Maintenance	• Load consolidation
• Operations outsourcing	• Deployment	• Cross-dock
• Administrative services	planning	planning

Routing/Scheduling		Warehouse management	
• Inventory management	• Receiving	• Metrics	
• Trailer capacity utilization	• Picking	• Cross-checking	
• Less-than-truckload shipments	• Put-away	• Sales planning coordination	
	• Load selection	• Returns management	

EXHIBIT 8.3   Key Factors in Optimizing a Logistics Network

with the targeted consumer groups. The solutions that are developed, however, must be designed for a network formation transition that enables the value chain constellation to perform excellently in the traditional physical channel as well as the rapidly growing cyber channel of response.

FACTORS IN OPTIMIZING A LOGISTICS NETWORK

Achieving network optimization in both dimensions, across a full logistics system, requires each constituent in the supply chain to demonstrate best practice in its area of linkage. To help in that endeavor, the channel partners have to work together and share resources to find the means to develop a total system of interaction that is seamless, flawless, and electronically enabled. That requires beginning at the upstream side of the network and working across each link toward the downstream side, scrutinizing each logistics factor along the way. Exhibit 8.3 is a generalized list of factors that could help a network group begin tracking logistics improvement factors. Additions can be inserted, as appropriate, for the network being constructed.

Starting with the area of freight costs and service management, each network member should consider the factors listed as opportunities for establishing the desired optimized conditions. As the process steps are considered, the idea is to determine which player is best suited for the function and, if necessary, where to outsource the function into more reliable hands. The next consideration is how inbound materials, outbound products, and warehouse deliveries can be consolidated into one transportation system that can be handled by the most effective entity. That move takes the constituents into Stage 2 of e–supply chain. Administrative services should be included, as these necessities can be a burden if not automated.

Moving to fleet management, a typical supply chain network is loaded with transportation equipment, particularly tractors and trailers. What is the total cost, how is the equipment being utilized, who does the maintenance, and how are deployment and back hauls planned are typical questions that bring a focus group to the point of making valid recommendations. The task is to determine which is the best constituent provider, through both channels of response, and thereby to make optimum use of the available assets without detriment to service levels. As the consideration goes forward, it becomes a time to look at the possibility of using a third-party logistics (3PL) firm or a lead logistics provider to handle the transportation services.

Across the bottom of the exhibit are factors relating to load planning, routing and scheduling, and warehouse management. These logistics elements should be considered as the focus teams analyze how the network can use best practices and e-commerce to move toward optimum conditions.

Throughout the entire planning process, the value chain members should be considering how the process steps could be automated or enhanced through technology. The complication of communicating through disparate software systems being used by network members should be dealt with as well as deciding on what data are needed and how it should be communicated. A major data consideration will be the information that will be communicated via the extranet. In the same way that advance shipping notices (ASNs) allow buyers to anticipate arrival of orders, the flow of information enables better decisions to be made faster. In this manner, information replaces inventory.

E-COMMERCE AS THE CATALYST ACROSS NETWORK LOGISTICS

E-commerce is having an enormous impact on the logistics function in most companies as the distance between suppliers, manufacturers, distributors, customers, and consumers continues to shrink. It is causing organizations to redefine their market assumptions, value propositions, and value delivery systems. It is also forcing firms to take on new value chain roles and responsibilities. In today's environment, most products flow through delivery systems that move bulk. E-commerce changes that situation by dramatically adding growth in small-parcel deliveries to homes and businesses.

The time required to arrange, manage, track, and monitor shipments in transit has gone from weeks or days to hours. Leading supply chain networks are equipped with total visibility across the entire logistics system, relying on connected extranets that include global positioning satellite (GPS) systems that pinpoint trucks, rail cars, and shipments in transit. The best of this group, with full network connectivity, can accurately track and monitor their transportation assets and the cargo they contain, from origin to destination, around the world. Some carriers in these networks can ensure the integrity of the shipment by monitoring it for temperature, shock, internal pressure, leakage, and forced entry. They report in-transit shipment status to customers on a near real-time basis and integrate all trade partners, giving them access to useful shipment data. The result is typically better on-time delivery, less damage, better order fill rates, lower levels of emergency inventory, fewer rush shipments, lower insurance costs, and improved use of transportation assets.

The Association of American Railroads (AAR), for example, has made Internet-based logistics a standard for the railroad industry. This Web-based solution provides a complete online interface that enables supply chain partners to check the location of their shipments, get updates, contact troubleshooters, be alerted to schedule changes, request price quotations, place orders, look at equipment specifications, and manage fleets.

With the emergence of cyber business, a new breed of service providers is appearing that we'll call "cyber logistics outsourcers." Their offering may not be applicable for all networks, but they provide a way to analyze where technology logistics systems are headed. These organizations, such as FedEx Logistics and GATX Logistics, offer to manage the entire breadth of the supply chain. They actually provide services beyond transportation and warehousing for those networks that feel they lack the competence to come close to optimum conditions. The outsourcer can be a 3PL, such as Schneider Logistics, and handle the transfer of goods with their vast fleet of tractors, trailers and piggy-back railroad equipment.

It can be a lead logistics provider (LLP) that prefers not to have any physical assets. Instead, this type of provider will do the scheduling, arranging, and tracking of shipments through other companies having open capacity with their equipment. Via a computer-to-computer system, these firms take advantage of open space on cargo containers, trailers, rail cars, barges, and the like, to move goods across an entire supply chain network. Examples include Ryder Logistics, Menlo Logistics, Exel Logistics, and large consulting outsourcing firms such as Computer Sciences Corporation (CSC) and Andersen Consulting.

These companies manage the physical needs of a cyber business, for example, from the moment an order is taken. Following that action, they can offer services covering order management, assemble-to-order requests, repairs and returns processing, multimodal transportation, global supply chain infrastructure, and fulfillment management. We'll use the approach taken by these cyber logistics outsourcers as an example of what a network system looks like for a cyber logistics supply chain.

Exhibit 8.4 diagrams the potential role of such outsourcers in both channels of supply. In the lower track, for physical distribution, the movement is through what is now being called a *hub,* a focal point for consolidating and matching loads for specific destinations. In the cyber channel, the manufacturer's products may be picked up and taken directly to the consumer's residence or delivered from stocks in the physical hub. The purpose of the hub moves from a center to create full truck loads or create a traffic pattern that

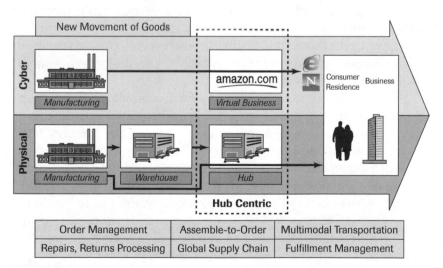

EXHIBIT 8.4 Cyber Logistics Outsourcing

makes best use of the carrier's equipment to breaking down loads so small packages can be accommodated. Using its hub, the provider could receive orders from Amazon.com or Disney.com and make delivery to a business customer or a consumer residence.

For the physical channel, the delivery could be to the manufacturer or a business customer's warehouse. It could also be made directly to the hub, from which loads will be aggregated and sent on to customers or consumers. Along the way, all of the functions mentioned are accommodated. Order management is facilitated if not performed outright, as the outsourcer might also assemble the final product and arrange for repairs and return processing, or perform minor repairs in addition to making the product delivery. Global deliveries are accomplished, including all of the necessary documentation and cross-border details. Fulfillment management becomes a feature as the outsourcer takes care of all final details, including tracking of the shipments and handling global and domestic deliveries that require multimodal transportation. The information provided by the outsourcer on what is happening in the system becomes one of the vital provisions. Many companies are not in a position to gather demand information effectively from their customer base, so providing this data becomes one more value offered by the cyber logistics outsourcer.

In Exhibit 8.5, we elaborate on the model being developed. Whether the network members choose an outsourcer or not, they must combine logistics efforts into a highly reliable system of response

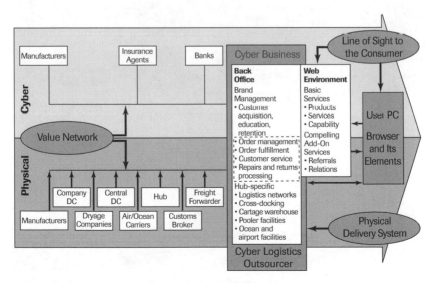

EXHIBIT 8.5 Cyber/Physical Logistics Example

to consumer consumption. As the exhibit details, that combination connects the cyber and physical channels into what becomes the value network. As this system is set up to handle many types of responses in the most efficient manner, the network creates options for different buyers. Existing warehousing is combined with the outsourcer's hub, and the total capability rationalized, but it retains the flexibility necessary to establish a market advantage. A variety of distribution mediums are included so global commitments can be met. Back-office functions are merged with order-processing needs and the hub-specific activities. Using the Web environment provided over the network's extranet, the business customer or consumer could browse the Web site and find the inventory of finished or partially finished goods. Business customers can divert shipments based on market conditions and arrange for returns and repairs. The line of sight between these customers and consumers will be dramatically improved as the clarity of the pipeline is now enhanced and placed online.

The hub becomes a crucial element in this logistics system for cyber sellers. It can be under the direction and control of an outsourcer, or the network members can share control, but usually they place one member in charge of operations. The purpose is to

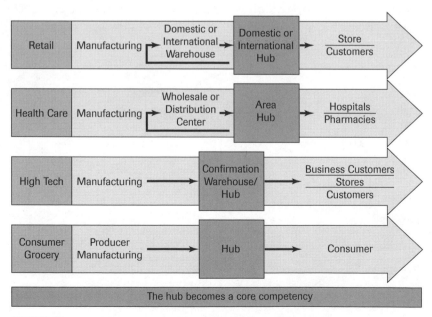

EXHIBIT 8.6 The Hub as a Key Supply Chain Component

streamline the delivery function while bringing innovative e-commerce features into play, so the network constituents all save costs while satisfying the intended consumers. Exhibit 8.6 illustrates how using this logistics factor will quickly place the hub as a key component in supply chain logistics. The hub becomes a crucial element for moving products to the appropriate location in the most efficient manner. When the costs of the hub are shared across network members, the effect on total delivered price is kept to a practical minimum while service levels reach what the consumer desires.

ELECTRONIC COMMERCE'S REDEFINITION OF ROLES

As we continue our look at the impact of e-commerce and supply chain on logistics in Level IV, we should consider how the electronic impact is going to alter and redefine some traditional roles. Exhibit 8.7 illustrates four areas where significant changes are taking

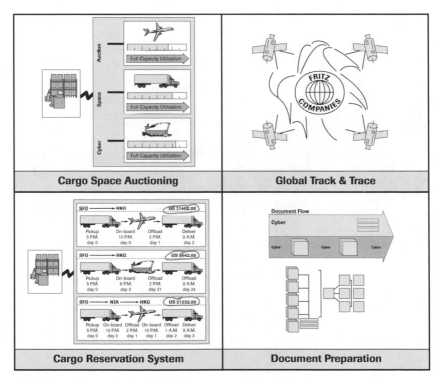

EXHIBIT 8.7   E-commerce Logistical Features

place: cargo reservation systems, cargo space auctioning, global track and trace, and enterprise-wide documentation. Each topic will be considered.

Cargo Reservation System

The business scenario in this sector could include an international logistics company that contracts space on aircraft flights, ocean vessels, rail cars, and trucks, such as the Fritz Company. The contracting firms focus their sales forces on customer segments where they understand the needs. Also, the company, as the shipper of the products, allows the customer a choice of rates, routes, and service levels and allows twenty-four-hour access to this information, utilizing the logistics resources of the full value chain.

Consider a shipment that has to move from San Francisco to Hong Kong as described in Exhibit 8.8. In this case, the options could include picking up the shipment at 5:00 P.M. on the first day, moving the goods to an airplane by 10:00, having the cargo offloaded by 2:00 P.M. the second day, and delivered by 9:00 A.M. on the second day (keep in mind the shipment would've crossed the

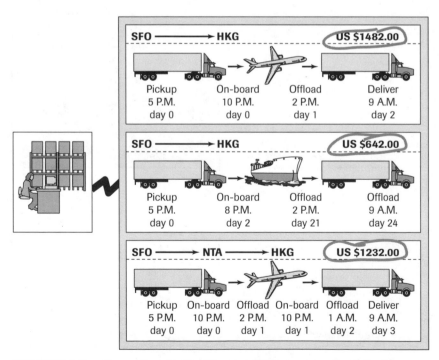

EXHIBIT 8.8 Cargo Reservation System: E-Commerce Opportunity

International Date Line). We start the timing on day 0, so the days listed refer to the time of the delivery cycle. The cost of using this mode is listed at $1,482.00. Now consider an alternative in which the goods are picked up at 5:00 P.M. on the first day, put on board a ship by 8:00 the second day, offloaded after the ocean voyage at 2:00 P.M. on day 21 and delivered by 9:00 A.M. on day 24. For this mode, the cost is $642.00, but the time is twelve times slower, which may or may not be a factor in the decision. The analyst will also have to consider the inventory carrying costs and the import/export costs before making the final decision. In the third scenario, the goods are picked up at 5:00 on the first day, switched through a series of open spaces on airplanes en route to the destination, and delivered by 9:00 A.M. on the third day. This cost is $1,232.00.

These three options can be viewed and a decision made electronically through the current cargo reservation systems being offered. The customer has twenty-four-hour access to the system and can select the best transport rate and route for the specific shipment. The business customer can decide on the value of the earlier delivery versus the extra cost and make an informed decision. As the logistics company allows rates to be adjusted to volumes and capacity, the customer can make plans based on the different options and how much can be charged to the end consumer for the higher cost alternatives.

Cargo Space Auctioning

The business case scenario here is best described by considering a transportation company that has a flight between San Francisco and Hong Kong this evening (see Exhibit 8.9). The firm expects to fill two of these positions with existing shipments. To fill the balance, they make two pallet positions available for auction with twenty-four-hour notice and with a minimum dimension and weight specification. The bid is closed out four to six hours in advance of pickup, and bidders are advised of decisions by e-mail and a telesales confirmation call.

The shipper is able to ship last-minute extra cargo, often responding to unexpected market demand, and obtains a real-time competitive price. The transportation company fills out volume contract commitments and protects margins that enhance profits and supports both forwarders and direct shippers. Cost of sales is lower, and customers are pleased with the prompt reaction to special needs. This system can also be used to integrate multiple modes of transportation along the route. National Transportation

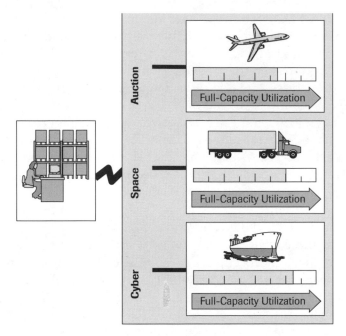

EXHIBIT 8.9   Cargo Space Auctioning: E-commerce Opportunity

Exchange, a dot-com firm located in Downers Grove, Illinois, is one firm focusing on open less-than-truckload (LTL) capacity opportunities. Nistevo Company is another dot-com, located in Minneapolis, dealing in freight exchange for full cargo shipments.

Global Track and Trace

In this area, the transportation company makes the progress of transportation visible by reporting on status across the entire delivery network. The firm provides tracking by purchase order number, order number, shipment number, bill of loading number, and so forth. It also provides connection to other supply chain partners for updated information exchange. The shipper utilizes one-stop track and trace for all modes of freight via currently available technology and allows the customer to see a visual status and location of the transported goods. Some firms even allow hold and diversion orders to be issued. Celarix is a dot-com located in Boston offering end-to-end tracking and visibility of shipment. FedEx and UPS are also expected to introduce services in this area.

The benefits are improved customer service by virtue of being able to give reliable shipment times. The system reduces much of the telephone tracking that goes on today and improves the visibility of problems as they occur rather than after the fact. The tracking and tracing can be done by the customer who can track online cargo across the entire network, including affiliate agents and contract carriers. It provides operational intimacy with information that is available twenty-four hours a day. Current systems can be linked with the Internet being used, and a single access point is provided for tracing and tracking.

Enterprise-wide Documentation

Small shippers can use the Web to prepare documents, and volume shippers can apply a systems interface. The transportation company has all documents, including international customers, generated online or scanned. These documents can be transmitted to the appropriate destination in advance, enabling easy document retention and recovery, if necessary. The shipper coordinates all activities with import and export personnel in advance of the shipment, coordinates receiving schedules, and works with inbound materials to stage receipts. Greatly improved service results by eliminating a problem that plagues international shipments—lost documents. The benefits include improved customer service and improved pass-through of information across the network and to government agencies. The reduction of duplication, distribution, and retention of physical documents provides some further savings.

Logistics Coordination

Logistics coordination has two dimensions: the information process used to plan and the physical activity where actual delivery of products and services is coordinated and managed. The goal is to establish long-term customer relationships. A key strategy is to track the activities of all supply chain members on a real-time basis. The desired results include the highest possible fill rates, on-time delivery excellence, minimal inventory, and zero obsolescence. Greater flexibility in the manufacturing and delivery processes and high customer service ratings ice the cake. The focus is moving to the reduction of time to market, with revenue growth, and optimum asset utilization. The financial goal, based on our research and experience, is 3 to 7 percent improvement of net revenue as the logistics cost advantage over a competing network. That target is feasible for members of a value chain constellation that has moved to full network connectivity.

A CASE EXAMPLE

Schneider National Inc., a major transportation company headquartered in Green Bay, Wisconsin, is installing tracking devices in some forty thousand freight trailers so it can pinpoint their whereabouts by satellite. Knowing where the equipment is at any time can save companies money and improve delivery to customers. The idea is to track the trailers once they have been dropped off at warehouses or other freight handlers. Tractors have been equipped with tracking devices for some time, but not the trailers they haul. Instead of waiting for calls to tell the driver where to go to get a trailer, the truckers can now send messages and dispatch instructions to the drivers in their cabs.

The firm will use Orbcomm Global LP's new satellite system. Besides tracking the location of the trailers, the system can determine when trailers are loaded or empty, hooked or unhooked to a truck cab, and when doors are opened or closed. It can also help with finding stolen trailers and keeping an eye on customers who keep the trailers too long. A typical result is a customer calling to track an order only to find out it is already sitting in his dock. The time wasted looking for phantom trailers should be an ancillary benefit (Machalaba 1999, p. A2).

Leaders have learned that advanced supply chain management should focus on sales growth, market share, and increased profitability for the internal company and its major supply chain partners. Treating your network suppliers as competitive partners is a key in the battle of supply chain versus supply chain. A global network enterprise emerges with the customer and consumer at the center of the new universe. Properly measuring the results of that enterprise, in terms meaningful to the customers and consumers, will be what makes the effort pay off.

REVERSE LOGISTICS

The best supply chain system would operate without any returns. Unfortunately, such conditions are rare. A reality of most supply chains is the existence of a small but growing percentage of returns in the business-to-consumer channel. In the high-technology sector, where new products are introduced at a rapid rate, that percentage can grow to 20 to 25 percent. Under those conditions, a returns management system is required. Also, many manufacturers are shifting to reusable packaging for moving components from suppliers to their factories. This packaging must be recirculated in a timely fashion. This area of supply chain is termed *reverse logistics*.

Fortunately, in a vein similar to what we have been considering for an e-commerce-based logistics system, features are available to enhance the return process. In the best of these systems, the manufacturer or retailer knows exactly what is being sent back and when it is going to be delivered to a warehouse, distribution center, or manufacturer. The company can control the service level used on the return transportation. When the returned shipment arrives at the designated location, a return material authorization (RMA) number, with bar coding, is clearly marked on every package address label. The manufacturer has provided an ASN for the returned packaging to the supplier, allowing that firm to balance its packaging needs and alert its dock to the shipment. L. L. Bean provides this type of service, and a firm called Genco is a 3PL in reverse logistics.

Such a service is also offered by Federal Express through its "NetReturn" system, an Internet application that integrates all merchandise return characteristics into a single system. It functions through a linkage between the manufacturer or retailer and the FedEx dispatch and tracking system. With this system, a customer contacts the sales/service rep to request an RMA number for a return. The customer service representative enters information online, into the NetReturn order screen, and schedules a time for the same-day or next-business-day pickup. Data on the action are transmitted electronically to FedEx systems. IBM uses such a service for "Thinkpad" repairs.

A FedEx courier is dispatched directly to the customer location for the pickup. The courier retrieves the goods and tracks all information about the shipment until it is back at its destination. For firms wanting to reroute the returns to a location where the products can be repaired, reworked and repackaged, FedEx offers a return and repair service whereby the goods go to a depot for repair and shipment to another customer. A replacement to a malfunctioning or damaged product can also be accommodated, including the retrieval of the product from the point of return, and necessary replacement parts. The product is repaired and returned to inventory. Companies are moving their warehouses into their computers using virtual reality features. With simulation techniques, they can move about within the computer-generated image. The viewer can visually track everything as it happens, from forklifts to stock items to shipment.

SUMMARY

Managing a global supply chain network demands a level of expertise, agility, and responsiveness beyond what has been required in contemporary models of local manufacturing and delivery. The value chain constellation that develops will only be as strong as the logistical system supporting it. Partners across that total network will have to work together on their new model to find the most competent constituent at each point of interaction. Optimization of that model will only come when each partner links itself solidly to the focus on end consumers, using e-commerce features, so a seamless flow of goods and services arrives via the physical stores or the cyber-based response preferred by those consumers.

9

The Impact on Marketing, Sales, and Customer Service

Arthur Miller's renowned play *Death of a Salesman* is witnessing a revival, after its initial presentation fifty years ago. In that play, the despondent salesman struggling with the end of his career, Willy Loman, concludes, "Selling ain't what it used to be." This tragic hero just couldn't seem to adjust to a changing environment. Now, half a century later, we could again remark that selling isn't what it used to be. Nor is marketing. Nor is the concept of service to a customer. In the new era, selling, marketing, and service are undergoing transformations that are bringing new definitions to these disciplines and forcing innovative restructuring to meet the business demands of the new century.

With business customers and end consumers firmly in control of consumption, the concept of servicing those constituents has become an obsession for firms intent on creating and sustaining a leadership position in their industries and markets. These firms know that customers and consumers expect superior attention and service and will quickly move to another supplier if their expectations are not met. While the importance of maintaining a high level of customer and consumer satisfaction has never been greater, the complexity of accomplishing this task effectively has also never been more daunting. Therein lies the new challenge for sales, marketing, and servicing forces.

A NECESSARY CHANGE IN TASKS FOR PROPER CUSTOMER RESPONSE

If the task for management has been to cultivate and retain satisfied customers, the new requirement is to develop and retain the best

149

consumers in designated profitable growth markets. This task must be accomplished on a network basis, through two channels of response—physical and cyber—and where the two channels converge in stores and on the Web.

Referring to Exhibit 9.1, we see that this understanding is not present in Level I/II. As firms complete those levels of supply chain, they tend to stay focused on internally developed programs. As the company turns its attention to the use of external resources to enhance the success of marketing and sales activities and enters the network formation stage, it discovers a wealth of new, extra data. With the help of suppliers and one or two strategic business customers, the firm is now ready to assume the nucleus position and develop initiatives, collaboratively with its partners, that are focused on specific customer and consumer groups.

The joint tasks that develop to pursue these initiatives may seem similar to those of a traditional model that insists the customers receive satisfaction, but with the proper technology systems, it becomes decidedly different. Buying and selling become critical elements of that management process. They combine with marketing, communications, and support/care, so the relationship flourishes and moves toward joint objectives. Customer relationship management becomes a network effort.

The necessary production and organization elements are created jointly with members of the supply chain network. Important knowledge is delivered to the point of need instantly. Products are matched to the targeted business customers and end consumers that the creators of the network know have the most ultimate value in terms of lifelong transactions. Business commerce transactions are accomplished in the most effective manner possible. Service requests are handled either directly or through instruction for self-as-

Progression ⟍ Business Application	Level I/II	Level III	Level IV	Level IV+
	Internal Supply Chain Optimization	Network Formation	Value Chain Constellation	Full Network Connectivity
	Stage 0	*Stage 1*	*Stage 2*	*Stage 3*
Marketing, sales, customer service	Internally developed programs, promotions	Customer-focused, data-based initiatives	Collaborative development for focused consumer base	Consumer response system across the value chain

EXHIBIT 9.1   E-Business Development Framework: Marketing, Sales, and Customer Service

sistance, and future needs are anticipated before they become crises. This merging of activities has been suggested for some time, but a Level III network demands that it becomes a reality.

As the merging effort proceeds, business-to-business-to-consumer connections provide a two-channel world of response to consumer needs. Industrial products manufacturers and their strategic suppliers will be focusing on a market strategy that gives global accessibility and delivery, while appearing to be tailored for local response. These suppliers must be linked to other network partners by an online extranet that receives consumption data as the trigger for response. Operations will function so as to avoid having the supplied products labeled as commodities, by virtue of value-adding features such as flexible and rapid collaborative design, digital manufacturing interfaces, and the potential of help in developing downstream delivery models.

Consumer goods firms will be hard at work rethinking their channel strategies to offer both a physical and cyber response. These companies will want to protect brand values but will do so by rapidly responding to electronic impulses detailing actual consumption. Inventory velocity will be at industry-high standards, as the companies replenish what is being consumed. The marketing and sales forces will be reoriented to incorporate the consumer-direct thinking brought back by their e-commerce-equipped sales representatives. Both marketing and sales personnel will work with key retailers to determine how to build a joint response system or how to work with the new electronic retailers that seem to appear on a monthly basis. In the former case, branding has to be settled regarding the retailer's private label appearing on the products. In the latter case, the obvious objections of long-time retail customers voicing their concern over splitting the market must be resolved.

Retailers will be equally busy creating newer, stronger demands. Access to current information on trends and consumption will define the necessary moves toward the most appropriate consumers. Using store- or cyber-based channels for securing orders, these retailers will customize their inventory assortments for these consumers while reducing investments in physical assets. Those stores needed for the physical response will be modernized and supported with e-commerce enhancements, while arrangements will be made to handle the third of the business that will be fulfilled over the Web. Methods and systems to counter or collaborate with the encroachment of the new cyber retailers (Amazon.com, Drugstore.com, Home Grocer.com) will be worked out cooperatively.

The physical demand channel will require timely and accurate information on what consumers want, a streamlined store delivery system that has the right inventories at the right place, and a feedback loop to upstream suppliers needing consumption data to determine delivery requirements, so inventories are kept to necessary minimums. The cyber-based demand system will need direct lines of communication to the ultimate consumers, with a high-speed efficient system of delivery. This latter channel will be unencumbered with the typical hierarchical management structure, require less working capital, have a global reach, but will be absolutely dependent on its distribution network to respond to the burgeoning number of Web-based orders it receives. Retailers will have to face the obvious disadvantage they have versus the cyber retailers, who benefit from direct 1:1 conversation with the consumer.

Smart retailers are realizing that new intermediaries, the dot-com creations (*attack.com* is the specific term often used to describe this new breed of retailer), are entering their markets, inserting themselves between traditional partners in the supply chain. We refer to the new cyber-based organizations having little to no physical facilities but a new business model and an active Web site that attracts specific consumers. These new retailers want the manufacturers to continue making products for their consumers, but they want to deliver these products to individual consumers. With their direct access and 1:1 interface with these consumers, they have a distinct advantage over traditional retailers and are forcing many of the latter to consider their own Web sites as channels for securing orders.

Consider an example of what not having an e-commerce response can do to a firm. A textbook case is provided by Toys 'R' Us. This firm struggled for years to carve out the largest market share in the toy business, competing with such giants as Wal-Mart and Target. It also sold toys online beginning in mid-1998, but its Web site offered only selected items and had little marketing support. Suddenly, the company found its very secure niche challenged by an upstart—an online e-commerce retailer called eToys. This Internet-based firm had sales in 1998 of a mere $30 million, equal to what would normally be pulled through a few Toys 'R' Us outlets.

Nonetheless, the fervor for cyber-based companies took over, and at the end of its first stock trading day, eToys scored a market capitalization value of $7.8 billion, dwarfing Toys 'R' Us's $5.6 billion. Investors were apparently willing to provide a large capitalization to help the upstart company develop its market share against the more established megafirm. Faced with the prospect of losing revenues to this newcomer catering to consumers interested in a cyber-based response, Toys 'R' Us had no choice but to establish toysrus.com (Byrnes and Judge 1999, p. 79). Their reaction follows a trend of smart offline retailers becoming adept as online players, so their leadership position is not eroded.

The trend is rapidly expanding in the business-to-consumer area, but it is expected to be much larger in the business-to-business arena, the latter becoming eight to ten times greater than the former. In the former area, some unusual new marketers are leading the way, and examples point out how companies in traditional channels of distribution are finding strange competitors. Bradirect.com is now outselling famed London-based department store Harrod's in bras. Netgrocer.com has groceries delivered to the home by Federal Express for $2.99. Valuestar.com offers help with attorneys, aluminum products, accounting, acupuncture, alarm services, and air conditioning, among their "A" listings. Sephora is taking its successful cosmetic stores, where you can select from leading brands in an alphabetical display in the store arrangement, to online access.

As the concept of mass customization—creating basic products and tailoring them for a specific consumer at the last moment—becomes more prevalent, the trend accelerates. You can now buy a personal computer assembled to your precise specification. You can order a pair of jeans that meet your physical dimensions or buy pills with the exact blend of vitamins, minerals, and herbs that you like. Glasses molded to the configuration of your face are available, as are CDs with music tracks that you select. Cosmetics matched to your skin tone, textbooks whose chapters are selected by your professor, or a night at a hotel where the employees know your favorite wine are all applications that demand an electronically enabled system of response. We are calling this system a *technology-enabled value chain constellation*.

THE DEMAND FOR NEW ROLES IN SALES, MARKETING, AND SERVICES

As an organization moves into the area being described, it progresses into the era of *effective sales response*. This must be a network response, so it's a time for solidifying the external alliances that will assure the value chain has the capability of giving an accurate and timely response to the orders that it gets. During this phase, the marketing, sales, and servicing organizations must shift their focus to how to develop profitable revenues from customers and consumers who will choose to make their deals through both channels of response. They must take on new roles consistent with the responses required from physical and cyber-based patterns.

This transition requires the sales representative, with the assistance of a focused marketing and servicing support group, to move from a role of information provider, sales counselor, and order taker to one of a valued external resource for accomplishing interorganizational objectives and jointly developing new business. If you accept the fact that the consumer or business customer drives your business, then you have to build a sales response that is providing what those consumer/customers are seeking. Under conditions prevalent in a time when buyer-seller alliances are defining new advantages, the sales representative becomes

- a voice of the customer/consumer, operating as a consumer advocate to his or her firm, bringing news on what is needed at the consumption end of the supply chain network, and working closely with internal resources to fashion an appropriate response;

- the initiator of crucial responses and improvement opportunities from the firm back to the customer/consumers, much in the manner of a business consultant, offering advice on how the interchange between the firms can be enriched to secure mutual objectives;

- a person empowered to help network improvement, through the supply of important resources—marketing information, team members, training, logistics opportunities, customer and network diagnostics, collaborative planning opportunities, and so forth—that enhance the total network response;

- a mechanism for shortening cycle response time, reducing mutual costs and better utilizing joint assets, with innovative suggestions, particularly of an e-commerce nature; and

- a person who becomes intimate with the customer and adds value at numerous points of need through an effective extranet of communication, which he or she has been instrumental in creating.

In short, the new salesperson will leave Willy Loman in the dust. He or she will be equipped to help customers with solutions that require the absolute latest in technology enhancement. The only alternative is to have two sales forces, one trained for the physical channel response and one equipped for the Web-based channel. Since the physical channel will also be technology enabled, however, this possibility is unlikely to endure. In any event, the buyer-seller relationship is moving toward high-tech features, and that demands retooling the sales force so it adapts to the new role of *technical business adviser.*

The marketing representative must coordinate more closely with the sales function, so the customer-centric effort is developed and supported. There is generally too much separation between what marketing thinks is important from an overall business development perspective and what the sales representative believes is needed in current customer situations. This gap has to be closed so both disciplines are working for the good of the customer/consumer and the total value chain constellation. From a marketing perspective, that requires

- a greater sensitivity to what is happening in the targeted network markets and how a total effort across the constellation can have benefits in terms of greater customer satisfaction and development of new revenues;
- more collaborative planning with the best customers on promotional, advertising, and other support efforts, which have meaning from end to end of the supply chain network;
- joint working sessions (focus groups, diagnostic labs, intercompany sharing sessions) with customers identified by the sales group as being key and strategic in nature and willing to invest resources in fashioning network solutions for the designated consumer market;
- development of innovative marketing efforts that complement the kind of network solutions being sought by the value chain constellation, including the design of Web sites that pull new revenues through for the network. Marketing will be especially busy in this area helping manufacturers and retailers determine how to cope with the influx of new retail intermediaries in traditional markets.

CUSTOMER SERVICE OFFERS A SPECIAL SOURCE OF HELP

From a service representative's perspective, it's time for management and business model designers to tap into the wealth of knowledge residing in the heads of customer service reps and sales personnel, those front-line connections with the customers and consumers. No other group in a business has as much daily contact with end users as the service organization, but we find they are generally the last to be contacted for information on what is happening in the market. At a time when most firms are trying to get hold of meaningful information on what customers complain about, what they want fixed, how they can be better satisfied, and how the systems bringing solutions to them can be enhanced, the service group generally has most of the answers. The new business model demands this source of knowledge be utilized to enhance the systems of customer and consumer response. Representatives have to be present at future model design sessions. We will elaborate on this subject in Chapter 10.

THE NEW ROLES ACCOMPANYING E-COMMERCE FEATURES

As the development groups are formed with people from member companies in the network, in an effort to jointly build the new business models, the best technology features must be applied. The e–supply chain processes such as order entry, tracking service delivery, technical support, inventory management, logistics optimization, display of available-to-promise goods and services, and automation of payments must now be supported with the best technology on a full-network basis. That is the objective of building a specific focused value chain constellation.

An in-depth study by H. B. Chally Co., on "Customer-Selected World Class Excellence," reports the number one factor distinguishing a sales representative in the view of the customer is "Personally manages my satisfaction"(Chally 1999, p. 5). There can be no greater call for the new sales role than this virtual demand that "an effective sales representative is not only intimate with my business, but can offer advice and solutions that increases my overall satisfaction." In the emerging world of technology-enabled business, that means the customer wants salespeople in the network representing key sources of supply, which can effectively help with the design of the requisite e–supply chain mechanisms.

We translate this call for response into three critical areas:

- The need for the sales representative to be a factor in helping increase the productivity and efficiency of the business customers in the supply chain network

- The need for a supply system that is equally adept at providing an electronic response when needed and not slowing the cycle time or increasing the delivered cost of supply

- The ability to provide useful information that enhances the opportunity to secure the designated final business customers and consumers, who are the targets of the value chain constellation of which the supplying firm is a key constituent

Properly equipping the new sales force requires arming them with features of e-commerce and data that span the full connectivity of the extended enterprises in the value chain. The first feature must be direct access to information that leads them to the best customers and consumers. Market and customer segmentation has to be brought online, so the representative can apply his or her time most appropriately.

Since the sales representative will be providing a valuable service by helping the customers with their business models, he or she will also need accurate information on best practices in an industry. As the process of quickly switching volumes to new suppliers becomes less of a problem in the new business relationships, the sales rep has to assure the buyer of the values being added in the relationship and the importance of continuing a long-term position. That means mitigating fears born of the traditional mistrust associated with buying and selling. Cost structures, margins, and pricing, for example, will soon be transparent, and these old concerns will be replaced with how to develop the best solutions. A special feature of that type of new relationship, requiring special knowledge, will be how to connect the ERP systems (covered in the preceding chapter).

The need is for a new set of sales tools that can handle complex, dual-channel input and sales configuration requirements, while linking to front-office activities for customer information. Trilogy Software offers a suite of software solutions in this respect, including help desk functions, assisted selling, procurement, personalization, and management of complex sales channels. The concept is to provide the salesperson with an end-to-end visibility of customer interactions. It should be possible, for example, for a buyer and seller to go to a site and see what is available from all the constituents in a network, which materials are in transit, and when they will arrive at specific destinations. These players should be able to divert necessary critical supplies and not destroy shipment integrity to the total network. Only with full network connectivity is this action feasible.

Additionally, management must play a key role in helping the sales force adapt to the new technical environment. Charles Schwab offers an interesting situation to illustrate this point. When the firm realized in 1995 the potential of using the Web for stock trading, managers also knew they had to deal with the threats that would be perceived by the existing branch sales staff. This staff was accustomed to direct trading and would clearly feel threatened by the online sales unit. Frequent e-mails were used to highlight the rapid growth and inevitability of online trading. Branch staff were trained first, so they, not the new technically oriented staff, could teach customers how to execute online services. In an allied move designed to maintain consistency, the firm reacted to feedback from its customers through both sales forces. The regular traders were charging customers $65.00 per trade. The online group charged $29.95. In January 1998, all trades were charged at $29.95. There was a short-term drop in revenues of $150 million, which was quickly recovered as new volume soared.

RESPONDING TO WHAT THE CUSTOMER WANTS AND REALLY NEEDS

It is important to begin with what the customer is seeking from its sales representatives. In the current business environment, the customer has two themes for the supplier's sales, service, and marketing teams: add value as you bring me goods and services, and help me with total solutions across the supply chain, not just temporary point solutions. These themes derive from three specific customer expectations:

- Business customers want to focus their main energies and resources on core competencies, and turn over the balance of responsibilities to network partners more capable of performing those functions.

- Suppliers that achieve the position of key, strategic sources must understand the buyer's business and be intimate enough with the operations to provide improvement opportunities and solutions to problems, in addition to the normal products and services.

- Suppliers must bring an element of continuous improvement to the relationship, through which the added value is constantly substantiated.

Buyers and sellers must realize that it is in their collective best interests to form alliances, particularly with organizations that offer strategic future value. We have stressed that the future does not belong to a single firm, no matter how massive or how many brands it owns. Optimization occurs when the total network operates in a precise manner. That requires finding best practices from end-to-end in the supply chain network. With so many companies being at such a variation in stages of progress, it becomes imperative to work with partners having some advantage to contribute. The value chain constellation forms best when each party can contribute to the new going-to-market model by sharing better practices and removing unnecessary process steps.

The ideal model will be one that includes shared values and visions, as a result of a collaborative design effort. The alliances have to be built on trust, engendered through the exchange of previously guarded information and best practices. The medium of exchange becomes face-to-face working sessions and electronic commerce, the vital extranet of communication. It's a time when transaction processing and low-level customer service are being automated. It's a time when the sales force should be playing a central role, not passively waiting for orders on how to progress. That means they are proactive in helping the buyers decide what are core competencies and what should be outsourced. With their marketing and IT allies, they provide counsel on how to develop the best overall electronic commerce features by drawing out the best practices across the total network.

In this sense, the effectiveness of the sales representative becomes as important to the customer as the quality of the product or service provided. Furthermore, the salesperson has to play a dual role, as a representative of the supplying firm and as an advocate for the buying organization and developer of the long-term business alliance sought by both firms. To meet these increasing customer expectations, sellers face a complex situation, requiring a new definition of effective customer response. This response must include the recognition of a customer-driven culture across the selling company, and the sales force has to become the voice for creating this effective culture, as they are the points of direct contact. The sellers must assist in providing the resources necessary to plan and execute the information systems collaboratively so necessary in a high-technology era. They must be instrumental in setting up consumer and customer feedback loops that go all the way to the beginning of the supply chain. The goal is to have response tuned to actual consumption, so the consumer is not disappointed and inventories do not become an excessive burden for replenishment. In short, the new role must include providing resources to the network that help transform the collection of interacting firms into a technology-enabled value chain constellation.

ESTABLISHING A CUSTOMER-CENTRIC CULTURE

The central focus of a customer-centric culture is the absolute necessity to provide added value across the total network of response (see Exhibit 9.2). Increasing the effectiveness of each buyer-seller link in the network will be what differentiates the value chain in the eyes of the final consumer. The customer-facing areas, those instances when there is some form of direct contact between buyer and seller, will be enhanced with sales force automation features. The customer service organization will be using computer telephony to reduce dissatisfaction and to proactively help the customer resolve problems and increase pull-through ordering. Much of this contact will be moving to a Web site, where automated order entry and fulfillment take place.

In the area around customer knowledge management, an enormous increase in availability of useful information will occur. Using a variety of codeveloped software and interface techniques, the partners will be mining each other's databases for information crucial to ensuring customer and consumer satisfaction and building new revenues together. Web filters will be at work to screen out nonessential and proprietary data. The best parts of legacy systems will be maintained

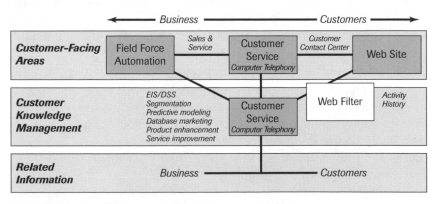

EXHIBIT 9.2   Customer-Centric Business Model

as external connection with key suppliers and customers creates the virtual data-processing center necessary for network activities.

Responding to the specific needs of the designated consumers, who are the ultimate target for the network, becomes the new business of the collective marketing and sales organizations across the total supply chain. The transition will not be as easy as might be presumed. In spite of a near universal cry for more customer devotion, a survey of three hundred companies conducted in 1999 by *Industry Week* magazine revealed that only ninety-eight met the magazine's definition of a customer-centric organization (Sweat 1999a, p.50).

One firm moving to the use of e-commerce features to rebuild a customer-centric focus is airline giant Delta. Under the strong influence of its IT group, Delta began a concerted effort working from data on the incidences when customers got upset with the airline. Problems and delays affect 20 percent of Delta's one hundred million annual customers. With a desire to focus on taking care of some of those customers in times of difficulty, as individuals, Delta developed a customer care system for gate agents that links a Windows NT graphical seating chart to a mainframe airline reservation system and a data warehouse. It can now track in real time which passengers are on board, regardless of where they checked in, reducing standby confirmation time. When planes are delayed, the system kicks in crucial information. The operations control center can tell which planes are delayed, and the reservation system can identify which passengers are going to miss connecting flights. The system uses an event manager that warns of such problems in real time, so agents can deal with them. These agents can clear unfilled seats on other flights, rebook the late passengers, and send an agent to the arriving gate to tell travelers where to go for their new connections (Sweat 1999a, p. 50).

If the new customer-centric culture is to be realized, another important element must be present. Marketing, sales, and service must make a definite alliance internally and externally with the network IT functions. In the customer-centric organization and network, it will be information technology that becomes the engine driving success.

SALES FORCE AUTOMATION ENHANCING THE CAPABILITY

A common ingredient for those firms making higher-level progress is efficient implementation and continuous management of consumer and customer data, product and service specifications demanded by the best customers, and collective purchasing data. When these data are put into the hands of a motivated sales force, they are better able to manage change, appropriately segment the designated markets and end consumers, and bring an effective customer-centric focus to their efforts. Using technology to facilitate interactions allows for increased, higher-quality face-to-face time between buyer and seller. The key, of course, is tailoring the technology to the organization and customers' specific needs.

This development requires specialists equipped with modern equipment. That means they have information that aids in uncovering problems, defining solutions, and bringing added value that would not typically be found in the traditional buying and selling relationship. Together, the new sales agent and his or her buying counterpart have to mine their databases to find useful information that enhances the relationship and generates new revenues. Together, they move from being product specialists to becoming solutions specialists. General Electric's Industrial Control Systems (ICS), for example, mined its database to identify customers in a given market that were operating motors fifteen years old or more. They then devised a plan to assist these customers in analyzing the inefficiencies and associated costs with the old motors as compared to operating with new. This created a model the entire sales force could utilize (Chally 1999, p. 35).

Boise Cascade Office Products uses a number of software programs that enable it to store, sort, and analyze data efficiently. Among those is Activity Based Cost Management (ABCM), which measures cost by activity, customer, and product and enables the company to directly assign over 90 percent of actual costs to specific customer-related activities. Information on cost savings possibilities can be developed and presented to key customers. The end result is typically improved financial results for both the buyer and seller. ABCM also allows for the sharing of business knowledge and flowchart processes with Boise's customers (Chally 1999, p. 35).

Advanced organizations have taken a keen interest and a deliberate path toward customer collaboration, often including elements of what is termed sales force automation (SFA). It is now clear that an automated sales force is necessary to reach Levels III and IV. The added need is to improve the sales, servicing, and marketing processes from an external, customer-centric perspective and then go about automating these processes through developing improvements. This technique avoids the misstep of automating weak or unnecessary processes.

In its version of SFA, Allegiance Healthcare Corporation has added an important tool to its sales and marketing efforts. Account managers and sales representatives use their laptops for interoffice communication. They primarily use their PCs for information transfer, pulling down pricing information or data on their customers. In addition to e-mail, voice mail is a commonly used communication tool for relaying internal messages and for keeping up with customer accounts. Other automation tools available to the sales force include these:

- Electronic catalog (E2)—can be used for customer quotes; also available to Allegiance customers, providing information on Allegiance products by catalog number as well as by competitor catalog number.

- Sales Rep Tool kit (SRTK)—a trend history system used to analyze a territory by sorting it into broad product category divisions or to analyze a customer's business. As one rep remarks, "I spend a great deal of time with this tool because I literally break down the top ten customers in every segment of my business. I want to know if my margin is where it should be, to know if my sales are growing at the same rate. SRTK gives me a clear snapshot of what my customers are buying, what their pricing is, what my cost is, and what kind of contract is out there."

- Automated Pricing Tool (PX)—enables representatives to be proactive with pricing by providing the options to notify customers of price changes. According to another rep, "For instance, I control a lot of my business because it's locally priced, but there's also a great deal of my business that is priced via national contracts over which I have no control. This tool gives me access to their national price. This allows the customer to be more proactive when they know what's happening in their account" (Chally 1999, p. 66).

Software suppliers are stepping up to the need for assistance in the area of automating a sales force. Some are now offering a variety of products that combine e-commerce and customer relationship management (CRM) capabilities. CRM is the deployment of strategies, processes, and technologies that acquire, develop, and retain customers and consumers. Core to this new way of thinking is to create an environment in which every interaction with a customer or consumer fully leverages the information known about that entity or person. It requires technologies and business processes to ensure these interactions are effective. Moreover, the data must be used to add value, no matter what medium the customer or consumer chooses to use—in person, via a call center, or over the Web.

The leading software firms are offering integration of customer interaction and Internet transactions. Oracle now offers Oracle 3I, a front-office suite of applications for billing and payment. Siebel's eBusiness is another suite that combines front office capabilities with e-commerce features such as product configurators, guided selling, and order processing—modules for electronic sales, marketing, service, and channel management. Two of these modules, eMarketing and eService, add capabilities such as a "call me" feature that lets Web customers initiate a live chat session with a customer service representative. The company's biggest feature is eSales, which includes an electronic catalog, price-quote technology, product configurating, and an ordering module that links to transaction-processing systems, credit card authentications, and payment services (Sweat 1999b, p. 18),

Salespeople without the proper electronic tools might not know what products and services their customers have ordered online. Combining customer management with e-commerce gives them a total view of this relationship. Hewlett Packard has introduced a set of its products, dubbed eCRM, that combines HP's call center, Smart Contract, with e-commerce and transaction-processing software from HP and partners such as Broadvision and BEA Systems, Inc. This suite merges traditional call centers and customer interaction capabilities with e-commerce functions. Essentially, CRM moves the management of customer information from the exclusivity of disparate databases (including the brains of sales- and service people) into centralized databases, accessible by the people and systems supporting customers and consumers.

MARKETING: A POSITION OF IMPORTANCE

Most of the recommendations in this chapter have been deployed toward the sales force of the future. This function will become far more technically enabled to help the key customers, but they will not be successful without the support of a focused marketing strategy that is part of a total business philosophy, as well as the kind of help that a resourceful marketing team can provide. A new definition is brought to the concept of customer and consumer in this regard. Companies upstream in the supply chain cannot think of their immediate business customers as the next firm in the linkage. They have to think all the way to the ultimate consumer and how they can play a role in increasing demand for the network of which they are a part. Du Pont, for example, cannot think of Milliken as the ultimate customer for fibers that end in clothing or carpeting. They have to think of Milliken as a wholesaler that takes converted goods downstream toward consumers. Together, the firms design a network solution that results in new revenues for both parties, by involving the downstream retailers of choice and focusing together on the best consumers, on a global basis.

The objective of the marketing group moves toward helping the constituents of the value chain constellation define their total channel strategy. In the example used, the players become inextricably linked through an extranet of communication. Now Milliken receives input on actual consumption from the retailers, so it can initiate resupply with the carpeting that is currently selling (in demand). Milliken then inputs online data to Du Pont, so the latter firm can keep the correct supply of nylon needed for daily production in the right places. Any new innovations are quickly relayed across the total network, and no excessive inventories are created during transitions because they are no longer needed. The result is a new form of just-in-time production and marketing, with greatly reduced cost, shorter cycle times, and rapid consumer response.

The traditional marketing thinking goes to the idea that marketers manage the demand side of the business equation, not the supply side. In the total network sense, that view is shortsighted and misses the opportunity others can play and the expanded effectiveness that could come through a total marketing effort. In the enlarged sense, many people can play a viable role in the marketing effort. Whirlpool offers a good example. Purchasing agents for this appliance manufacturer will work with Whirlpool's marketers to specify the quality and budget levels for steel and other components. Then the buyers will search for suppliers, who will qualify as "best strategic partners"—that is, those who can deliver the best combination of quality, technology, service, and price. The selected suppliers will be invited to participate with Whirlpool in further design and efficiency studies. The aim is to view Whirlpool and its suppliers as a "value delivery system" that can outperform its competitors in meeting target customer needs (Kotler 1992, p. 7).

Marketing will provide the vital link in the new interenterprise network models that bring market analysis together with manufacturing and planning to develop the decision support tools and make the proper channel selection. Ultimately, sales, customer service, and marketing will work as one uniform force, providing an integrated approach to selling, servicing, and sustaining customers across field sales, telesales, an extended selling network, telemarketing, and customer support. In this way, the supplier will merge with the customer and help the customer in its pursuit of the desired end consumer. The requirement is for heavy doses of technology, most of which is currently available, and an organizational restructuring that creates the integrated perspective necessary to meet the need of sophisticated customers and consumers, making their choices through two channels of response.

Customer Care Begins with Product and Service Support

A central thesis throughout this book is that a major degree of control in a supply network has passed downstream to the business customers and consumers. The bottom line of our statement is that these constituents hold the trump cards in the new game of business. The world has become a buyer's market, and we, as consumers, are gaining the upper hand in controlling the supply chains that bring us what we want.

From a satisfaction point of view, with this increased control come increased expectations. Quality, delivery, and service are the fundamental requisites in the game, with the customers/consumers expecting some form of superior attention as a major differentiating factor in making buying decisions. They also expect to receive what they want without having to return the product and wait for replacement. If they do not receive what they want, they will quickly turn to an alternative source. In terms of a supply chain, this situation translates to a necessity to satisfy the retail customers near the end of the chain, as they must satisfy the final consumers. It all becomes a game of how to provide initial products and services most efficiently and a postsale service that keeps the consumers coming back to the same network.

With that necessity in view, we now turn our attention to the secondary theme, or counterpoint, to advanced supply chain management and e-commerce. We'll consider how the real factor of differentiation in the future of business will be how well the supply chain network uses technology to create the desired elements of customer care that cannot be attained from another competing network.

A NEW MODEL TO LEVERAGE CUSTOMER CARE AND TECHNOLOGY

For those value chain constellations determined to forge a leadership position, two very difficult, awkward, but fundamental tenets must be observed:

- All customers or consumers do not warrant the same level of service or attention, nor do all want similar levels. Some business customers demand so much in the way of special services from their suppliers that when actual costs are applied to the relationship, we find no profit at all. In fact, many large-volume situations enter a loss position. Some consumers can fall in the same category as they refuse to pay anything extra for what really are beneficial services. To dismiss this tenet is to spend valuable time and resources on individuals and organizations that have little intention of developing a long-term and mutually rewarding relationship or of increasing sales for something they do not really value.

- To enhance profitability, maintain control of costs, and increase differentiation in the eyes of the targeted customer and consumer groups, customer service strategies must leverage technology. Some business customers and consumers want and need direct contact, and the value of the orders placed more than covers the provision of that contact. Others are more appropriate for an online, Internet system of interaction that meets individual needs, particularly when a business customer, for example, does not want to pay for any special services but accepts a reliable Web-based, self-service response as being adequate.

We cite these tenets as difficult because of the generally pervasive attitudes that all customers should be treated equally and whatever the customer wants should be provided. In the new business environment, those concepts come under attack, and our research overwhelmingly shows the leaders are moving to a position described by our tenets. In this chapter, we'll elaborate on the tenets and show a way to provide the satisfaction desired and needed by various groups of customers and still make a profit.

Internet Enhancement of Customer Care

In Exhibit 10.1, we show the route to matching the appropriate customer care with actual needs. Beginning in Level I/II, most firms

Progression Business Application	Level I/II Internal Supply Chain Optimization *Stage 0*	Level III Network Formation *Stage 1*	Level IV Value Chain Constellation *Stage 2*	Level IV+ Full Network Connectivity *Stage 3*
Customer care*	Customer service reaction	Focused service – call centers	Segmented response system, customer relationship management	Matched care – customer care automation

*Includes order management.

EXHIBIT 10.1   E-business Development Framework: Customer Care

focus their customer service efforts in a reactive mode. That is, they wait for a particular customer to have a problem and then react by searching for a quick solution. Some companies do this very well, but it's generally after the fact. It's not a proactive approach to anticipating and resolving problems before they happen. As a company completes Level II, there is a shift to a more proactive stance with a stronger customer-centric focus. A call center is usually established to provide more directed service. Unfortunately, we find little consistency across these centers, and a wide range of customer reactions results. As the electronic network starts to take shape, the constituents begin to share information on how to improve the effectiveness of these centers.

Generally, however, this stage does not show the same level of progress as that which occurs with other functions. Customer care tends to lag behind marketing and sales, for example, and awaits the results of ERP connectivity before going external. We find most progress is delayed until network partners move to the value chain constellation position and begin considering segmented response systems as part of a customer relationship management program. Use of full network connectivity comes very late in this discipline but does result in a matched care system that we call customer care automation. Each of these progressions requires far more application of information technology than is usually used in customer care departments.

While a number of technologies have application in this area, three stand out as a means for matching elements of customer service with customer needs:

- Technology-assisted selling, including management of identified opportunities with new and existing customers, development of telemarketing sales to focused groups, and more rapid and accurate quotation preparation and delivery to online inquiries

- Customer support and call center management that delivers product and service availability information online, provides access to order status (allowing changes where appropriate), and offers internal help desks for problem resolution
- Field service and logistics providing technical services support and field service and repair for those customers needing direct assistance

Via the Internet, these elements can be enhanced and made specific to particular customer groups. In fact, a new service format is possible that enables a business to provide more efficient, economical levels of service to selected customer and consumer segments, typically by removing the barriers to the access and utilization of important data. This service, moreover, can be extended to the entire customer base, but it will be done in a manner that matches the type and amount of service with value to the business network and actual customer need. Self-service, Internet-enabled customer support can dramatically improve the service experience (for those customers desiring that type of attention) and those willing to pay for the inherent benefits. It fits conveniently into the concept of customer relationship management (CRM), can create the measure of difference in today's crowded marketplace, and leads to a renewal of customer loyalty. Exhibit 10.2 illustrates the integration that occurs with CRM and the concepts to be considered.

Most companies that are not network members place human interfaces between their customers and the information they seek (e.g., new product offerings, order status, or technical services information). For those companies using people who are skilled at the role and enjoy the position, the experience can be mutually beneficial to customer *and* supplier. Unfortunately, our research indicates those who have little in the way of interpersonal skills often fill the jobs, and the pay scale is such that it attracts temporary personnel.

With the understanding that the service position could be enhanced and enabled to take advantage of improvements to the supply chain, firms have moved to a new model that emphasizes matching the degree of customer care with the particular customer and that customer's real needs and desire for service. For each customer type, moreover, some form of Internet response is applied to the desired service. With this model, customers who do not need direct contact can access the generic information they want more quickly and with less effort. They can get the data on orders, sched-

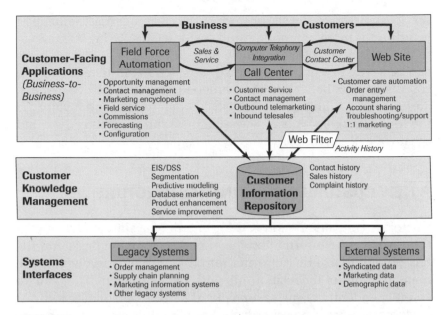

EXHIBIT 10.2   Customer Relationship Management with Internet Enhancement

ules, inventory, and shipments they want at the time they want it. The best customer service representatives find more time to interact with other customers and deal with more complex business situations. In the process, companies find they can generate a single, comprehensive customer knowledge base by automatically storing, accessing, interpreting, and cross-referencing all of the data received from customers during online interactions.

This information includes what customers order and when; the kinds of service they request; what they discuss when they are unhappy with the interaction; and the frequency, duration, and complexity of the interactions. This is a gold mine of information that has traditionally been left fallow as companies typically drove much harder for the sale, regardless of the capability to service the customers and keep them happy after the sale. When matched with the information flowing from the network extranet, customer service can dramatically resolve what is often an area of discontent. Customers with problems find a proactive business function determined to anticipate problems before they happen and offer solid solutions when they do.

The new model calls for fewer but more skilled people at the heart of the direct service effort. Those people must be trained in some level of supply chain response and activity-based costing so they know the value of making appropriate suggestions during the service transaction. For the balance of the customer base, something less direct is more appropriate and cost-effective. Using technology to meet the needs of what can be the larger segment of customers can be a way to significantly raise satisfaction while reducing the costs of service. Better and more efficient customer service that creates new opportunities to establish customer value and loyalty are the foundation blocks of a new e-business model designed around what we will call *customer care automation*.

A NEW CUSTOMER CARE INFRASTRUCTURE

Customer care automation (CCA) centers on a simple idea: If customers have the information they need on a timely basis and the technology to use that information, they can effectively manage many portions of the relationship with their suppliers. They can do so independently of salespeople, field service personnel, or direct customer service representatives. Applying this concept to the appropriate customers requires fundamentally new relationships between customers and suppliers. It dramatically changes the process of caring for customers in the most reasonable manner.

CCA is an infrastructure of technology and process change that allows customers and consumers to access and use the information they need to maintain a fruitful trading relationship with those supplying what they want. It can encompass order placement and intelligence (order entry, order inquiry, product availability, and pricing), as well as technical, functional, and marketing assistance (access to specifications, training information, performance records, and promotional materials). Within such a framework, a customer can

- interact with suppliers at any time to place orders, determine order status, access maintenance or repair information, and execute transactions;
- learn about new products, review performance specifications, change order requirements, and watch products perform; and
- obtain most forms of service without having to call or interact with salespeople or service center personnel.

In addition, suppliers can

- improve sales efficiency by freeing salespeople to concentrate on high-growth-potential customers and those who require personal involvement in formulating their purchasing decision;

- inform customers about promotions, sales product updates, and service and warranty issues more effectively than through traditional means of contact;

- lower the cost of training and maintaining sales and customer service personnel;

- reduce certain hardware, software, and other investments required by more traditional forms of customer relationship management;

- efficiently capture and assess customer data to better understand customer desires and grievances and develop product/service offerings to address them; and

- expand sales and marketing contacts through one-to-one interaction opportunities with the targeted, most desirable customer segment.

Customer care automation provides a simple, more profitable alternative to serving low-margin and infrequent customers by automating the interaction with these accounts. It can also be as complex as fully redesigning sales, marketing, and customer service processes to serve every customer uniquely. In some cases, CCA is used by larger companies (those having the technological capability), while personal interaction is used by the small firm. Most firms find the right value proposition somewhere along this continuum.

In general terms, a good customer care system enables a form of 1:1 marketing. In Exhibit 10.3, we show that such a process involves four steps. First, the service representative learns more about the

1. Profiling —
Learn about my customer
- Existing customer data
- User profiles
- Observation engine

4. Transactions —
Make the sale
- Commerce
  Shopping cart
  Pricing/tax/shipping
  Payments
- Finance
  Balances, transfers
  News, stock feeds
- Legacy system integration
- Alerts

One-to-One Marketing

2. Matching —
Understand customer interests and how they connect to my products and services
- Rule-based matching
- Taxonomy-based matching
- Targeted editorials, ads, products recommendations, incentives

3. Content —
Provide information based on these identified interests
- Page templates
- Editorials
- Products
- Incentives
- Advertising
- Discussion groups

EXHIBIT 10.3 Enabling 1:1 Marketing

customer and begins creating a useful profile. This profile becomes the observation engine. Next, the rep begins to understand the customer's interests and how they connect with products and services being provided. Now there is an opportunity to match rule-based decisions on ads, promotions, product introductions, and the like, with customer activities. Third, the content of the interactions is recorded and analyzed to provide information based on identified interests. In the final step, the rep can make a direct sale by completing a valuable transaction with the customer. In general terms, the eventual automation of the customer care function addresses the changing service expectations in three ways:

- Control and personalization of the entire process are matched with what different customers want to receive in the gathering of needed information, placing purchase requests in the most effective manner, and getting the service necessary to make the experience worthwhile.

- Access to information, sales representatives and account information, including product and price, order status, delivery status, payment status, and customer service, is available on a twenty-four-hour/seven-day basis.

- Customer interactions are measured by quality of service provided, including consistency and effectiveness, self-service when desired, and convenience without waste of time.

A HYPOTHETICAL EXAMPLE

To understand better the concept being discussed, let's consider a hypothetical situation in which a company has decided to develop a customer care automation system to assist with its rapid and profitable growth. Advanced Cyber Technologies (ACT) is a large manufacturer and distributor of computer parts and accessories, such as disk drives, modems, and other peripherals. ACT implemented the technology and process changes being considered and now uses customer care automation to address its entire customer base. While the company has always emphasized its service capability, it has expanded its focus to include customized marketing plans and more effective use of sales and customer service representatives.

One of ACT's most profitable customers, Global Overseas Operating Dynamics (GOOD), has recently completed the implementation of an enterprise resource planning system and has electronically linked its ordering and inventory management systems into an extranet system that includes a few key suppliers like ACT. Rather than having to call ACT's customer service center to discuss order status and delivery, GOOD's personnel can now view timely information at their own convenience. Although they have always placed a high percentage of orders electronically, they now receive instant updates on order status, product promotions, product substitutions, and new products. E-mail notification is sent when orders have been shipped. During the last busy season, the GOOD warehouse manager received regular updates about when critical orders were scheduled to arrive.

Nearly all of GOOD's communications with ACT now take place electronically, saving substantial time and energy. The data are accurate, comprehensive, customizable, and available twenty-four hours per day. When it needs to see a sales representative, GOOD uses a special access number to reach the appropriate sales agent's pager. Order expediters can call the ACT customer service center as needed to get additional information or make special inquiries. This process has improved now that ACT representatives have more time to discuss complex sales issues instead of resolving routine service problems. Also, visits by ACT representatives are more frequent and conversations more strategic since rudimentary data on products, promotions, and support are now delivered on request electronically.

Product managers now develop customer-specific marketing plans, based on size, geography, business type, and other pertinent characteristics. The more customers interact with ACT, the more the data accumulate and are analyzed, and the more comprehensive their profiles become, allowing ACT to further customize the approach taken to each customer. Marketing managers also receive automatically generated inventory and product movement information at their weekly operations planning meeting. They target particular customers for moving excess product and can specify substitutions electronically. The entire process is orderly, efficient, and exceptionally customer-friendly.

Significant changes have also occurred in the sales department. Low-volume accounts, which salespeople used to visit monthly, are largely addressed with the new technology and a small, centralized telemarketing group. Salespeople now have a smaller group of strategic accounts to which they allocate more of their time to become an advocate for solving problems, providing solutions, and helping these customers develop new revenues. The result is a more consultative style of selling in which partnering is used to meet mutual business objectives.

Customer service no longer has a large staff that deals with all accounts in a region but rather a small cadre of highly trained representatives. Each one is responsible for five to ten key accounts. Representatives can work closely with GOOD's account representatives to provide the kind of personal attention that was never feasible when they were inundated with calls from more than a thousand customers and fifty salespeople a day needing order status and new product information. Lastly, customer service now has customer retention and sales goals, which it shares with salespeople. A sizeable portion of the compensation paid to customer service representatives is now based on those goals.

CUSTOMER STRATIFICATION AS THE BASIS FOR CUSTOMER CARE AUTOMATION

As the company moves into Level III and leverages technology to improve customer service, it segments the customer and consumer base so each segment can be serviced appropriately. The idea is to match supply chain capabilities to the real needs of the customers. The alternate and traditional approach of providing uniform service for all segments ignores the varying levels of customer value and needs. If the supply chain constituents are in business to make a profit, delighting the least important customers (typically designated as C, D, and E customers) with outstanding services (but often without a profitable return for the effort) creates happy customers but generally unhappy stockholders. Providing outstanding service to large customers that view the service indifferently can also be a waste of valuable time and effort. Customer stratification should be based on the following criteria:

1. *The volume of a customer's purchases.* Often, the volume of orders can create economies for companies, making better use of their capacities and driving profits because of sheer size. This size also allows the firm to cover much of its fixed costs in a small number of customers. This situation is not uniform, however, and we always find a few of the largest customers are also among the least profitable because of the demand for special services for which they are unwilling to pay.

2. *The strategic value of the customer.* Just because a customer is not highly profitable *now* does not mean that it won't be in

the future. Strategically valuable customers may require an investment in order to grow into tomorrow's best customers. Consider the suppliers that did not take Wal-Mart seriously in their early stages, only to watch the firm exceed $150 billion in retail sales in 1999.

3. *The profitability of the customer.* Volume alone does not drive profits. Smaller customers are sometimes willing to pay more for a unique product or capability. Also, market conditions sometimes allow a premium to be charged for certain products and services.

Exhibit 10.4 is a simple illustration of the type of segmentation being considered. In this diagram the customers have been divided into four categories:

- The "super" customers might be small in numbers but are typically large in volume and have been deemed profitable and strategic. The criteria for this designation will be worked out with the marketing and sales function, with help from the accounting department, providing activity-based costing data, and valued members of the supply chain network. Some checking will be done with key partners to make sure these customers have full supply chain network value. Proprietary information does not have to be shared during this activity, but vital information on the costs of doing business with specific categories of customers must be shared so a valid determination can be made of what criteria will be met to receive this highest rating. In a business-to-business situation, most of the customers will be large, fully developed accounts that are

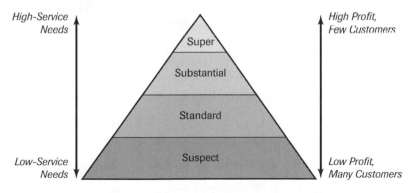

EXHIBIT 10.4 Customer Segmentation

looking to automate or improve the way they transact business with suppliers. Or they may be smaller in volume but extremely profitable when all cost factors are considered. In a business-to-consumer situation, the volume is not as important as the loyalty and the anticipated margin per transaction.

- The "substantial" customers may also buy from competitors or have other divisions or complementary businesses that could be served. Depending on their potential strategic value, some of these customers will be best served by the incremental customer care time freed up as personnel concentrate on the super category customers. Service is not curtailed in this area, simply matched with what the analysts decide is appropriate. A substantial customer is typically a midvolume account that has demonstrated loyalty over a reasonable time frame, pays for services rendered, does not have barriers to doing business or extraneous costs associated with servicing, and requires minimal sales contact.

- The "standard" customers generally represent the largest group in terms of numbers of accounts, but cumulatively they generate a small portion of the supplier's total revenues. These customers may be very price-sensitive and not particularly loyal. They are often unprofitable because they require an inordinate amount of attention relative to the revenue they contribute. We find in this category many accounts that deserve the designation "wannabe." The sales representative is spending an inordinate amount of time trying to cultivate relationships because these firms want to be a substantial account, but many times the reality is the investment has little chance of moving up in a category.

- The last category contains the usual "suspects." Here we find what is typically a large number of accounts that collectively represent a small amount of annual business. If these customers are kept, they are definite candidates for an automated servicing system with minimal time and cost. Most of these customers are often better served by another network.

In a large supply chain, other categories might be added, but staying with our simple four-level pyramid is usually sufficient for beginning the kind of diagnosis that leads to a reasonable segmentation. Each of the groups characterized will have its own service profile and potential for the implementation of customer care automation.

Customer Care Focus	Customer Segment	Objectives

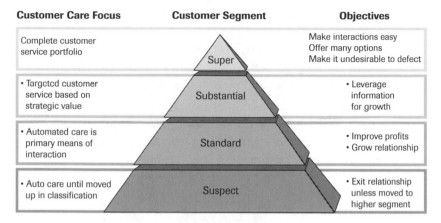

Complete customer service portfolio	**Super**	Make interactions easy Offer many options Make it undesirable to defect
• Targeted customer service based on strategic value	**Substantial**	• Leverage information for growth
• Automated care is primary means of interaction	**Standard**	• Improve profits • Grow relationship
• Auto care until moved up in classification	**Suspect**	• Exit relationship unless moved to higher segment

EXHIBIT 10.5 Creating a Customer Profile

Using Exhibit 10.5 as a guide, the customer care focus is then matched with the designated customer segments, along with specific objectives for each category. Suppliers may find it difficult to accept that each of these groups requires and deserves differing levels of customer service. However, companies cannot afford to devote the same resources to low-profitability, transaction-oriented customers as they must devote to more profitable or potentially strategic relationships. In some cases, the customers will prefer the differentiated service level, particularly if it meets their needs and there is less buying contact on their part.

MAKING SENSE OF CUSTOMER CARE AUTOMATION

As companies complete the primary stage of e–supply chain, often with the help of external constituents, and they see the value chain constellation taking shape, they make a belated effort to move into Stage 2 and take advantage of interenterprise resources. This delay is generally caused by the reluctance to share direct information on customers. Always fearful that these data will fall into the wrong hands, most firms continue to pursue customer service on an internal basis, even if augmented by external information. This approach misses the chance to build a stronger, total system of response, so some firms move to the next stage of progress and consider the automation of customer service. Intent on completing their service matrix, they seek answers to a series of questions:

- What level of customer service should we provide? What services mean the most to our best customers? Does the value received from continuing relationships with our customers vary substantially, and do we believe there is inherent value in treating different segments of customers differently?

- Are the specific real needs of the customers diverse enough that we can determine the variation in appropriate response? How can we differentiate our firm based on service in our market? Do our customers expect some form of customization in the way goods and services are delivered? Do some of them especially value the supplier's ability to satisfy their most unique needs?

- Are we dealing with customers with whom there is no real measure of differentiation? Do our customers regard the products and services received from us on a purely commodity basis? How can we translate improved service for some customers into profitable growth?

Exhibit 10.6 depicts two types of variation among customers, still from a supplier's perspective. Strong value variations among customers (the situation shown on the left of the exhibit) increase the desirability of a customer care automation system. With a shallow distribution, there is little to differentiate the supplier, and more standard, uniform style and level of service are probably appropriate.

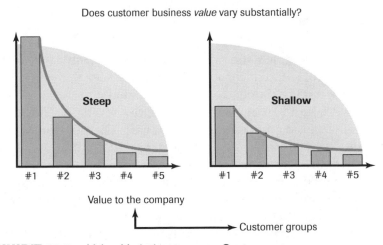

EXHIBIT 10.6   Value Variations among Customers

Companies that have customers with diverse service needs are also generally more appropriate for a customer care automation process. In Exhibit 10.7, we see that the firm on the left has a wide diversity of needs as expressed by the customers and confirmed by the in-depth analysis that goes into customer care evaluations. On the right, we notice the needs are relatively uniform. This situation would indicate the firm on the left is more likely to benefit from a segmented care approach than is the firm on the right.

By considering the variations and implications they suggest for a marketing and sales strategy, the firm can help itself and its best customers by designating the type of service most appropriate for the situation. Exhibit 10.8 can be used to array the customer values against the customer needs and more easily come to a conclusion regarding where to apply customer care automation. Where the customer value is shallow and the need uniform, mass marketing is probably most appropriate. Where the customer value is steep and the need still uniform, a key account strategy generally works best, in which the customer receives direct attention from an account executive and the necessary supporting service infrastructure.

Where the customer needs are diverse and the values are low, a niche marketing approach in which the attention is specific to the need on an as-needed basis is more appropriate. Finally, if the analysis indicates the customer value is steep and the need diverse, customer care automation is definitely called for. Now the firm goes online with what becomes a customized response system for

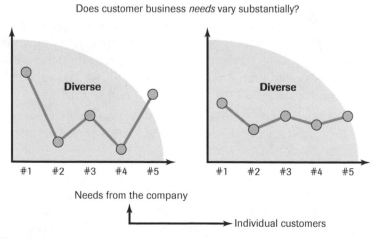

EXHIBIT 10.7   Variation in Customer Needs

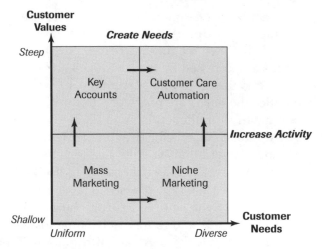

EXHIBIT 10.8   Need/Value Continuum

customers not needing the direct attention of a conventional service system.

Understanding the relative value and diverse needs of customers will give a company a clearer picture of how it should allocate customer care resources. The next step is to determine the level of customer care automation capability required as suppliers must balance the real needs of their customers against the underlying technology and process capabilities inherently required to enable the change. Based on a thorough assessment, the firm may choose to implement any number of capabilities, some rudimentary and some highly advanced, including the following:

- *Technical, functional, and marketing expertise*—specifications, training information, applications, warranty information, material safety sheets, performance records, promotional materials, options available, operating instructions, forms, substitute/ alternative data, ISO documentation, and so forth
- *Order intelligence*—order entry, order inquiry, product availability, product pricing, contract inquiry, service request status, and order history inquiries

The appropriate level of capability should be driven by the number of customers relative to their value and need, as well as their potential for growth, their buying motive, and the costs required to serve them effectively. The capabilities implemented must be consistent with the supplier's overall business strategy. A firm that is driven by operational efficiency, for example, might benefit more significantly from customer care automation than a highly specialized company with a small, partnership-driven clientele. Companies that exhibit the following characteristics typically benefit from segmentation and allocated customer care procedures:

- A high percentage of the dollar volume comes from customers that are technologically sophisticated and want to use that technology to make transactions as easily, inexpensively, and quickly as possible.

- A strong opportunity exists to improve some customers' strategic value. Ideally, these customers are looking for a profitable bundling of pricing and service. Responding to that need will require suppliers to use a variety of customer care resources to cement a long-term, profitable relationship. To do this, they must ensure resources are effectively deployed against the most strategic customers.

- A large percentage of their customers have relatively low value. Their purchases, for example, are often small or unprofitable due to high transaction costs. For the most part, the company neither desires nor can afford to commit serious customer care time to this group, yet it cannot afford to lose the volume of sales that these customers represent as a category.

TECHNOLOGY CONSIDERATIONS

Some very large companies are still not paying the proper attention to the primacy of the customer and equally failing to build the technological basis to deal properly with the best of those customers. Others are using new techniques to forge stronger relationships with the most desirable customers. At Sears, Roebuck and Co., customer data quality is considered to be key to this firm's efforts to increase cross-selling opportunities among multiple businesses, including retail, home services, credit, specialty catalog, and e-commerce operations. The company encountered a major problem along the way to its solution, however. Each business has its own IT system, making it nearly impossible for Sears to develop one single customer list (Wallace 1999, p. 63).

Sears is now developing a data warehouse that will include information on its credit and home service customers—237 million individual customer records totaling four terabytes of data. The information will be cleansed to assure a high level of accuracy, giving the company a "better picture of what the customer means to Sears as an enterprise and what potential business opportunities exist." With the data warehouse, for example, marketers can identify customers who bought appliances on credit and may be good prospects for purchasing extended warranties or maintenance services (Wallace 1999, p. 67).

The Internet is CCA's medium for dialogue, so customers, suppliers, and distributors can be linked for basically the cost of a personal or network computer, modem, and Internet service provider. Customer care applications are built into this extranet of communication with the business logic separate from the application. A Web development team creates the building blocks of the application, but business managers determine what content should be available to the Web site and how it is targeted to different customer segments and site visitors. The content of a basic site might include any combination of product or service profiles and advertisements; an incentive system to influence the customer to act in certain ways; editorial content, including text, audio, and video; and discussion groups.

To be most effective, the constituents decide collaboratively to build the appropriate customer care automation technology, taking care to fulfill the following requirements:

1. It must use a common mechanism for dialogue that is inexpensive for the customer and supplier.

2. Its content must be controlled by the business manager(s) responsible for the demand chain

3. It should be easily expanded to accommodate new products and services.

4. It should use a rules-based system in which rules can be added, modified, or phased out, independent of the products or applications.

5. It must be able to remember and learn from the customer, both through active means such as transaction history, registration, and feedback, as well as through passive means such as observations and generalizations based on the totality of a customer's input.

6. It should be scalable to ensure higher performance levels as the business grows.

7. It should integrate easily with the supplier's existing business systems.

KEY CHALLENGES

Companies entering into customer care automation face two significant challenges: resistance to adoption and concerns about security and reliability. Predictably, the two groups most dramatically affected by—and most resistant to—the adoption of customer care automation are salespeople and long-term customers. Salespeople and sales management will be concerned that CCA means fewer sales representatives and a diminished role for the sales professional. From experience, salespeople are vitally important in the new model, albeit with one significant difference: emphasis will now be on closing sales and developing relationships with key customers, instead of taking orders or providing after-sales support. A salesperson's greatest attribute will be the ability to convince a target audience that the product or service being represented has greater value than its alternatives.

Customers, too, may be reluctant to adopt the new customer care relationships. Suppliers need to help them understand the tangible benefits—most important, that service should improve in all aspects, even though there may be less personal contact. If personal contact is critical and the customer is valuable enough, customer care automation should be offered along with other options.

SUMMARY

The ultimate goal of a customer care automation system is twofold:

- Attain more profitable growth by servicing less valuable customers more efficiently, but no less effectively by matching service with value and need.

- Acquire more high-value customers or greater sales volume with these customers through the more effective use of focused customer care resources and improved utilization of the information being gathered from customers.

Suppliers can achieve these goals by creating automated sales and service opportunities that produce a stable, satisfied base of less valuable customers. They can make a greater proportion of customer care resources and dollars available to target higher-potential customers. In addition, they can leverage customer information to deepen relationships, thereby creating a more loyal customer base and greater long-term value for both the customer and supplier.

The end result can be an automated, value-added relationship in which suppliers become superior sources of customer support by

- learning from each transaction to provide progressively better service;

- receiving, storing, analyzing, and responding to real-time customer input about the need for new products and services;

- becoming better promoters by using technology to construct economical, one-to-one marketing models with automatic response mechanisms;

- supporting all customers more effectively, creating more genuine sales opportunities, and ensuring better field support for the sales staff; and

- enabling customers to get their own information and place their own orders, twenty-four hours per day/seven days per week, and thus lowering overall customer service costs.

The concept of customer care automation clearly illustrates how Internet-enabled processes can contribute to profitable growth. The challenge for companies adopting the concept is to build around what is right for their customers and for their company as a whole, not just what appeals to individual constituencies. With the correct perspective—and the integrated application of technologies and business processes—a new level of customer service and profitable growth can be attained.

The Need for Connectivity
with Human Resources

In spite of the dramatic drive toward our brave, new digital world, the impact on business will not be meaningful unless leaders recognize a critical need. There is a collective urgency, on a global basis, to connect what is occurring in the e-business arena with vital human resources—the people who will make the right things happen. While information technology will be at the center of e–supply chain applications, unless proper connectivity exists between the new technology and the people implementing the wave of change, the effort will not contain enduring benefits. That connectivity begins with having a sufficient supply of technically trained personnel and extends to training them further in the new cyber techniques and providing them with a meaningful association with what they will be implementing—the most dramatic change to business commerce since the industrial revolution.

The key understanding that must permeate the new business culture is that digital technology and the changes to be fostered by e–supply chain in the new economy are the tools to be used by people to enhance their skills and abilities to perform jobs better. The business results so desired by business managers will then be the offspring of this greater productivity and efficiency. As recent trends have clearly shown, the new technology is not replacing people; it is enhancing their performance. In a time of unprecedented prosperity and high employment, we are witnessing a revolution in how people find data, use data, and function in the new information era. With an expected shortage of people able to perform in technical positions, the need to pay attention to the human resource side of the business technology issue has never been more important.

In this chapter, we'll continue our counterpoint to supply chain and e-commerce as we take a look at how firms are going to find sufficient, skilled talent to implement the kind of changes we've discussed. We'll consider the need to enlarge that talent base and bring them training in the advanced concepts and applications so they can apply their skills in a meaningful and satisfactory manner.

RESPONDING TO BASIC REQUIREMENTS

Firms not yet involved in electronic network formation concentrate on internal supply chain training. A growing body of resources—universities, internal training courses, and consultants—is available to assist in this area. As the practice matures, so does the training and the volume of helpful material expand. The value chain concept is still so new, however, that most companies are struggling with how to raise awareness and enhance skills with their personnel in this area. As human resource (HR) managers begin to recognize that certain HR processes must be improved and automated through e-business applications, they also realize a lot of activity is needed to assist in the formation of e-networks. Job postings, the application process, benefits administration, and general recruiting processes move onto intranets in the typical firm. These moves help acclimate the employees to use the computer for business purposes by making it easy for them to gain access to opportunities.

In an early move intended to help employees, Ford Motor Company maintained a facility in Highland, Michigan, as a document site. Using this location, personnel could find important information, but it could take up to six months to locate a particular document. As a result, most people did not access the site. They re-

Progression / Business Application	Level I/II	Level III	Level IV	Level IV+
	Internal Supply Chain Optimization	Network Formation	Value Chain Constellation	Full Network Connectivity
	Stage 0	Stage 1	Stage 2	Stage 3
Human resources	Internal supply chain training	Provide network resources, training	Interenterprise resource utilization	Full network alignment and capability provision

EXHIBIT 11.1 E-Business Development Framework: Human Resources

created the work, bringing marginal effect to the efficiency planned. Even the use of computers did little to help. If some valuable information was on a personal computer, no one else had access. When Ford employees were surveyed in 1994 and 1995, it was no surprise that half felt they did not have access to information that would help them do their jobs.

With the introduction of its intranet, Ford can now share information around the world, reducing cycle times and allowing its people to leverage intellectual capital. Reflecting on the results, Bud Mathiesal, as Ford's CIO, stated that the Ford intranet had overtaken Ford's mainframe computer assets in importance to Ford's business execution. Now a larger need must be met—helping people progress into the new digital economy and benefit from the use of the Internet. It is in this area that we find gaps in availability and training.

The cyber field is awash with recruiting firms, headhunters, and company-sponsored sites designed to make it simple for the prospective IT recruit to search for and find suitable employment. Job searching, quite simply, has moved onto the Internet. In a counter-effort to keep the employee satisfied, some companies now let employees surf their internal bulletin boards to find the latest information on company activities and performance. Firms generally allow employees to purchase products made by the company and other goods.

Some employers have allowed workers to shop at work. Microsoft, Nordstrom, 3M, Northwest Airlines and others have introduced programs that let workers buy discounted products and services, from their company and external partners, from their desktop computers. Delivering benefits directly to employees' computers is just one of the tactics being used to retain and reward workers in today's very competitive workplace. Other employees can arrange flexible hours of work and care for their workers' children. In short, these firms have made a means of external and internal contact available to their workers over an internal channel of communication.

As companies complete Level I/II, other features are introduced that enhance the worker's ability. When First Union Corporation wanted to get the bank's financial information more quickly into the hands of employees, it built a special portal. This report portal is designed to allow more than one thousand First Union employees to view hundreds of thousands of pages, reports on everything from employee reimbursement to the monthly budget. These portals are becoming more common. They generally rely on a host of supporting technologies, including databases, transactional systems, online analytical processing software, query and reporting tools, data mining, search engines, Web browsers, and publishing delivery mechanisms. The objective is to make report distribution more efficient and effective.

When the company achieves sufficient internal competency to begin external network development and begins building the e-commerce capability needed to move to Stage 1 of e–supply chain, a more fundamental and critical application appears, requiring considerably greater HR attention. Now the organization has to face the generally universal difficulty of finding a sufficient technical talent pool and training this pool to perform a viable role as the value chain constellation is constructed and expands. This need is met on an internal basis first but quickly expands to determining how to develop sufficient skilled talent across the full supply chain network. As the problem is addressed, most firms discover a lack of skill and training. This problem is so critical that it has been recognized on a national basis.

In a report released by the U.S. Department of Commerce, *The Digital Workforce: Building Info Tech Skills at the Speed of Innovation*, Secretary of Commerce William Daley comments on the growing shortage of skilled workers and the need for training. "There's no question," he says, "that if you don't have people properly training for the future, it will affect our economy. If the need for IT workers isn't addressed, it could have a sizable impact on our economy because information technology, such as e-commerce, is playing such a tremendous part in our economic explosion" (Mateyaschuk 1999b, p. 44).

The report next discusses how the computer industry views the problem as a shortage of workers. That is one side of the issue, but the problem is more than just meeting the shortage. From our experiences, we find most industries are not properly utilizing the resources once they are recruited. The IT workforce challenge is to meet the demands of the dramatic rise in e-commerce-related events, which will only accelerate. Whether the global market for this talent will establish some sort of equilibrium between demand and supply is not clear to us. The Commerce Department report concludes that the problem is more complex than any individual view. In any event, there is a shortage of skilled workers, and we see an important need to connect these people more correctly to the action they must take to move a firm and its partners through an e–supply chain progression.

The challenge is pervasive and global and moving at Mach speed. The solution must involve getting the right number of qualified people, keeping them in satisfying positions, properly training them to stay abreast of what promises to be an ever-changing environment, and providing them with a solid understanding of their role in the new e-business world. That means not ushering them into a back-office environment for years of a Chaplinesque dedication to making the electronic machinery work. Rather, they must have a clear understanding of how to apply their skills effectively and be given roles of advocacy for how the technology is to be applied and how the results will be beneficial to all of the stakeholders affected. As the network increases in scope and applications, there will be a need to share the best talent and training across that network.

The need for a solution is pervasive. It must be addressed by a coalition of business, government, and educational institutions. Their joint purpose has to begin with finding and training more people with the interest in this burgeoning field in technology and business skills—people who want to play a role of significance in the new cyber-based revolution. Fortunately, there are signs of recognition of the dilemma and action is being taken. In one example of how such a movement can be created, the University of Nebraska has formed the Peter Kiewit Institute in Omaha. The $70 million state-of-the-art computer science facility comprises the university's new College of Information Science and Technology and its Lincoln College of Engineering and Technology. Two-thirds of the funding was raised from businesses within the Omaha community. The state of Nebraska contributed the balance. Local businesses also funded scholarship programs and internships for the institute. First Data Resources, a provider of transaction-processing products and services, donated the land for the project (Mateyaschuk 1999a, p. 92).

At a time when nearly two thousand positions for IT workers are open, the institute is a sign that business and industry can join forces with government and education to deal with what could only become a larger problem. A special feature will be an "experts-in-residence" program, which will allow executives from high-tech companies around the world to spend a year or more teaching and mentoring students at the Omaha facility. Boeing and IBM have already committed to participate. Cisco Systems and US West have donated technology to help deliver distance-learning capabilities. According to Walter Scott, chairman of the institute's board, "Colleges have a reputation for being slow to adapt to change. This institute will be an example of education being responsive to the needs of business" (Mateyaschuk 1999a, p. 92).

In a similar move, Pennsylvania State University now has a new college dedicated to information science and technology. Working with business and government assistance, Penn State also has a new research center for e-business. This university is also rapidly expanding its capabilities to answer the call we are citing.

For businesses to gain the competitive advantage offered by taking a lead in the e-business race, talented people will be the key ingredient. Firms can raise capital and copy strategies and tactics applied by others. What will stall progress is a lack of skilled and motivated human resources. As Jeffrey Bezos, CEO of Amazon.com, explains the situation, "The thing that has constrained us for the last four years has always been people bandwidth. Just having enough smart, hard-working, talented, passionate people to execute against our vision" (Byrne 1999, p. 112).

The need for solutions is also moving at breakneck speed. As more and more companies progress into advanced levels of e–supply chain, they're going to discover keeping up with the changing technology becomes a major challenge. A new business issue is emerging for managers—applying the correct technology to their particular applications in time to have meaning in their market. This new dimension of concern only heightens the problem of keeping business units abreast of what is the best technology and application for the business environment being faced. As this technology is moving at speeds never before seen in business commerce, the nontechnically skilled managers have a real problem to face. Staying ahead of the competition completes the puzzle as business needs and technologies converge, and the firm discovers a whole new array of problems. A solution not only has to meet current needs, but it must also keep pace with the rapidity of innovation in this new and dynamic business discipline.

CONNECTING COMPETENCY AND BUSINESS STRATEGY WITH PERSONAL VALUES

To satisfy the needs of all stakeholders, including employees, a company has to start with determining at what business processes must the organization and its network excel. We have stressed the need for advanced-level firms to have certain core competencies to gain a competitive advantage. A Level III firm will have identified those competencies and will be diverting key resources and talent into those areas. As these organizations then focus on human resources and the necessary connectivity with network strategy and purpose, they will begin asking the following questions:

- How do we motivate people to execute the critical processes that make our core competencies special? How do we keep them motivated following what could be major redesign or redirection? How will we get them to understand the network concept and the need for external sharing?

- To achieve our vision, how must our people learn, communicate, and work together? How will we use this understanding to sustain our ability to change the total organization and improve across the critical technology support functions? How will we extend this understanding to enhance working with external resources dedicated to the same objectives?

- How do we share responsibilities and roles within our organization and with our key network constituents? How do we build in the enabling systems and data transfer at each critical point of interchange?

The ultimate HR goal has to be giving every employee a meaningful role in the implementation of the strategies and activities that support the central vision and purposes of the value chain constellation. That will become the driving force behind the move to Level III and the means of gaining the insights and dedication necessary to make such a pervasive change in the way a network functions. The key to execution will be finding new, innovative ways to do the necessary work better and with less physical effort and to take advantage of interenterprise resources across the value chain. Done correctly, the work is efficient and satisfying.

In essence, achieving these results requires linking vision with strategy and employee execution. Exhibit 11.2 illustrates this connection. The process improvement on an external basis begins with

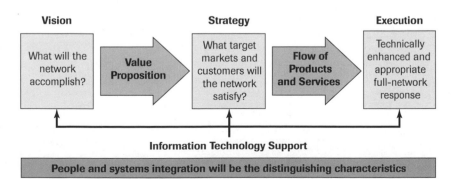

Vision	Strategy	Execution
What will the network accomplish?	**Value Proposition** → What target markets and customers will the network satisfy?	**Flow of Products and Services** → Technically enhanced and appropriate full-network response

Information Technology Support

People and systems integration will be the distinguishing characteristics

EXHIBIT 11.2 Attaining a Level III Network Position

a vision that succinctly spells out the value proposition that will drive the network effort. It then establishes the target market and the products and services to be taken to the designated customers and consumers. Then the collective supply chain competencies are organized and technically enabled to respond. Completing the loop, information technology support enables the right people to bring the purported value to those customers and consumers by properly integrating people with systems. That integration becomes the distinguishing characteristic of the network. One important caveat is that all of this must be done in a way that brings clarity—and not confusion—to the people charged with executing the activities that will achieve the purposes of vision and strategy.

Level III networks work on bringing distinctively better responses to focused markets and customers. Building the enabling technical infrastructure must follow that same intention. It must be focused and relevant to those doing the execution.

Exhibit 11.3 is a strategy map intended to guide the building of network alignment in Level III. The process begins with a definition of what constitutes customer or end consumer satisfaction. What

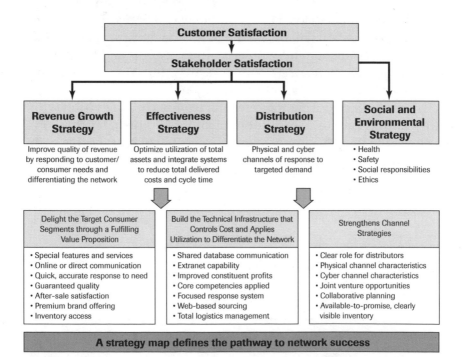

EXHIBIT 11.3   A Strategy Map for Network Alignment

exactly will establish the difference in securing the desired new revenues from the targeted consumption base has to be clearly articulated for members of the total value chain constellation that is emerging. A complete and succinct value proposition should be included, spelling out the roles for distributors, if appropriate, and employee roles and responsibilities. A statement of what will constitute stakeholder satisfaction follows this information. Now management of the supply chain constituents will work out a meaningful vision to guide the effort. This vision moves to specific strategies, calling for action by the people charged with execution.

In the exhibit, we have listed four types of strategy that normally have supply chain significance. Others may be added for companies and networks having special aspects and customers. First and most important, the network members work out a revenue growth strategy that will detail how future profitable revenue will be enhanced through the system of response that will appeal to the targeted customers and consumers. Second, there must be an effectiveness strategy. This element will be of special importance to the technology people who will play a major role in establishing the integration of systems and applications to reduce the total delivered costs in the shortest feasible cycle time. Third, we have included a distribution strategy to be consistent with the thesis that future networks will have both a physical and cyber-based mode of delivery. This strategy will provide answers to how the network will respond to the targeted audiences with an appropriate dual-channel system. Fourth, a properly designed strategy will include a social and environmental plank, spelling out at least the fundamentals in health, safety, social concern, and ethics to be observed as the value chain constellation takes shape.

Beneath each of the three key strategy categories, we have listed many of the elements that will have to be executed in order for the network to become distinguished in the eyes of the targeted consumer base. The list is not meant to be definitive, but it is directional so the constituent members can work out a series of actions that make the most sense in terms of the vision and value proposition guiding execution. This exhibit also shows in general terms the type of processes and activities that have to be effective and properly supported by IT to achieve the network intentions and vision.

The means to accomplish the strategy should determine the characteristics of the business model to be followed. Most business visions are intended to be customer-centric, as the authors put together the words and distribute them to employees. Most of the business strategies we have read combine customer-centric intentions with profitable revenue growth. Our experience, however, is that most business tactics are oriented toward cost reduction, regardless of the effect on customers and consumers.

A GUIDING MODEL

The ability to execute supply chain strategy is ultimately based on the network's ability to learn, adapt, and grow through its collective human resources. This ability is embedded in the infrastructure of the collective value chain organizations. The secret is to move to Stage 2 and build a network capability that has Level IV features in the entire concept of human resource utilization. Exhibit 11.4 diagrams the features that need to be embedded in the firm's personnel as the network moves to advanced supply chain levels. That connection is helping build the network infrastructure, defining and helping enable the core competency employee skills, and providing access to critical information.

With the understanding of the importance of participation and a sufficient level of motivation, the people involved will play a major role in moving the internal orientation to an external perspective. The exhibit details some of the important strategies in both the internal and external levels of progress. As the company finds itself

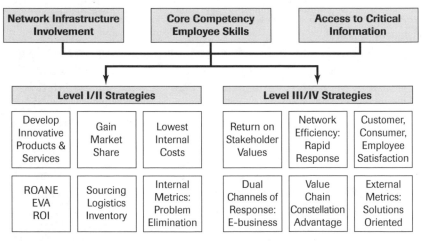

EXHIBIT 11.4 Learning and Growth: Keys to Levels III and IV Performance

really ready for a movement to Levels III and IV, the strategies change, and the workers find a dramatic increase in the need for enabling technology. We cannot overstress the need during this transition for knowledge workers who are determined to play an important role in the transformation.

We have given calls to action throughout this book for functions to accept new roles so workers can move from back-office orientations to take a more proactive position in defining new value propositions. Now we issue a major call to the human resources profession. It is time to take a front-office role in defining the connection among vision, strategy, and e-business and network supply chain capabilities. Such a connection is virtually nonexistent today.

The action call will necessitate a coalition between information technology and human resources, much as progression requires an alliance between supply chain management and the CIO's office. This coalition works to bring the full model of connectivity among HR, IT, ASCM, and e-commerce together so the value chain constellation can forge a competitive advantage. Exhibit 11.5 illustrates such a comprehensive model of how understanding and training have to be focused on doing the right things across the full network.

The model begins with an understandable and motivating vision, a defining strategy, and a call for execution from the collective management across the supply chain network. With this direction, HR and IT work together on the four elements of success. The right

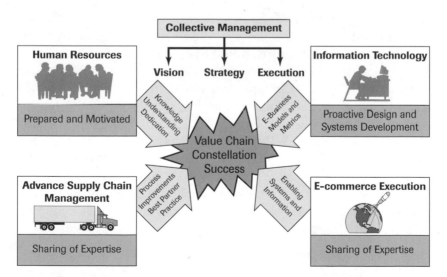

EXHIBIT 11.5 Aligning Network Needs with Information Technology

number of correctly trained personnel is focused on building the value chain constellation. When this group is prepared and motivated, they bring the knowledge, understanding, leadership, and dedication to make the constellation succeed. Concurrently, the information technology group should be proactive in the design and development of what will be the necessary technical aspects of network success. From this group will flow the enabling systems and critical technical information.

The elements brought to bear on process redesign and network fulfillment will come from advanced supply chain management as explained in the preceding chapters. Now the sharing of expertise across the network will be beneficial, as the collective groups bring process improvements and best practices for the most competent partner to each point of interaction. At the same time, e-commerce features are being introduced with a specific customer and consumer focus. This group is providing the e-business models for the future and the metrics to measure performance from a customer-centric perspective. This model can be adjusted for any network application, but it captures the elements of success that will make the effort worthwhile.

INTEGRATING PEOPLE AND TECHNOLOGY IN SUPPLY CHAIN MANAGEMENT TO COMPLETE THE LOOP

The process starts with keeping workers satisfied and motivated in their jobs. According to Robert A. Zawacki, professor emeritus of management and international business at the University of Colorado, writing for *Information Week* magazine, "The shortage of programmers, network engineers, technicians, and other IT workers is arguably worse than ever, and competition for limited resources is great." Keeping these workers motivated and focused has never been more challenging. Zawacki cites a term provided by Professor D. D. Warrick at the University of Colorado, who now calls these talented people "gold-collar" workers. Zawacki lists six key factors that HR managers should consider in any motivational program designed to increase productivity and help reduce staff turnover:

- *Make certain people perceive that what they do on the job is meaningful work.*

- *Provide strong leadership during periods of rapid and random change.*
- *Provide for workers' personal development, allow people to attend technology conferences and give them a clearly defined career path.*
- *Allow people to learn new technologies as they emerge.*
- *Give people the resources they need to do their job well.*
- *Be competitive in terms of salary and benefits; consider annual salary surveys to keep abreast of salary levels (Zawacki 1999, p. 319).*

Today, managers have to recognize the need for flexible organizations with employees dedicated to making quick and accurate responses in a global marketplace struggling to keep up with dynamic changes. The traditional model, constrained by layers of managers acting as bottlenecks to decision making and action, has to be replaced with one that fosters decisions that are responsive to customer and consumer needs. The new model is typified by what CEO Jorma Ollila of Finland's telecom giant, Nokia, says is "flexibility, an open mind, and transparency of organization" (Byrne 1999, p. 110). It will have to be designed by moving HR and IT into the front office and working with senior management to define and create a feasible twenty-first century model.

This model will be customer-centric, global in scope, and fully supported by technology. Its people could come from anywhere in the world. Let's consider an example: Planet-Intra.com Ltd., a new software company nominally based in Mountain View, California. The founder, Canadian Alan McMillan, works in Hong Kong; a software team in Croatia wrote the company's product; the vice president for technology is Russian; and the VP of international sales is a German living in Tokyo. They use the Internet to collaborate across borders (Byrne 1999, p. 110).

If we accept the premise that the use of qualified IT resources in support of business strategies is critical to achieving the benefits of the e-business wave, then we must also accept the need to find the means to integrate people and technology effectively. These people will have diverse backgrounds and come from many cultures. They will also be the keys to future success. In supply chain and e-commerce, complex situations arise requiring quick and accurate response. People need rapid access to the information behind the situation and the data that will influence their decisions. Therein lies the new role of the IT professional.

The new Level IV and V e-business models do not yet exist from an HR perspective. They have to be designed and include the need for cyber-based talent, those capable of using the Internet to the advantage of the full-network organization. The central elements include enhancing the way people work, identifying the key business process and support with IT, balancing the roles of people and technology, managing multi-enterprise processes flexibly and dynamically, managing knowledge strategically, and promoting individual effectiveness.

The improvement system is basic. Identify the core competencies across the supply chain network, focus on the business processes critical to gaining an advantage, and redesign, with the help of IT, to make them discernibly better. The result will be more effective total performance, shorter cycle time, less errors, and greater customer responsiveness.

The need is for integrated supply chain systems (ISCS) across the full value chain constellation designed by the IT specialists for the business users. Each constituent might bring its own Internet response to its segment of the value chain, but the total effectiveness is only enhanced when the network shares talent and resources to define the full system of response that beats any other network. When the best talent is used collaboratively to design a total system of response, the network optimizes in terms of full network alignment and capability provision. Efficiency and customer satisfaction are natural results of this collaborative effort. Such collaboration, furthermore, includes ERP, inventory management, order fulfillment, logistics, and all of the other supply functions that cry out for optimization.

SUMMARY

Internet businesses become virtual communities as they participate in value chain constellations. To make these communities as effective as possible, the people within them must feel they have helped create the infrastructure and have a strong relationship with the business and customers/consumers. This feeling requires interaction with the end customers of the supply chain, something most IT people never get. As the IT workers are exposed to advanced training, it must include interfaces with at least a few of the important customers. A viable program would include two-way communication that benefits buyer and seller. Face-to-face meetings, telecommunication interactions, and electronic mail can also be used. Eventually, the virtual community becomes real as the interfaces span suppliers, manufacturers, distributors, retailers, and some group of end consumers.

The need is for development of interenterprise sharing and solution development that is just beginning to appear. The means to get at best practices and create the trust so important for success will become the ends for network superiority. We call for an alliance between the information technology and human resources functions to forge the new models that will recruit, train, and motivate the new employees who will enable the transition to the models of the twenty-first century.

A Guide to the Future

We are witnessing a global revolution that is midway to conclusion—and many people are not aware of its presence or its intentions. The revolution was started about five years ago, by an unusual set of mercenaries intent on seizing an opportunity—using the Internet as the new weapon for business attack. It has been promulgated with the help of an incredible number of allies who contributed the capital funding to create the strategies, tactics, and means to gain victory. The first battles in the revolution have already been won. The clear victors include us, the consumers, who now have the ability to use alternative means of buying to satisfy our consumption needs. Through these alternatives, we are making the opposing forces in the revolution rethink their plans and develop new guides to the future.

Those leading the revolution are not desperate for aid and sustenance or concealed in some camouflaged hideaway. They are a part of the new, and very visible, business power elite. This elite includes some very familiar Internet stars who have found the formula to mount the change and generate new capitalization to support their revolution on a scale never seen before. They lead companies such as Amazon.com, AOL, Buy.com, Charles Schwab, Dell Computer, eBay, eToys, Microsoft, Netscape, Oracle, Priceline.com, RealNetworks, Sun Microsystems, Women.com, and Yahoo! They are generally young, irreverent, not beholden to traditional business models, and intent on forging a totally new way of conducting business. They have their maps, have tested their business models, and are equipped with the necessary technology to carry away victory.

The revolutionary winners are being rewarded with huge market capitalization and a new consumer base, which marches to a new form of loyalty—won by rapid, custom responses delivered over the Internet. These cyber winners may or may not make money selling to their consumer base, as they conduct their campaigns for dominance of particular business sectors. But that doesn't deter their ardor, their ambitions, or the investors eager to give them more funds. They move forward relentlessly, developing their new business models and changing the way a significant number of consumers shop. They're defining the new guides for business success, and they scoff at those pursuing the battle with outdated frameworks and models. The battlefield is being drawn between these cyber entrepreneurs and the traditional businesses that want to enhance profits and not lose valued customers, while combating the new adversaries.

A truce will be declared in this revolution in about five years—when we predict a 67/33 overall equilibrium is reached between the sponsors of the traditional, physical channels of distribution and those fomenting the movement toward cyber-based shopping. While the actual ratio will vary by industry, the consequence of not realizing this changing ratio is to risk current positions and be left out of a significant portion of future revenues. The benefits of realizing the intent of the battle and mobilizing a successful attack will include protecting existing turf, gaining new consumers, growing revenues, and creating the means to sustain future viability.

REVOLUTIONARY IMPLICATIONS

The guide to the future is already in front of us, and the roadways are under construction. These elements have been present for five years or more. Those paving the new highway system come from the power elite and the new breed of entrepreneurs who want to take advantage of the greatest opportunity to gain new wealth in the history of the planet. This group has discarded tradition in favor of cyber space and the growing, unstoppable proliferation of computers and cyber communication systems and their complementary applications. Fueled by an enormous flow of investment capital and enabling technology and software, these new leaders are showing how to create a change as dynamic and impactful as the industrial revolution. They are leading the new cyber revolution.

Let's consider one example. Borders, Inc., and Barnes & Noble introduced a new model for purchasing books, when they brought us large stores with lots of titles and a comfortable setting. Jeff Bezos, CEO of Amazon.com, is one of the new mercenaries who saw an opportunity to introduce a newer, cyber business model and capture a portion of the book business. His business model was built on the concept that some readers would shop over the Web, accessing millions of titles. The idea changed the way some books are bought and forced a reaction by his two largest physical competitors. While most of us are familiar with his new business model, some may be less familiar with his guide to the future.

Bezos determined five years ago that there was a new way to bring books to the consumer via the Internet. In a time span measured in months, Amazon has gone through an amazing evolution. Without making a profit during that time, the company generated greater capital value than its two largest rivals did. With a portion of that capital the company has built a virtual consumer response empire. On the morning of September 29, 1999, Bezos gave a preview of his future plans to a crowd in the Versailles room of the New York Sheraton Hotel. "Sixteen months ago," he told the anxious listeners, "Amazon.com was a place where you could find books. Tomorrow, Amazon.com will be a place where you can find anything" (Brooker 1999, p. 120). With those words, this revolutionary introduced the most recent installment of his map to the future, his plan to corner a significant portion of the e-business world.

Katrina Brooker of *Fortune* magazine has detailed the progress of Bezos's plan. Her report shows the extent of ambition one of the revolutionaries is planning to carry forward:

> *Throughout the year, Amazon has been on the move. On average, it has announced a major initiative every six weeks. In February it bought 46 percent of Drugstore.com; in March it launched online auctions; in May the company took a 35 percent piece of HomeGrocer.com; in June, 54 percent of Pets.com. That same month, Amazon opened two new online shops: toys and electronics. Last month's announcement was Z-shops (an online mall) and All Product Search (a product browser).* (BROOKER 1999, P. 121)

Asked whether he intended to become the Wal-Mart of the Web, Bezos responded, "The truth is, we're not trying to be anything on the Web. We're genetically pioneers." Pioneer, yes, but Bezos is a pioneer intent on dominating a major sector of the e-commerce world. He is one of the new entrepreneurial breeds determined to take the Internet to whatever level of exploitation is possible. He is winning the battle over traditional rivals, and imitators are copying his strategy.

The battle is for consumers, and smart companies are constructing guide maps, models, and roadways to find and respond to consumers, regardless of whether the pathfinder companies are traditional organizations or part of the new entrepreneurial breed. Procter & Gamble, a 162-year-old company in Cincinnati, for example, is taking steps to create its guide to lead that venerable organization to future success. This company is not one of the newly hatched cyber businesses; it is a traditional firm vowing not to be lost in the battle. As one element of its new business strategy, P&G is building a roadway focused on a particular sector of end consumers. The chosen route crosses over the traditional channels of distribution and is designed to deal directly with the targeted audience. The designers call the effort "reflect.com," and it is targeted at selling cosmetics and hair products (traditional high-margin items) that are customized to the looks and perceptions of each woman who shops on the Internet (Himelstein and Galzuka 1999, p. 87).

Their goal is to give each cyber shopper a product so personalized that no two individuals will get the same items. To pursue this novel venture, the company formed an alliance with Institutional Venture Partners, a Menlo Park, California, firm to create a separate entity to be based in San Francisco. When in use, the personalized Web site applies an interactive question-and-answer process to determine each woman's needs. With this data, using P&G's research and development lab for mixing technologies, a truly personalized product will be created and packaged per the specifications determined for each order. The vision is to offer as many as fifty thousand unique hair, skin, and makeup combinations. The cost of the products is expected to be no more than the consumer would pay at a department store cosmetics counter.

Not wanting to stop at this point with its cyber adventure, P&G has also announced a deal with Yahoo! Through this revolutionary Internet sponsor, the company will showcase a number of its brands—Pringles, Pepto-Bismol, Pampers, and a variety of home care and laundry products. P&G will act as sponsors of popular types of cyber programming, as well as cyber soap operas (a traditional role for the company). Obviously, this well-established, traditionally physical channel marketer is willing to at least test the cyber waters and try an Internet adventure.

As other firms, new and old, construct their version of this concept, a few revolutionary facts need to be kept in mind:

- The spoils from the revolution will be saving existing territory, while building future growth and profit. Failure to participate in the war can be devastating as the new soldiers march through your territory and take away your customers. Firms in commodity industries, for example, may assume there is no application for them. That could be a very bad assumption, particularly if a cyber entrepreneur finds the way to market its commodity on a global Web basis. As these commodities firms find their products being auctioned on the Internet and going at lower prices, the opportunity to be proactive with the Web will have been missed.

- New strategies and generals are needed to win this revolution. Most traditional firms lack the necessary armaments to do battle or mount a counteroffensive in the revolution. The revolution will be won with new and amended business strategies, new business models, and alliances with other firms determined to create the future routes to success. The generals must be visionary and capable of leading the troops through territory that will be unfamiliar to most of them. They must also recruit some new soldiers from nontraditional fields who are not tied to old business designs.

- If your business model is two years old, it either is out-of-date or needs some serious modifications. The new mercenaries are well armed with the new communications weaponry and are backed by the near hysteria from supporters promoting the use of these weapons. Defense might delay losing battles, but it will not ensure victory. The new generals need a viable model to define their means of attack and support their vision to lead and win those attacks.

THE CONVERGENCE OF BUSINESS AND TECHNOLOGY

As the new models and guides are being planned, some companies have made the strategic decision to embrace the new discipline of integrating advanced supply chain and e-commerce. The result is a gap that can now be measured in years in some industries. The good news for those organizations that have not yet made e–supply chain a part of their business imperative, and have not yet formulated a new e-business model, is that there's still time to get into the action. So few organizations have found the way to the advanced levels that there is still an opportunity to make up for lost ground and even to move to a position of leadership. Doing so requires the participation of willing, able, and trusted partners. In the electronic age and the digital economy, that means having supply chain constituents with sophisticated e-business capabilities for building network solutions.

The formula for success should be clear. The future of business is inextricably linked with electronic collaboration across a network of enterprises working closely and continually to provide the best consumer response. Within specific industries, dominance is going to pass into the hands of the value chain constellation winners. These will be alliances of companies linked in a supply chain network that applies collective resources in a collaborative manner. The unwavering focus will be on specific industries, markets, customers, and end consumers that will deliver the highest yield on effort. The constellation constituents will align their strategies and work in a spirit of trust to develop new and profitable revenues. At the same time, they will deliver above-industry levels of satisfaction to the targeted customer/consumer base. These constellations will display greater overall effectiveness than any competing supply chain network.

To enjoy sustained success, these alliances will go to market through a physical channel and a cyber-based channel of customer fulfillment. Both channels will have to accentuate e-business features that distinguish the constellation. Furthermore, the supporting network has to reach all the way to the primary suppliers in order to be totally enabled. With anything less, the supply chain response will be diminished and consumers will be lost.

An example helps illustrate this point. One of the most successful of the new breed of companies is Cisco Systems. Cisco teamed with another leader, Federal Express, to define a new business model that is beneficial to both firms and enhances the building of the desired customer base. FDX, the parent company of FedEx, is scheduled to coordinate Cisco's shipping in the next two years, 80 percent of which comes from orders received over the Internet. In the following three years, the plan calls for the elimination of Cisco's warehousing.

Parts for Cisco's familiar line of routers, connectors, and other communication systems products are made in the United States, Mexico, Scotland, Taiwan, and Malaysia. Products, including partial orders, are held at local warehouses, so complete orders can be shipped to business customers at one time. With 40 percent annual growth, Cisco decided it couldn't build enough warehouses to handle its demand, hold inventory, and pay reshipping costs. In a page from the advanced supply chain management handbook, they decided to introduce a new concept and model. They would merge the parts and orders in transit.

Under the alliance with FDX, as many as one hundred packages for one customer will be shipped when manufactured. The packaged products will be coordinated to arrive at the customer site within hours of each other. The final assemblies will then be made on site, by a Cisco team that normally handles that part of the delivery. This new system will result in the need for zero warehousing by Cisco.

Showing you can merge new technology with old but good systems, FedEx created the new model using parts of its existing infrastructure. Routes to the customer are selected automatically for the nearly endless Cisco shipment possibilities, but every shipment will essentially be custom planned. Existing software programs will select the best possible transportation mode, meaning air, ship, train, or plane delivery will be chosen based on the parameters defined by customer, location, and need. Customs controls across national boundaries will also be handled as part of the process. Real-time status checking will be available via the extranet established between the companies.

In the emerging business environment of electronically enabled commerce and value chain constellations, collaboration and technology convergence will be the keys to success. That is, the ability of the constellation members to combine business strategies and information technology with a focus on consumption will become a defining characteristic of the industry leaders. The confluence of these two dimensions flowing products and services to the specified customers and consumers will lead to success and sustenance in the new millennium. In this age of convergence, companies will have to combine business growth, profit, and customer/consumer satisfaction strategies with state-of-the-art technology to develop a cohesive business plan. Importantly, this cooperative action must be done across a full value chain of partners that have formed the constellation of choice for the most desired consumers.

As the value chain constellation builds new, profitable revenues with the intended consumer groups through a clearly superior e-business capability, true business-to-business-to-consumer commerce becomes a reality. The additional profits that derive from these revenues will ratify the e–supply chain effort as a business discipline. Constructing this future roadway will require a new level of business trust and cooperation. This means getting the supply chain partners' collective professionals to work together, much as an army group determined to win a major battle. They must determine a game plan and develop an execution strategy. Then they must design and build the necessary future systems supporting the strategy. The requirement goes beyond any single process area or individual company. It must include the collaboration of designers and IT groups across the breadth of the total supply chain network. This kind of inclusiveness can help avoid any weak links in the ultimate network design.

MAKING A BET ON THE FUTURE

As we progress in the twenty-first century, two types of organizations will likely emerge. One will continue to pursue the old business models; the other will recognize the new e-business realities. The first group will be characterized by

- a refusal to collaboratively build a network of optimized business partners to provide the most effective physical and electronic response to both business and consumer demands,
- a hesitancy to build any type of cyber-based response system, and
- an insistence on dominating and controlling the movement of products and services to consumers—even if that means having less able partners in their value chain.

The second group of companies will demonstrate an entirely different set of traits. They will work diligently to forge an end-to-end value chain constellation that is optimized at every link of interchange. Their strategic and operational response to business customers and commercial consumers will include both physical and cyber-based components. Finally, these industry leaders will serve as a nucleus for the network partners. They will champion the effort to provide the best channel response to the best customers and consumers—physically or electronically.

It is on this second group that we will place our future wagers. They recognize the essential truth that in the future every company will be a technology company, responding to the ultimate consumer in the manner those consumers want their needs met. Business strategy and technology have converged—whether some companies want it to happen or not. The process has been an inevitable one. Now is the time to begin fashioning the future networks that will capitalize on this convergence. Those already behind the progress curve need to accelerate the pace. All of their efforts should be geared toward the ultimate conclusion of the supply chain vision, to create a business-to-business-to-consumer system of response that is unequaled by any competing network.

Business professionals are faced with at least three mandates in helping their organizations realize the desired future state. First, they need to make their internal constituents aware of the inevitability of the business-technology convergence and the enormous opportunity it affords the business. Second, they must be catalysts in moving their companies to the necessary external perspective so an advanced supply chain network can be constructed. Third, they have to create the forums, workshops, and pilots through which the value chain constellations can eventually be constructed. Throughout the process, they must bring their allies in information technology along on the trip. An effective alliance will make certain the applications developed take full advantage of the existing systems that are best adaptable for the network and that will provide a leading-edge dimension to the final plans, and models. If the alliance capitalizes on the opportunity, today's business professionals and their allies can lead the way to tomorrow's e-business future.

Glossary

ABC analysis—The classification of items in an inventory according to importance defined in terms of criteria such as sales volume and purchase volume

Advanced cost models—The development of costing analyses that span a total supply chain network, in which network constituents pinpoint the values at each point of connection, from initial supplies to final consumption and postsale servicing

Advanced supply chain management—The creation and maintenance of a network of organizations dedicated to building and constantly improving a value chain constellation focused on a particular industry, market segments and consumer groups. This concept is the culmination of supply chain management in which a trusting network of suppliers, manufacturers, distributors, and sales and support specialists works interdependently to achieve market dominance.

Available-to-promise (API) inventory—An online display of the goods in inventory, throughout a full supply chain network, offering the viewer the opportunity to determine what is available for immediate delivery, where any particular order has progressed, and what back-up supplies can be accessed to complete an intended order

Benchmarking—A management tool for comparing performance against an organization that is widely regarded as outstanding in one or more areas, to improve performance in those areas

Capital—The resources, usually cash or credit, available for investing in assets that produce output

Cash-to-cash cycles—The time accumulated between the expenditure for necessary raw materials and supplies until the receipt of payment from the customer for receipt of the finished goods

Collaborative planning—The process through which a firm works together with its suppliers and customers to design and forecast demand for products

Continuous replenishment process (CRP)—A system used to reduce inventories and safety stocks while improving service to customers and consumers

Cross docking—The holding and movement of goods directly from a receiving position to accumulation of full order and direct loading to an outbound carrier, to eliminate storage and handling expense

Customer service—Activities occurring between the buyer and seller that enhance or facilitate the sale or use of seller's products and services

Cycle time—The time it takes to complete an organizational process

Database mining—The analysis of information residing in collective databases across a supply chain network, to develop information for sales groups, who can then offer opportunities and solutions for specific business customers and consumer groups

Direct store delivery—A logistics system designed to improve services and lower warehouse inventories by having the seller move the ordered goods directly to the retail outlet

Distribution—The transfer of goods from a manufacturer, producer, or distributor to a business customer or end consumer

Downstream—The processes in a supply chain that occur after manufacturing or conversion that are dedicated to getting goods and services to customers and consumers, usually involving warehousing and distribution with subsequent transportation to retail outlets

E-business—The use and application of electronic commerce models and techniques to improve internal and external processes that impact on the creation, manufacture, storage, and delivery of products across a full supply chain system

E-commerce—The use of computer-to-computer technology to transfer information important to the buying, manufacture, selling, distribution, servicing, and accounting processes inherent in supply chain activities

E-networks—The system of collaborating firms, linked electronically across a full supply chain system, so the business customer or final consumer perceives that a seamless system of response is at work delivering the desired goods and services

E-supply chain—Systems designed to create the necessary Internet-enabled links among data, communications, and network effectiveness

Economic value added (EVA)—The calculation of real return on assets employed

Electronic data interchange (EDI)—Computer-to-computer communication between two or more companies so such entities can enter purchase orders, generate bills of lading, expedite orders, and pay invoices. EDI enables a firm to access the information systems of suppliers, customers, and carriers and to determine the current status of inventory, orders, and shipments.

Enterprise-wide resource planning (ERP)—An advanced planning and scheduling system through which orders are entered directly into the company's planning systems, and manufacturing is coordinated to take advantage of full systems integration, from material supply through final goods production. Various systems will include a menu of possible applications.

Extranet—A network based on Internet technologies that provides private and proprietary connections. Computer-to-computer technology between external partners to a supply chain network is used to transfer information important to the buying, selling, manufacture, distribution, and accounting processes inherent in supply chain activities.

Fill rate—The percentage of order items that are completely delivered in one shipment

Finished goods inventory (FGI)—The products completely manufactured, packaged, stored, and prepared for distribution to a business customer or end consumer

Fixed costs—Costs that do not fluctuate with the volume of business in the short term

Forecasting—A prediction of future levels of business commerce, particularly in terms of anticipated volumes of product orders, demanded by customers in specific time unit (week, month) in a forthcoming time period (quarter, year)

Information systems (IS)—The management of the flow of data within an organization and between its external partners in a systematic, structured, and effective manner, to assist in planning, implementing, and controlling all of the process involved

Information technology (IT)—The systems, procedures, software, and hardware involved in establishing an effective and leading-edge methodology for enabling a total supply chain network of response, from incoming materials through delivery and satisfaction with finished goods and services

Integrated enterprise resource planning (I-ERP)—The integration of ERP systems across a full value chain constellation, whereby the network constituents share demand and supply information to optimize the use of total assets and achieve above–industry average standards of customer satisfaction

Internet—The worldwide public electronic network, a relatively inexpensive forum where value chain constellation information can be presented, in a manner appropriate for improving the system of supply and for transferring important data on product, costs, availability, specification, and ordering possibilities. Use of the Internet is best focused on specific consumer groups that will find the network advantages of importance in their buying decisions.

Intranet—A private network based on Internet technologies that provides an inexpensive electronic network, through which a nucleus organization and its internal constituents are given access to privileged information permitting them to add value to supply chain processing

Inventory—The number and cost of units a company holds to satisfy internal production needs while providing acceptable levels of customer satisfaction

Inventory management—Administration of the amount of inventory and safety stocks required meeting or exceeding current actual customer demands. This process includes proper planning, adequate stock positioning, monitoring of stock levels, and ensuring of product availability at the point of need to meet current demand

Just-in-time inventory system (JIT)—An inventory control system that reduces inventory levels by coordinating demand and supply to the point where the correct amounts of the desired items arrive just in time for use

Kitting—The process through which individual items are grouped or packaged to create a single shipment

Logistics—The processes involved in transferring goods through manufacture, storage, and transportation to business customers and end consumers

Logistics channel—The network of intermediaries engaged in the transfer, storage, handling, and communications that contribute to the efficient flow of goods to customers

Materials requirement planning (MRP)—A decision-making technique used to determine how much material to purchase and when to purchase it, so it meets the needs of the manufacturing plan

Network-focused metrics—Measurements that are based on the performance of the entire supply chain network from raw materials to end consumer, such as total cycle time or returns from the entire chain

Order cycle time—The time that elapses from placement of order until receipt of order, including time for order transmittal, processing, preparation, and shipping

Order fulfillment—The processes involved in receiving and entering orders, passing the orders through planning, and scheduling and completing delivery of the orders after manufacture

Partial alliances—Limited financial investments with suppliers, distributors, or customers, designed to achieve revenues for all members of the alliance

Point-of-sale information (POS)—Price and quantity data from the retail outlet as sales transactions occur, reflecting the actual consumption of specific items

Process mapping—The drawing out of the process steps involved in a particular portion of a supply chain or the totality of the supply chain network, with particular depiction of the hand-off that occurs between members of the supply chain

Project logistics—Specific internal warehouse, transportation, or distribution projects

Purchasing—The functions associated with acquiring the goods and services a firm needs to operate its business

Quick response—A method of maximizing the efficiency of the supply chain by rapidly responding to specific orders with the correct amount of product drawn from a minimized inventory

Reengineering—A fundamental rethinking and radical redesign of business processes to achieve dramatic improvements in performance

Reverse logistics—The process of collecting, moving, and storing used, damaged, or outdated products and/or packaging from end users

Safety stock—The inventory a company holds beyond normal projected needs, as a buffer against delays of receipt of orders or changes in customer buying patterns

Sourcing—The methodology involved in procuring the necessary materials, supplies, and services necessary to sustain a supply chain system

Stock-keeping unit (SKU)—A single unit of a manufacturer's line of products, such as a particular size of bar soap or cereal

Supply chain—The core business processes that allow a company to create and deliver a product or service from concept through development and manufacture or conversion into a market for consumption

Supply chain management—The methods, systems, and leadership that continuously improve an organization's integrated processes for product and service design, purchasing, inventory management, manufacturing or production, order management, logistics, distribution, and customer satisfaction. Implementing supply chain management principles involves such techniques as working with suppliers to optimize the cost of supply, introducing flexible manufacturing strategies and systems, and using process redesign to streamline systems throughout the full supply chain network.

Supply chain network—The linkage of business firms into a concerted effort to apply mutual resources for achieving mutual benefits across the full supply chain system, from primary raw materials through consumption and recycling. Firms might be part of several such networks.

Supply chain optimization—The development of the lowest-cost and most effective system of supply chain interactions, through sharing of best practices between constituents, resulting in virtually no wastes across the network and above-industry levels of customer satisfaction

Supply-demand linkage—The connection of a demand chain (forecasted buying patterns modified by the flow of incoming orders) with a supply chain (flow of products and services in response to actual orders), whereby replenishment is in response to actual pull-through consumption

Third-party logistics provider—(3PL) A firm that supplies logistics services (particularly transportation and warehousing) to other companies

Total quality management (TQM)—A management approach in which managers constantly communicate with all organizational stakeholders, to emphasize the importance of continuous quality improvement and total elimination of waste

Upstream—The processes that occur before manufacturing or conversion into a deliverable product or service, usually dedicated to getting raw materials from suppliers

Value-based metrics—Measurements that catalog the network's ability to optimize total systems cost, while delivering the highest possible customer satisfaction

Value chain—The result of transforming a full supply chain system, through the application of activity-based costing techniques, into a process map that includes all significant costs at each step in the process, so the total cost of delivering the final product or service to a satisfied customer is determined

Value chain constellation—A consortium of companies linked together to build a superior supply chain network with a focus on specific markets, customers, products, and end consumers. The purpose of the constellation is to use collective assets and resources to build a seamless network of supply that will distinguish the network from any competing group.

Variable cost—A cost that fluctuates with the volume of business

Vendor-managed inventory (VMI)—A customer service strategy used to manage inventory for customers to lower cost and react more directly to customer demand

Virtual inventory systems—An online network in which one can find the location of inventory anywhere in the entire supply chain network (in manufacturing, warehouses, or in transit) and divert it, if necessary

World Wide Web (WWW)—A collection of systems/sites available through the Internet. The Web is the graphical successor to the Internet as well as a huge online market where buying, selling, and information gathering take place. The Web has hundreds of millions of users worldwide. It is the basis for the e-business revolution currently under way.

Work-in-process (WIP)—Parts and subassemblies in the process of becoming completed assembly components

List of Abbreviations

3PL	Third-party logistics provider
4PL	Fourth-party logistics (Andersen Consulting proprietary name)
A/P	Accounts payable
A/R	Accounts receivable
ABC	Activity-based costing
ABC-M	Activity-based cost management
AEI	Automatic equipment identification
AMR	Advanced manufacturing research
ANSI	American National Standards Institute
ANX	Automotive Network Exchange
APS	Advanced planning and scheduling
ASCM	Advanced supply chain management
ASN	Advance shipping notice
ASP	Application service provider
B2B	Business-to-business
B2C	Business-to-consumer
BOM	Bill of materials
CAD	Computer-aided design
CAM	Computer-aided manufacture
CLM	Council of Logistics Management
CPFR	Collaborative planning, forecasting, and replenishment
CPG	Consumer packaged goods
CRM	Customer relationship management
CRP	Continuous replenishment program
DRAM	Dynamic random access memory

DRP	Distribution resources planning
EAI	Enterprise application integration
ECO	Engineering change order
ECR	Efficient consumer response
EDI	Electronic data interchange
EPS	Earnings per share
ERP	Enterprise resource planning
EVA	Economic value added
FGI	Finished goods inventory
FMS	Freight management systems
GLS	Global logistics system
GMA	Grocery Manufacturers Association
GUI	Graphical user interface
IES	Interenterprise solutions
ISO	International Standards Organization
JIT	Just-in-time (manufacture and distribution)
KPI	Key performance indicators
LAN	Local area (computer) network
LDI	Logistics development incentive
LLS	Lead logistics provider
LTL	Less than truckload
MAP	Manufacturers assembly pilot
MRO	Manufacturing, repair, and operating (supplies)
MRP	Material requirements planning
MRP II	Material resources planning
OEM	Original equipment manufacturer
ORM	Operating resource management
PCA	Printed circuits assemblies
POS	Point of sale
RFP	Request for proposal
RFQ	Request for quotation
ROA	Return on assets
ROIC	Return on invested capital
SCCI	Supply Chain Council International
SCM	Supply chain management
SCO	Supply chain optimization
SCOR	Supply chain operations reference model
SCP	Supply chain planning
SKU	Stock keeping unit
SRM	Supplier relationship management
TCO	Total cost of ownership

TMS	Transportation management system
TOC	Theory of constraints
UCC	Uniform Code Council
VAN	Value-added network
VICS	Voluntary Inter-Industry Commerce Standards
VMI	Vendor-managed inventory
WAN	Wide-area (computer) network
WMS	Warehouse management system
XML	Extensible markup language

Bibliography

Adhikari, Richard. "The ERP-to-ERP Connection." *Information Week*, October 19, 1998, pp. 12SS–18SS.

Alsop, Stewart. "E or Be Eaten." *Fortune*, November 18, 1999, pp. 86–86.

Anderson, David, and Hau Lee. "Synchronized Supply Chains: The New Frontier," online: http://anderson.ascet.com, 1998.

Anonymous. "Pericom Story." *Infoworld*, November 9, 1998, p. 78.

Arntzen, Bruce C. "Designing Global and Time-Critical Supply Chains." Unpublished paper, Insight, Inc., Maynard, MA, online: www.gsca.com, 1998.

Baron, Talila. "One Vendor, One Solution." *Information Week*, November 8, 1999, pp. 108–112.

Bernstein, R. "A Leaner, Cleaner Supply Chain." *Consumer Goods*, September/October 1998, pp. 12–14.

Blum, Scott. "Meet Mister.buy(everything).com." *Fortune*, March 29, 1999, pp. 119–124.

Brooker, Katrina. "Amazon vs. Everybody." *Fortune*, November 8, 1999, pp. 120–128.

Brown, Eryn. "Nine Ways to Win on the Web." *Fortune*, May 24, 1999, pp. 112–125.

Byrne, John. "The Search for the Young and the Gifted." *Business Week*, October 4, 1999, pp. 108–116.

Byrnes, Nanette, and Paul Judge. "Internet Anxiety." *Business Week*, June 28, 1999, pp. 79–88.

Chabrow, Eric. "Seeking the Deeper Path to E-success." *Information Week*, March 6, 2000, pp. 49–64.

Cone, Edward. "Cautious Automation." *Information Week*, October 19, 1998, pp. 2SS–6SS,

Dalton, Gregory. "FedEx Keeps an Eye on Supply." *Information Week*, October 25, 1999a, p. 97.

———. "Going, Going, Gone." *Information Week*, October 4, 1999b, pp. 45–50.

DeSisto, Robert. "Supply Chain Management and the Front Office." Paper presented at the Gartner Group I/T Symposium, Orlando, FL, October 1998.

Durtsche, David, James Keebler, Michael Ledyard, and Karl Manrodt. *Keeping Score; Measuring the Business Value of Logistics in the Supply Chain*. Oak Brook, IL: Council of Logistics Management, 1999.

Enslow, Beth. "Supply Chain Management Scenario." Paper presented at the Gartner Group Symposium, Orlando, FL, October 1998.

Esper, Zachary. "Assemble Your E-business Team." *e-Business Advisor*, December 1999, pp. 30–34.

Ferguson, Kevin. "Purchasing in Packs." *Business Week*, November 1, 1999, pp. EB33–EB38.

Fine, Charles H. *Clock Speed: Winning Industry Control in the Age of Temporary Advantage*. Reading, MA: Perseus, 1998.

Foley, John, B. Bacheldor, and B. Wallace. "E-markets Are Expanding." *Information Week*, February 28, 2000, pp. 22–24.

Gerdel, T. "LTV to Sell Excess and Damaged Steel on Web Site." *Cleveland Plain Dealer*, August 19, 1998.

Gilbert, Alorie. "Exchanges Get into Gear." *Information Week*, November, 8, 1999, pp. 20–22.

Gilbert, Alorie, and Jeff Sweat. "Reinventing ERP." *Industry Week*, September 13, 1999, pp. 18–20.

Gill, Philip J. "ERP: Keep It Simple." *Information Week*, August 9, 1999, pp. 87–92.

Gould, Janet. "WebPlus EDI Equals Better E-commerce." *IDS*, April 1999, pp. 18–21.

Hamel, Gary. "Bringing Silicon Valley Inside." *Harvard Business Review*, September–October 1999, pp. 71–84.

Hamm, Steve, and Marcia Stepanik. "From Reengineering to E-engineering." *Business Week E.Biz*, March 22, 1999, pp. EB14–18.

Hardin, A. "Eaton Corporation Looking to Expand E-commerce." *Crain's Cleveland Business*, October 5, 1998.

Hax, Arnoldo, and Dean Wilde. "The Delta Model: Adaptive Management for a Changing World." *Sloan Management Review*, Winter 1999, pp. 11–27.

Henkoff, Ronald. "Delivering the Goods." *Fortune*, November 28, 1994.

Himelstein, Linda, and Peter Galzuka. "P&G Gives Birth to a Web Baby." *Business Week*, September 27, 1999, pp. 87–88.

Hof, Robert D. "The Net Is Open for Business–Big Time." *Business Week*, August 31, 1998, pp. 108–109.

Hof, Robert D. "Electronic Business—A Survival Game." *Business Week E.Biz*, March 22, 1999, pp. EB9–12.

Hof, Robert D., and H. Green. "Going, Going, Gone." *Business Week*, April 12, 1999, pp. 30–32.

Holt, Stannie. "Back on the Supply-Chain Gang." *Infoworld*, November 9, 1998, pp. 78–83.

H. R. Chally Group. "The Customer-Selected World Class Sales Excellence Research Report." Dayton, OH: Author, 1999.

Kotler, Philip. "It's Time for Total Marketing." Executive brief, McGraw-Hill, 1992, p. 7.

Lee, Louise. "An E-commerce Cautionary Tale." *Business Week,* March 20, 2000, pp. 46–48.

Leibs, Scott. "E-commerce Diplomacy." *Industry Week,* February 7, 2000a, p. 27.

———. "World of Difference." *Industry Week,* January 7, 2000b, pp. 23–26.

Levitt, Jason. "The Internet Presents." *Information Week,* September 15, 1997, pp. 61–70.

Machalaba, Daniel. "Schneider National to Outfit Trailers with Tracking Device to Map Locations." *Wall Street Journal,* May 7, 1999, pp. A2 and A6.

Manheim, Martin. "Integrating People and Technology for Supply Chain Advantage." *Information Week,* September 27, 1999, pp. 304–313.

Martin, James D. "CEOs and Logistics." *Inbound Logistics,* June 1997.

Mateyaschuk, Jennifer. "IT Skills Gap Demands Action." *Information Week,* July 5, 1999a, pp. 44–46.

Mateyaschuk, Jennifer. "Foreign Aid for IT." *Information Week,* August 9, 1999b, pp. 108–110.

———. "Partners in Education." *Information Week,* August 23, 1999c, p. 92.

McCullough, Stacie S. "Dynamic Supply Chains Alter Traditional Models," on-line: http://mccullough.ascet.com, 1999.

———. "Mastering Commerce Logistics." *Forrester Report,* August 1999.

McHugh, Josh. "The $29 Billion Flea Market." *Forbes,* November 1, 1999, pp. 66–68.

McKendrick, Joseph. "The Rise of the Market-Makers." *EC World,* November 1999, pp. 24–28.

Murphy, Jean. "Satisfying the 21st Century Consumer: Supply Chain Challenges." *Global Sites and Logistics,* May 1999, pp. 24–89.

Navas, Deb. "E-commerce and E-tail Trends Predict Big Changes." IDS, April 1999a, pp. 24–34.

———. "The Scoop on ASNs and Amazing Goop." *IDS,* April 1999b, pp. 36–43.

Porter, Michael. "What Is Strategy?" *Harvard Business Review,* November–December 1996, p. 77.

Reardon, Marguerite. "Sizzling Cisco." *Information Week,* February 28, 2000, pp. 47–60.

Roth, Daniel. "Dell's Big New Act." *Fortune,* December 6, 1999, pp. 152–166.

Schonfeld, Erick. "The Customized, Digitized, Have-It-Your-Way Economy." *Fortune,* April 28, 1998.

Selland, Christopher S. "Integrated Logistics and Supply Chain Management." Yankee Group white paper, Boston, 1999.

Shepherd, James. *Achieving Supply Chain Excellence through Technology.* San Francisco: Montgomery Research, 1999.

Stein, Tom. "ERP's Future Linked to E–supply Chain." *Industry Week,* October 19, 1998 pp. 20SS–22SS.

Sweat, Jeff. "Customer-Centricity in the Post Y2K Era." *Industry Week,* May 17, 1999a, pp. 46–62.

———. "E-commerce and the Customers." *Industry Week,* May 17, 1999b, pp. 18–20.

———. "When Customers Are King." *Information Week,* September 27, 1999c, pp. 362–370.

Taylor, Dave. "Developing an E-business Strategy." Paper presented at the Gartner Group I/T Symposium, Orlando, FL, October 1998.

Tully, Shawn. "The B2B Tool That Really Is Changing the World." *Fortune*, March 20, 2000, pp. 132–145.

Useem, Jerry. "Internet Defense Strategy: Cannabalize Yourself." *Fortune*, September 6, 1999, pp. 121–134.

Violino, Bob. "Pricing Shakeout: The Internet and E-business Are Reshaping IT Purchasing." *Information Week*, March 6, 2000, pp. 79–90.

Wallace, Bob. "Data Quality Moves to the Forefront." *Information Week*, September 20, 1999, pp. 52–67.

White, Andrew. "Value Chain Management and the Internet." Paper presented at Distribution/Computer Seminar, Anaheim, CA, February 9, 1999.

Wilder, Clinton. "New Market Makers." *Information Week*, March 13, 2000, pp. 22–24.

Windham, Laurie. "The Customer Loyalty Puzzle." *e-Business Advisor*, December 1999, pp. 10–16.

Yang, Catherine. "No Web Site Is an Island." *Business Week E.Biz*, March 22, 1999, pp. EB38–40.

Zawacki, Robert. "Gold-Collar Standard." *Information Week*, September 27, 1999, pp. 320–323.

Zellner, Wendy, and Stephanie Anderson. "The Big Guys Go Online." *Business Week*, September 6, 1999, pp. 30–32.

About the Authors

C harles C. Poirier is a partner with the Net Management Practice of Computer Sciences Corporation (CSC), one of the world's largest information technology and management consulting firms. He is a regular contributor to domestic and international conferences and seminars on subjects ranging from supply chain optimization and electronic commerce to finding value throughout business interenterprises and associated partnering opportunities.

Poirier has held a variety of management positions, including senior vice president of manufacturing and marketing at Packaging Corporation of America. He was also group manager of a major business unit of that company. His background includes direct management experience in productivity, quality, cost containment, business strategy, mergers and acquisitions, training, sales and marketing, and information technology. His previous publications include *Business Partnering for Continuous Improvement* (Berrett-Koehler), *Avoiding the Pitfalls of Total Quality Management* (ASQC Press), and *Supply Chain Optimization* and *Advanced Supply Chain Management* (Berrett-Koehler).

M ichael J. Bauer is a partner in Computer Science Corporation's Electronic Business Practice, where he brings best practices in new business models and market enhancements to his clients. His work in this exciting technological development, e-commerce, gives him an insight into the strategic opportunities for revenue growth, operational efficiency, and effective asset utilization, while his experience affords him the caution necessary to be successful with new ventures. Mr. Bauer has worked with some of the largest and most successful companies in the world, collaborating with manufacturers, distributors, and service providers to add value, increase marketability, and raise profitability across their business processes, especially demand creation, order fulfillment, and application of advanced technology. He is a frequent speaker and author and has appeared on radio and television.

Mr. Bauer has achieved national recognition as a business and technical strategist for many industries, specializing in manufacturing and telecommunications. His career has taken him to all parts of the world where he develops and assists in the implementation of business and technical strategies in product development, marketing, sales, customer service, and distribution to establish new market opportunities. Mr. Bauer has experiences in strategy, operations, and consulting. His hands-on background gives him a unique perspective that allows him to navigate shop floors as easily as boardrooms.

Index